ANGLO-AMERICAN SUPPORT FOR JORDAN

ANGLO-AMERICAN SUPPORT FOR JORDAN: THE CAREER OF KING HUSSEIN

Miriam Joyce

palgrave
macmillan

First published in 2008 by
PALGRAVE MACMILLAN™
175 Fifth Avenue, New York, N.Y. 10010 and
Houndmills, Basingstoke, Hampshire, England RG21 6XS.
Companies and representatives throughout the world.

PALGRAVE MACMILLAN is the global academic imprint of the Palgrave Macmillan division of St. Martin's Press, LLC and of Palgrave Macmillan Ltd. Macmillan® is a registered trademark in the United States, United Kingdom and other countries. Palgrave is a registered trademark in the European Union and other countries.

ISBN-13: 978-0-230-60451-3
ISBN-10: 0-230-60451-X

Library of Congress Cataloging-in-Publication Data

Joyce, Miriam.
    Anglo-America support for Jordan : the career of King Hussein / Miriam Joyce.
        p. cm.
    Includes bibliographical references and index.
    ISBN 0-230-60451-X
    1. Jordan—Politics and government—1952–1999. 2. Hussein, King of Jordan, 1935–1999. 3. Great Britain—Foreign relations—Jordan. 4. Jordan—Foreign relations—Great Britain. 5. Great Britain—Foreign relations—1945–6. United States—Foreign relations—Jordan. 7. Jordan—Foreign relations—United States. 8. United States—Foreign relations—1945–1989. I. Title.

DS154.55.J79 2008
327.569504109'045—dc22   2007039541

A catalogue record of the book is available from the British Library.

Design by Scribe Inc.

First edition: May 2008

10 9 8 7 6 5 4 3 2 1

Printed in the United States of America.

CONTENTS

ACKNOWLEDGMENTS

I had considerable support while writing this book. I am especially grateful to my friend, American diplomat Alexandra Sundquist, who used her connections at Diplomatic and Consular Officers Retired (DACOR) to locate Americans who had served in Jordan and were willing to be interviewed. I am also indebted to retired diplomat Sir Harold Walker, who provided British diplomatic contacts. In addition, I deeply appreciate the role former British Consul General in Jerusalem John Snodgrass played in his timely appearance in the audience at London's National Theatre. Finally, I wish to acknowledge the help of my student research assistant, Adam Raven, who understood my passion for primary sources.

Figure 1. King Hussein in traditional Bedouin dress.
Photograph courtesy of the Embassy of Jordan.

INTRODUCTION

Hussein bin Talal, born in 1935, was heir to the throne of the Hashemite Kingdom of Jordan. He was educated to assume the responsibility of safeguarding the Hashemite family legacy. Although he was often unpopular with Palestinians and Arab nationalists, he maintained the firm loyalty of his Bedouin tribesmen. At the same time, he understood the importance of his Western connections, and as Great Britain lost influence in the Middle East he worked diligently to form close ties with the United States. Although during King Hussein's reign there were numerous events that caused tension between Jordan and its Anglo-American allies, both London and Washington agreed that support for Hussein served their interests. The Hashemite Kingdom stood as a barrier to Soviet expansion, radical Arab nationalism, and militant Islam.

Hussein's small kingdom had been created after World War I, when the League of Nations granted Great Britain mandates for both Mesopotamia and Palestine. After accepting these mandates London had an opportunity to fulfill its obligation to the Hashemite family for rebelling against the Ottoman Empire and cooperating with the British during the Great War. Throughout World War I Hussein's great-grandfather, Sharif Hussein of Mecca, led the Hashemites. As members of the Prophet's Al Quraish tribe, Sharif Hussein and his sons were recognized as direct descendants of the Prophet Mohammad—descendents of the Prophet's daughter Fatima and her husband Ali. Thus, the Hashemites retained considerable prestige in the Muslim world.[1]

Prior to Turkey's decision to join the Central Powers, Sharif Hussein sent his son Abdullah to Egypt to contact British officials. In Cairo Abdullah discussed the possibility of a Hashemite-British alliance in the event of war between Great Britain and Turkey. After Turkey joined the Central Powers, the Sultan issued a call to *Jihad* (holy war), insisting that all Muslims join their Turkish coreligionists in the conflict against the Allied Powers. His Majesty's Government was concerned about the impact the sultan's call might have on the

Figure 2. King Hussein, greeting his eldest son, the future King Abdullah. Photograph courtesy of the Embassy of Jordan.

Muslim population of its vast empire, which included both India and Egypt. Discussion between the Hashemites and the British continued. Putting himself forward as the representative of the Arab nation, on July 15, 1915, Sharif Hussein agreed to lead an Arab revolt against the Turks. In return he expected British support for the independence of the Arabic-speaking territories east of Suez.[2]

The Arab revolt began in the Hejaz in June 1916. Bedouin units fought together with their British allies, and in October 1918 Abdullah's brother Feisal marched into Damascus with the victorious British Army. Soon after, a Syrian Assembly elected Feisal king of Syria. However, in 1916 London had not only discussed the future of the Middle East with the Hashemites but had also reached an understanding with France. During a meeting between British representative Sir Mark Sykes and French official, M. F. Georges-Picot the two secretly worked out a plan to divide the Middle East, known as the Sykes-Picot Agreement. Disregarding Arab wishes, this plan gave Syria and Lebanon to France, and Iraq and Palestine to Britain.[3]

Further complicating the future of the Middle East, in the midst of the war Great Britain had made yet another commitment concerning the future of Ottoman territory. In November 1917 Foreign Secretary Lord Arthur Balfour issued the Balfour Declaration, promising British support for the establishment of a Jewish homeland in Palestine. The declaration also stipulated that "nothing should be done which might prejudice the civil and religious rights of existing non-Jewish communities in Palestine."[4]

At the postwar San Remo Conference in April 1920, the British government agreed to honor the Sykes-Picot Agreement. As a result, in June 1920 the French occupied Damascus and expelled Feisal. The embarrassed British later provided the ousted king with the Iraqi throne.[5]

After the French had expelled his brother Feisal from Syria, in November 1920 Abdullah and three hundred Bedouin moved from Mecca to Ma'an, still part of the Hejaz. According to historian Philip Robins, Abdullah's move "embodied a symbolic restatement of Hashemite political ambitions in greater Syria and beyond."[6] Abdullah announced that he intended to drive the French from Syria and return his brother to Damascus. Abdullah attracted the attention of the area's sheikhs and notables, who visited Ma'an and pledged their loyalty to him.[7] Accompanied by his supporters, in February 1921 Abdullah traveled from Ma'an to Amman where he received an enthusiastic welcome.

Colonial Secretary Winston Churchill visited Jerusalem in March 1921 and, following the advice of Colonel T. E. Lawrence, asked Abdullah to meet him there. Churchill assured Abdullah that the provisions of the Balfour Declaration would not be applied to Transjordan. As a result of these discussions, Abdullah agreed to serve as governor of Transjordan for a six-month trial period. In return for his acquiescence, he was provided with a subsidy.[8]

Although Churchill assured the new governor of Transjordan of British support for the Hashemite family, he underlined the caveat that such support excluded Hashemite rule of Syria, Palestine west of the Jordan River, and Arabia. During his visit to Jerusalem Churchill also met with Jewish leaders. He told a Zionist delegation that the British government supported their cause but also warned that it was necessary to eliminate Arab suspicion.[9] In addition, Churchill received an unhappy Palestinian Arab delegation. He underlined to the disgruntled Palestinians that the British, not the Arabs, had liberated Palestine from the Turks, and he pointed out that the graves of thousands of British soldiers were located nearby.[10]

In a final distribution of what had been Ottoman territory, the British installed Feisal as king of Iraq, and Abdullah as Amir of Transjordan—the area of Palestine east of the Jordan River, from which London had excluded Jewish settlers. Abdullah's territory covered less than forty thousand square miles, and had little water and no valuable mineral resources.[11] Historian Elizabeth Monroe later referred to the small Hashemite kingdom as "the vacant lot which the British christened the Amirate of Transjordan."[12]

Amir Abdullah formed his first government in April 1921. From the outset he remained loyal to his British connection and depended on British officers to build a reliable Bedouin military force—the Arab Legion. In 1930, John Bagot Glubb, a British officer serving in Iraq, was sent to Transjordan to organize the Legion. Abdullah and Glubb established a warm relationship.[13] In his memoirs Amir Abdullah expressed his appreciation of the Legion: "I thank God that I am able to say that I owe the greatest share of my success to this army, which does not disgrace its leaders, discourage its commanders, disappoint its people, or shirk or flinch from the defence of either its rights or those of it country. It is courageous and intrepid as well as obedient and faithful to its orders."[14]

Although Abdullah and his brother Feisal now both ruled kingdoms, in 1924 their father Sharif Hussein lost control of the Hejaz to Abdul Aziz Ibn Saud.[15] Robert Graves, the biographer of Lawrence of Arabia, noted that the Saudis, members of the puritan Wahhabi branch of Islam, had expanded their control over the entire Arabian Peninsula. Graves compared Arabia under Abdul Aziz Ibn Saud to England under Oliver Cromwell, "except that Ibn Saud is far more strict than Cromwell in keeping religious virtue among his followers." Although Great Britain had not yet interfered in Arabia, in 1922, when Ibn Saud's forces raided a village south of Amman, British airplanes frightened off the invaders in order to support Hashemite rule in Transjordan.[16]

After Sharif Hussein was forced out of the Hejaz, the British insisted that he leave the region. He was only permitted to return from exile in Cyprus to settle in Amman in 1929, after he became ill. When his father died in 1931, Abdullah's brother Ali asked the British-appointed mufti of Jerusalem, Haj Amin al-Husseini, for permission to bury his father in Jerusalem. The mufti then requested London's permission; it was granted. Arrangements for the burial of Sharif Hussein clearly underlined that Amir Abdullah lacked autonomy, that he depended on His Majesty's Government.[17]

As Abdullah established himself in Transjordan, a Palestinian national movement developed—a movement composed of several factions. Among the leaders of that movement was Haj Amin al-Husseini.

The mufti soon became Abdullah's rival for control of Palestine. Another Palestinian faction led by the Nashashibi family supported Abdullah's plan to unite Palestine and Jordan, a plan that would provide autonomy to the Palestinian Jewish community.[18]

According to historian Avi Shlaim, from the beginning of his tenure as Amir of Transjordan, Abdullah was realistic about the balance of power between the Zionist movement and the Arab national movement.[19] Following the publication of the 1930 British White Paper, limiting the sale of Palestinian land to Jews, Abdullah did not oppose permitting the Jewish Agency to purchase land in his Amirate. Transjordan always needed funds and the Jewish Agency in Palestine was a willing donor. In addition, Abdullah wanted the opportunity to illustrate that he had the ability to rule a kingdom that included a Jewish population. The British, however, interfered with Abdullah's plan insuring that the Hashemite government adopted a Nationalities Law, which prohibited the sale of land to non-nationals.[20]

Although he was sometimes annoyed by British interference with his plans, Abdullah maintained confidence in Great Britain's ability and its power. Ambassador Charles Johnston claimed that from the beginning of World War II, "Abdullah, alone of all the Arab rulers never lost faith in a British victory."[21] Upon learning that Great Britain had declared war, on September 3, 1939, Abdullah sent King George a message of support and offered his Arab Legion to His Majesty's Government.[22]

After the pro-Axis Rashid Ali al-Kailani took control of Baghdad in April 1941, political resident in Amman, Sir Alec Kirkbride, feared that the British would lose control of Transjordan because pragmatic tribal leaders would wish to move toward the Axis. Indeed, Haj Amin al-Husseini, announced his support for Hitler. The mufti fled first to Iraq and than to Berlin. However, the loyal Arab Legion fought with British forces in Iraq and achieved success. During the war the Legion expanded to include eight thousand soldiers, four times its pre-war size.[23]

Following World War II, Prime Minister Clement Attlee stated that his Labor government wished to assist the Arab states to achieve independence. At the same time, London did not want to leave a vacuum in the Middle East. Attlee had little respect for most Arab leaders, including Egypt's King Farouk. However, he considered Abdullah "an admirable man."[24]

Warm relations between London and Amman continued and in 1946 Abdullah negotiated a treaty with Great Britain. Under the provisions of the treaty Transjordan obtained independence and Abdullah assumed the title of king. Sir Alec Kirkbride, who had served as political resident from 1939 and had a very close relationship with Amir Abdullah (now King Abdullah), was appointed Great Britain's first ambassador to Jordan. Every winter Kirkbride spent weekends with the king at a royal residence in the Jordan Valley. The British ambassador later wrote that this arrangement enabled him to remain in close touch with Abdullah. In the afternoon the two men had tea, talked business, and played chess. They dined at eight o'clock and "gossiped for about an hour" before retiring.[25]

Unable to maintain order in Palestine, in February 1947 the frustrated British government decided to turn to the United Nations (UN) to decide the country's future. Publicly, every Arab leader refused to accept the possibility of the establishment of a Jewish State. Privately, alone among Arab leaders, King Abdullah was willing to work with Palestine's Zionist leadership. However, rather than acquiesce to an independent Palestinian State, Abdullah wanted to enlarge his own kingdom. Hence, both the Hashemite ruler and the Zionists shared a common enemy: Palestinian leader, Haj Amin-al Husseini. As a result, secretly Abdullah was willing to cooperate with the Zionists. "He may not have fully understood the ideology that propelled the Jews to strive so relentlessly for an independent state in Palestine, but he knew a going concern when he saw one. Abdullah and the Zionists saw in each other a means to an end."[26]

As members of the UN discussed a plan to partition Palestine and establish two independent States—a Jewish and a Palestinian—on November 10, 1947, head of the Political Department of the Jewish Agency, Golda Meyerson (later Golda Meir), visited the king. During their meeting Abdullah called Palestinian leader Haj Amin Husseini their common enemy and explained his intention to annex all of the Palestinian territory that the UN would allocate to the Arabs. In addition, he promised that Jordan would under no circumstances attack the Jews. According to Ambassador Kirkbride, sending a woman to represent Palestinian Jewry was a mistake. The king did not consider women equal to men. Hence, "his dignity would have been better served if the other side had been represented by a man."[27]

Then on November 29 the UN passed a resolution calling for the partition of Palestine, the establishment of both a Jewish State and a Palestinian State. Under pressure to maintain solidarity with his Arab brothers, the king broke his promise. Jordan joined the war against the newly established State of Israel. As the mandate ended, on May 14, 1948, Abdullah stood at the head of his troops at the eastern side of the Allenby Bridge, drew his revolver, and fired into the air shouting, "forward."[28]

Despite the UN vote to establish an independent Palestinian State, the British government was willing to support Abdullah's annexation of the territory designated for the Palestinians.[29] The additional territory that King Abdullah acquired increased the population under Hashemite rule from 400,000 to 900,000. The new population included, not only Palestinians living on the West Bank but also refugees from the regions of Palestine that became part of Israel.[30]

After the British left Palestine in May 1948, the Arab States had immediately attempted to destroy the newly proclaimed State of Israel. However, the Jewish State emerged from the hostilities with more territory than had been envisioned in the UN partition plan— but no Palestinian State was created. After discussions on the Island of Rhodes under the chairmanship of UN mediator Ralph Bunche, Amman and Tel Aviv signed an armistice agreement. Despite the earlier UN call for the internationalization of the city, Jerusalem was divided between Israel and Jordan, with the demarcation line corresponding to the November 30, 1948, cease-fire line. This line gave control of the ancient eastern section of the city to Jordan and the new western section to Israel.[31] Because the UN partition plan had called for the internationalization of Jerusalem, when Abdullah initially had moved the Arab Legion into the city, Great Britain suspended aid to the Hashemite Kingdom. In addition, Ambassador Kirkbride received instructions from London to remove all of the seconded British officers serving in the Arab Legion from active military roles in Palestine and to order their withdrawal to the East Bank of the Jordan River. Abdullah expressed his anger to Kirkbride.[32]

Under UN auspices Egypt and Israel signed an armistice agreement on February 24, 1949, and on April 3 Jordan and Israel also signed an armistice agreement. While official meetings between Jordanian and Israeli representatives took place on Rhodes, secretly the king received Israeli negotiators at his Shuneh palace. General

Moshe Dayan, who participated in the secret negotiation, stated that the king had obtained Great Britain's blessing to move directly from an armistice agreement to a peace agreement. Abdullah wanted these negotiations to be made public. London said, "no." The king complained, "in the eyes of his people he was king, but the British treated him as though they were his masters."[33]

Abdullah did not relinquish his goal: control of both East Jerusalem and the West Bank. Finally, with a nod from Tel Aviv, Washington's acceptance, and London's approval, in April 1950 the union of Arab Palestine and Jordan was announced. Hence, no Palestinian State was created.[34] Israel celebrated its second independence day on April 23, 1949, as Jordanian troops sat on the stone wall surrounding the Old City and watched through their binoculars.[35]

Approximately 600,000 to 760,000 Palestinians, 50 percent of the population, was displaced by the 1948 war. Half of those who were uprooted settled in Jordan, most on the West Bank. Large numbers were housed in refugee camps, 20 on the West Bank, and 5 on the East Bank. Palestinian refugees who entered the Hashemite Kingdom received Jordanian citizenship. Nevertheless, the displaced Palestinians in Jordan suffered from discrimination. They were not accepted into the Jordanian army's combat units or into the officers' corp. The unhappy Palestinians considered the Hashemites London's protégés, who relied on British subsidies.[36]

While, initially the United States had been actively involved in seeking resolution of the Palestinian problem, in 1949, after China fell to Mao, Washington became preoccupied with the Far East. Then, the 1950 North Korean invasion of South Korea led to the Korean War, with American forces fighting under the UN mantle. But finally, in March 1951, Assistant Secretary of State George McGhee toured the Middle East. During McGhee's visit to Amman, underlining his commitment to the West, King Abdullah expressed regret that he was unable to send his Arab Legionnaires to fight communist aggression in Korea.[37]

While the king expressed concern about communist aggression, local interests were plotting against him. Enlargement of the Hashemite Kingdom had distressed Palestinians who longed for their own state. Distraught refugees, together with established West Bank Palestinians, resented King Abdullah. As a result, it was difficult for the king to negotiate with Israel. In April 1951, a British official

explained, "However much King Abdullah may want an accommo-
dation, he does not seem to control his government and subjects as
he did in the past, and we imagine that he cannot afford to disregard
the hostility which a premature settlement with Israel would arouse
both among his own people and in other Arab States."[38]

Worried about the possibility of an attempt to assassinate the
king, British Ambassador Kirkbride asked Abdullah to stop attending weekly Friday services in Jerusalem.[39] American officials also
warned the king to exercise caution.[40] The king ignored these warn-
ings. On Friday, July 20, 1951, together with his sixteen-year-old
grandson, Hussein bin Talal, the king traveled to Jerusalem to pray
at one of Islam's holiest sites, the al-Aqsa Mosque. At the mosque a
supporter of Palestinian leader Haj Amin al-Husseini assassinated
the Jordanian ruler.[41] The assassin also fired at the young Hussein.
Although Hussein was still a student, Abdullah had earlier given him
the honorary rank of captain.[42] The bullet hit a medal on the future
king's uniform and bounced off. As the stunned Hussein stood
alone, British Air Force officer Wing Commander Jock Dalgleish
approached him and gently said, "Come with me, sir. I'll look after
you." Dalgleish flew Hussein back to Amman. The two became
good friends, and the British officer later taught the young ruler how
to pilot his own plane.[43]

After Abdullah's assassination, on July 31, Jordan's new prime
minister, Tawfiq Pasha Abdul Uda, met with U.S. Ambassador
Gerald Drew. During their meeting the prime minister told Drew
that he considered both the United States and Great Britain to be
Jordan's most important allies. He requested that Ambassador Drew
stay in close touch and provide advice.[44] On September 6 Hussein's
father, Talal bin Abdullah, was proclaimed king of the Hashemite
Kingdom. Hussein did not return to Victorian College, his British
school in Alexandria, but was sent instead to study in England, first
at Harrow, where his young cousin Iraqi King Feisal was also a student. Then in September 1952, for six months prior to returning to
Jordan, he attended Sandhurst, where he became Officer Cadet
King Hussein. According to Hussein, years before, his father had
explained to him that it was impossible to rule a country without discipline, "and nowhere in the world do they teach men discipline like
they do at Sandhurst."[45]

Ambassador Drew, who called on King Talal shortly after his
accession, reported to Washington that although there had been

concerns about the new king's mental condition, he appeared to be completely normal. "He has carried off his royal functions with all the aplomb and dignity which he inherited from his late father." Insuring the succession, his court had quickly issued a royal decree, which named the new king's son, Hussein bin Talal, crown prince. There remained concern about the poor state of the economy and some apprehension about the possibility that nationalist members of the Jordanian parliament might agitate for the abrogation of the treaty with Britain and the ejection of British officers from the Arab Legion. Nevertheless, Jordan appeared calm. The commander of the Arab Legion, John Bagot Glubb, now known as Glubb Pasha, was taking a month's vacation and British Ambassador Sir Alec Kirkbride had plans for a fishing trip to Aqaba.[46]

Unfortunately, King Talal truly was mentally ill and could not long continue to function in office. After consulting specialists, on August 11, 1952, both houses of the Jordanian Parliament held a special session, where the members voted unanimously to depose King Talal and crown his son Hussein.[47] The deposed king left Jordan for Turkey.[48] Seventeen-year-old Hussein was on vacation with his mother in Switzerland when he received word that he was now Jordon's ruler. He was alone in his Beau Rivage Hotel room looking at the swans on Lake Geneva when a hotel page brought him a cablegram. Hussein picked up the envelope, which was addressed to "His Majesty, King Hussein."[49]

CHAPTER 1

THE YOUNG KING

Prior to King Hussein's return from England to assume the throne, British officials engaged in efforts to insure a stable government and, of course, continued British influence. Among the major issues of concern was who would serve as The young king's first prime minister. It appeared that Prime Minister Tewfiq Abdul Huda would resign and that the Jordanian establishment favored Fawzi Mulki as his replacement. According to one Foreign Office official, Mulki was regarded as pro-British but weak. Hence, he could easily "fall . . . victim to opposition, with harmful effects on our own position in Jordan."[1]

As expected, in March, Prime Minister Abdul Huda announced that he planned to retire. British Ambassador in Amman, Geoffrey Furlonge considered the possibility that Abdul Huda wished to be coaxed to remain in office. However, the British ambassador decided that it was, indeed, best for the prime minister to resign. Abdul Huda already had served eighteen months in office. According to Ambassador Furlonge, Jordanians wanted change. By Middle Eastern standards, for a prime minister who was not a dictator, twenty months in office was a long period. The issue was important to Whitehall because observers would assume that London had the "final say."[2]

Ambassador Furlonge began to speculate about possible candidates for prime minister. He discussed the issue with the Commander of the Arab Legion, General Glubb Pasha.[3] On March 19 Prime Minister Abdul Huda once again visited the British ambassador to confer about Jordan's future government. He said that the young king showed considerable promise, but because of his youth he might be tempted to keep his distance from foreigners in order to prove his patriotism. In addition, Abdul Huda warned that Hussein might be attracted to the wrong Arab states. Hence, the prime minister was convinced that it would be easier to guide Hussein if he was out of office, "an unofficial adviser proffering disinterested advice." After he explained his position to the king's mother, Queen Zein, she agreed with his approach. Furlonge now understood that Abdul Huda was not truly planning to retire, but rather he wanted to become the *eminence grise* until his successors stumbled and he would then be called upon to return to office to save the kingdom.[4]

When the new king returned from Sandhurst in early April, the entire diplomatic community greeted him at the airport where a tent was set up for the occasion. American diplomat Carter Hills recalled that he stood in front of the tent in order to have a better view of the event. The young American diplomat was especially impressed with the Arab Legionnaires who paraded before the assembled dignitaries astride their camels.[5]

During his first days in Jordan, King Hussein received long lines of notables, consulted with the regency council and with his prime minister. He also visited the principal government ministries, where he asked officials questions about their work. On April 12, the king left the capital, populated by 160,000 people, to tour other sections of his kingdom, including villages on the Israeli border. After returning to Amman, the king told Ambassador Furlonge that he spoke to one of his national guard members, a man who carried a rifle but had no ammunition. In addition, the king expressed distress at the poor condition of Jordan's roads.[6] Unfortunately, Jordan was "a wretchedly poor country": Only 8 percent of its 20,000 square miles received sufficient rain to permit farming, and it had no oil. The only available minerals were salts and phosphates from the Dead Sea.[7] As a result, throughout Hussein's reign the economic situation of his kingdom remained a source of substantial concern.

Due to the success of his goodwill journey, the king decided to prolong his tour of the country. Furlonge said that Hussein made an excellent impression. Nevertheless, the British Ambassador cautioned: "He is, however, evidently a young man in a hurry, and I hope that he will not fall into the error of saying too often "something must be done about this" when the something involves the expenditure of money which Jordan has not got."[8] During his early days as ruler, Hussein remained close to his British advisers but also made a good impression on the Americans who resided in his country. Among those who observed his performance at the beginning of his reign was American diplomat Talcott Seeyle, who served in Amman from 1952 to 1954. Earlier, Seeyle's father had taught at the American University in Beirut. Several members of the king's cabinet had been his father's students. As a result, the young political officer was very careful not to take advantage of his connections. Seeyle recalled that: "we were a little apprehensive about how things would go."[9]

Continuing the tour of his kingdom, Hussein insisted on driving his own car. On April 23 Hussein arrived in East Jerusalem where he visited victims of a recent Israeli assault. Because snipers occasionally fired along the border, General Glubb insisted that the king refrain from visiting the front line. Ambassador Furlonge reported that Queen Zein, who had an excellent relationship with her son, remained in the palace spending considerable time, "wringing her hands." Perhaps it was more difficult to pacify his mother, because during a luncheon the king instead attempted to soothe the nervous British ambassador. Hussein told Furlonge that in every area he hoped for the closest possible relationship between London and Amman.[10]

Led by Fawzi al-Mulki, on May 4, the new Jordanian cabinet was installed. The following evening at a dinner for the visiting Duke of Gloucester, Prime Minister al-Mulki emphasized his intention to cooperate fully with the British and to accept Glubb's guidance on defense. King Hussein reinforced his prime minister's position and told Ambassador Furlonge that he was welcome to visit the palace whenever he deemed it necessary.[11]

Among the urgent issues the king had to consider was Jordan's relationship with Israel. Since the armistice between the two countries, Palestinians had illegally crossed from the Hashemite Kingdom into the Jewish state—some to visit their old property, others to strike at Israelis. On October 12, 1953, an Israeli mother and her two children were killed after *fedayeen* (Palestinian guerillas) threw a grenade into their house in *Tirat Yehuda*. Two days later, Israeli forces moved into Jordan and destroyed forty-two houses in the village of Qibya, killing sixty-six people, among them women and children.[12] This was only one of many such incidents. As a result, according to Seeyle, members of the United Nations (UN) armistice commission "would arrive pro-Israel and would leave very anti-Israelis."[13] Seeyle also recalled that the U.S. Central Intelligence Agency (CIA) had direct contact with the king, which was the bane of the ambassador's existence. Hussein would talk first to the CIA rather than to the U.S. ambassador.[14]

Israel's October raid on Qibya had a negative impact on Great Britain's position in Jordan. The Jordanian press pointed to the Arab Legion's absence from Qibya and claimed that the British had failed as allies. Jordanians organized strikes and demonstrations, including an emotional meeting in Ramallah on October 18, 1953.[15]

General Glubb told Ambassador Furlonge

> [t]hat it would have been a military nonsense for the Brigadier in charge to send troops on a dark night to a village undergoing a pre-pared attack by the Israel armed forces, since previous experience has shown that the latter always prepare for a counter-attack by dig-ging in round the point of assault, erecting road blocks, and mining the roads, so that the rescuing force would probably have been badly cut up.[16]

Outside Glubb's office demonstrators shouted: "Down with Glubb Pasha." Glubb complained that it was difficult to serve the Palestinians. The Arab Legion had supported them; nevertheless, they were ungrateful. Rather than assemble to protest Israel, they gathered in the streets to condemn the very soldiers who earlier had defended them.[17]

Ambassador Furlonge was distressed that the Jordanian press now had the liberty to criticize British action, or rather the absence of action. Furlonge had hoped that the Jordanian government would control the press.[18] He was equally worried about growing tension on the Israeli-Jordanian border. In addition, Washington's support for Israel now served to inflame anti-American sentiment in Jordan. And to add to the ambassador's anxiety, Jordanians continued to criticize the British for their failure to respond to Qibya.[19]

Prime Minister al-Mulki read King Hussein's Speech from the Throne on November 1. Ambassador Furlonge claimed that the king had used the speech as a vehicle to appease irresponsible ele-ments. The British diplomat was offended that although the king discussed economic development programs, which had been made possible by British loans, he did not explain the source of these funds, nor did he directly mention Great Britain in any other context.

According to Furlonge, Hussein pointed to Jordan's "obligations toward allied and friendly Governments sandwiched between two references to the bonds of friendship with Moslem and Arab League Governments."[20]

Hussein remained concerned about the security of his kingdom. Despite the UN monitored truce between Israel and Jordan, violence continued along the border. In March 1954, after an incident in the Negev, Iraq offered Jordan military assistance. Iraqi military representatives arrived in Amman in early April willing to provide one brigade. Prime Minister al-Mulki reminded his Iraqi guests that since Baghdad had not signed an armistice agreement with Israel, the presence of Iraqi troops in Jordan would provoke the Israelis and perhaps even arouse jealousy in other Arab States. As a result, Iraq agreed to send troops only in the event of an emergency. British officials discussed what to do if Iraq moved its troops into Jordan. According to Whitehall, under the terms of Great Britain's Treaty of Alliance with Iraq, Baghdad would be obligated to consult with London prior to taking such action.[21]

As the king gained experience he continued to make decisions that did not always please his British advisers. After an inquiry into the Qibya incident, he fired several officers, including his commanding officer on the West Bank, British Brigadier Teal Ashton.[22] According to one British member of the Arab Legion, the Qibya massacre was a watershed in Anglo-Jordanian relation and if the Israelis had deliberately set out to wreck those relations, they could not have planned it better.[23]

Nevertheless, the king continued to rely on British officers and his policy provided fuel for Egyptian leader Abdul Gamal Nasser, who vigorously campaigned against Hashemite rule. Nasser had been among the nationalist officers who, in July 1952, toppled King Farouk. Later in November 1954, Nasser himself became president of Egypt. The British were convinced that Nasser's plan was to destroy Jordan or at the very least have Egyptian officers replace those British officers who commanded the Arab Legion. According to British intelligence, Egypt was training terrorists to murder key British and Jordanian officials, including General Glubb and his Private Secretary Major Saleem Qawar. At the same time, British sources were concerned that the king himself was a target. From Amman, British officials confirmed that the Egyptian military attaché was in charge of the anti-Hashemite, anti-British plots but that the Jordanian Government did not have sufficient courage to expel him.[24] London noted that anti-Jordanian sentiment was growing throughout the Arab world, even in Kuwait. Whitehall wanted Hussein to send a message to the Kuwaiti ruler, Shaikh Abdullah al-Sabah, protesting anti-Jordanian activity in his Shaikhdom. The king refused, suggesting that a message from London would have more influence.[25]

Determined to defend Western interests in the Middle East, in 1955, with Washington's blessing, London established a mutual security agreement known as the Baghdad Pact, signed by Great Britain, Turkey, Iran, Iraq, and Pakistan. The major goal of the Baghdad Pact was to block Soviet expansion into the Middle East. In December, Prime Minister Anthony Eden sent Field-Marshal Sir Gerald Templer to Amman to persuade Hussein to join the pact. For the king's agreement, London made a tempting offer in return, which included extensive military assistance, with an emphasis on establishing a Jordanian air force.[26]

The king declined to join the Baghdad Pact. Broadcasts from Egypt had referred to the Baghdad Pact as a Zionist plot, and demonstrations against the pact took place in several cities, including Amman, Jericho, Hebron, and Nablus.[27] Prime Minister Eden correctly concluded that Nasser was behind Hussein's rejection of the pact.[28] Indeed, Nasser's deputy, Anwar Sadat—who in 1955 served as secretary-general of the Islamic Congress—claimed credit for limiting the pact's success. Sadat had traveled to Amman where he effectively pressed the king to reject membership.[29] Thus, as Nasser's influence rose, British influence declined.

Nasser achieved an additional victory, on March 1, 1956, when the twenty-year-old king once again fired a number of British officers, including the long-serving chief of the general staff of the Arab Legion, General John Bagot Glubb: "The dismissal came like a thunderbolt for Glubb, for British Ambassador Charles Duke and for the British Government."[30] Glubb was ordered immediately to leave the country. The king was defensive about how he dismissed Glubb. In his autobiography Hussein wrote: "I would like to point out that, though he was dismissed, he was dismissed with full honors. He was driven to the airport in my own royal car. My Defense Minister represented the Cabinet and my Chief of Diwan represented me. They both bade him good-by."[31]

Jordan's prime minister told Ambassador Duke that he assumed Glubb's departure was temporary. He hoped that the king would soon request Glubb's return. However, Glubb considered the break final; he had no intention of returning to Jordan, after he had been dismissed in such an abrupt fashion.[32] On the evening of March 1, Ambassador Duke asked the king why he had delivered such a heavy blow to Great Britain. The king said that his Arab Legion officers were unhappy. In addition, he had to fight Egyptian attacks on Glubb. According to the king, there were all sorts of articles, some even in the British press, that represented Glubb "as everything that mattered in Jordan." The British ambassador was not satisfied with the king's explanation and told Hussein that after Glubb's many years of outstanding service in Jordan the loyal officer ought not to have been treated "like a pilfering house-hold servant."[33]

Clearly, the British were offended. On March 2, Prime Minister Eden sent a message to the king saying: "I feel it my duty to tell Your Majesty that the resentment in Britain at this action will be widespread and deep."[34] Later, Eden repeated Ambassador Duke's sentiment, that Glubb had been treated as if he was a "pilfering servant." Eden wrote in his memoirs: "I am convinced now, that part of the King's sentiment towards Glubb was based on jealousy of a younger man for an older one long established in a position of authority in the country."[35]

Although he had abruptly dismissed Glubb, the king assured Ambassador Duke that he wished to maintain strong ties to Her Majesty's Government (HMG). Hussein was convinced that in the final analysis Glubb's removal would serve the best interest of both Amman and London. In addition, the king wanted those British officers who had not been dismissed to remain in place.[36] Ambassador Duke's Military Adviser, Lieutenant-Colonel Gammon, now held talks with various Jordanian officers. According to Gammon, Ali Abu Nuwar, a member of a branch of the Egyptian inspired Free Officers Organization, had led the coup against Glubb. The British Military Adviser claimed that Abu Nuwar might attempt to move Jordan into Egypt's orbit. Gammon advised that the British try to cultivate moderate Jordanian officers. At the same time, he cautioned that if the support appeared obvious it would be a "kiss of death" for them.[37]

Hoping to preserve Great Britain's role in Jordan, Ambassador Duke suggested that London offer a two thousand–pound bribe to

Abu Nuwar. Aware that Abu Nuwar had a close relationship with the king, Prime Minister Eden agreed. The Jordanian officer accepted Great Britain's bribe. Nevertheless, he remained committed to Nasser.[38]

Of course, the departure of Glubb and his colleagues enhanced the king's prestige in the Arab world, pleased Egyptian leader Nasser, and placed the king in a favorable position later in the year during the brief Anglo-French-Israeli invasion of Egypt. Meanwhile, ongoing Israeli retaliation raids against his territory frustrated the king and offended both London and Washington. In response to Israeli raids, on September 14, 1956, the king invited Baghdad to send an Iraqi division into Jordan. The Iraqi government agreed. Officially, Iraq sent troops to Jordan to protect the Hashemite Kingdom from Israel. However, the British ambassador to Iraq reported to London that Iraq's most important goal was to distance Hussein from Nasser.[39]

Washington continued to object to Israeli military actions inside Jordan. On October 15, 1956, President Dwight Eisenhower wrote in his diary that he had asked Secretary of State John Foster Dulles to tell Israeli Ambassador Abba Eban that Tel Aviv must end attacks on the Hashemite Kingdom. President Eisenhower feared that Jordan was on the verge of breaking up, and that Israeli attacks would provide an opportunity for Moscow and eventually result in Soviet intervention.[40]

Eisenhower's concern increased when the Anglo-French-Israeli invasion of Egypt began on October 29. The king immediately distanced himself further from Great Britain. On November 27 the Jordanian parliament approved a declaration that called for the end of the Anglo-Jordanian Treaty. HMG did not attempt to delay termination of the treaty. Clearly London no longer had control over either the Arab Legion or the king's foreign-policy decisions.[41] Jordan now turned to Cairo and Damascus for financial assistance, "in spite of its clear absurdity (Egypt and Syria not having any money to contribute anyway)."[42]

The word on the Jordanian street was that the British were now villains, and not to be trusted. After the end of the invasion and the conclusion of negotiations to end the Anglo-Jordanian Treaty, a three-day holiday was declared. The celebration included parades organized by various groups, including school children, the Muslim Brotherhood, and communist advocates. Although the Communist

Party was banned in Jordan, for the first time supporters openly carried banners and shouted slogans. As a component of the celebration, hundreds of thousands of shots were fired into the air. Jordanian communists loudly proclaimed their opposition to Washington. These Jordanians no longer had Amman's British connection to attack and so quickly shifted focus to their next target: the United States.[43] Washington was not pleased·

During the October 1956 Suez campaign, all British officers had been withdrawn from Jordan. The outspo ken nationalist, Major-General Ali Abu Nuwar, replaced Major-General Radi Anab, who had initially assumed Glubb's position as commander of the Arab Legion. Many Jordanians cheered the departure of British soldiers. However, their removal resulted in a shortage of experienced officers.[44]

Nasser, who now relied on Moscow for assistance, became the great Arab hero. Fearing both Egyptian and Soviet intentions, Hussein did not wish to join Cairo and become a recipient of Soviet aid. The young king turned to Washington for support. He urged his fellow Arab leaders to beware of communism and to reject propaganda "that belied our beliefs, faiths[,] and religion."[45]

Concerned with the expansion of Soviet influence, on March 9, 1957, the U.S. Congress adopted a joint resolution, known as the Eisenhower Doctrine. Earlier on January 5, President Eisenhower had addressed a joint session of Congress, during which he warned that the Soviets posed a danger to the Middle East. Endorsed by Congress, the Eisenhower Doctrine proclaimed Washington's willingness to aid any country threatened by communist aggression and provided an opportunity for Hussein, whose country had so-long relied on Great Britain "to change his foreign policy orientation away from support for a has-been power and towards a super power."[46] The American ambassador to Jordan, Lester D. Mallory, told Washington that even if he lacked popular support, Hussein would be able to maintain control as long as the Jordanian army stood behind him.[47]

Shortly after the announcement of the Eisenhower Doctrine, a few Jordanian officers who were inspired by Nasser—including Abu Nuwar—attempted a mutiny, which was quickly put down by the king. On April 13, 1957, after the king was informed of unrest at the military base in Zarqa, he rushed to the base and personally took command. His brave and timely action ended the rebellion.[48]

Explaining that he did not wish to create a martyr, Hussein decided neither to execute nor to imprison Abu Nuwar. Instead, the king permitted him to leave Jordan.[49] President Eisenhower was impressed with Hussein. He observed that the young king showed "considerable spunk."[50]

Washington considered Jordan an important barrier to the spread of radical Arab influence and communist infiltration. Hence, the White House declared that the independence of Jordan was vital to the United States. In support of the Hashemite Kingdom, the American Sixth Fleet was ordered into the eastern Mediterranean. In addition, on April 29, 1957, Jordan received a $10 million–dollar grant from Washington. According to historian Uriel Dann, the payment to Amman was an indication that the United States had indeed replaced Great Britain in Jordan. However, unlike London, Washington did not suggest policy to the king, "aside from the general assumption that the objectives of both countries tallied."[51]

Two months after Washington's grant to Jordan, Saudi Arabia's ruler, King Saud, arrived in Amman for discussions with Hussein. The traditional Hashemite-Saudi animosity no long appeared relevant. The visiting Saudi monarch also agreed to provide funds to the struggling Hashemite Kingdom. However, after providing an initial payment, the Saudis failed to follow through.[52]

Saud's visit provided Hussein with little long-term benefit. Here once again was evidence that Jordan could not depend solely on the Arab world. Although throughout his long reign King Hussein wished to work with other Arab states, his primary goal was the survival of his kingdom. In order to accomplish that goal, he often had to turn away from neighboring Arab countries and look to London or Washington. Radio Cairo provided yet another reason for Hussein to seek Western support. Claiming that the king was soft on Israel, Egyptian journalists encouraged his assassination. In an effort to help Hussein, American Secretary of State Dulles insisted that Israelis stop entering their side of the Jordanian-Israeli neutral zone, where Israel had been engaged in a project to plant trees in order to prevent erosion. Dulles understood Jordanian sensibilities, and Washington wished to underline its support for the kingdom.[53]

Then in February 1958, Egypt and Syria announced plans to unite their two countries to establish the United Arab Republic (UAR). In response to the establishment of the UAR, King Hussein and his cousin, Iraqi King Feisal, signed an agreement to join their two countries and create an Arab Union. Four years earlier when King Hussein had visited the Iraqi ruler, the British ambassador to Iraq noted that the two young men appeared truly to enjoy each other's company.[54]

Membership in the Jordanian-Iraqi Arab Union was to be open to other Arab states. Each ruler retained constitutional powers in his own kingdom, but Iraq's Feisal was designated to serve as the head of the Union. Later, referring to the two young kings, the British ambassador to Jordan, Charles Johnston wrote, "As I watched them I could not help wishing that the two cousins had been born for each others thrones. Hussein's qualities were, I felt, wasted on his troubled little kingdom. Under his rule Iraq would have really gone ahead and prospered. Whereas Iraq under Feisal . . . ? My reflections were all too soon to be borne out in practice."[55]

President Nasser sent a telegram to King Feisal congratulating him on the union. No such message was sent to King Hussein, who speculated that the absence of congratulations was Nasser's method of suggesting that "Jordan as a country and I as a king no longer counted."[56] However, the duration of the Union was brief. It was dramatically cut short after a bloody coup on July 14, 1958, resulted in the overthrow of Iraq's Hashemite monarchy. There is no evidence that Abdul Nasser personally knew in advance about it; however, there is evidence that the coup was supported by Syria, which provided the necessary financing.[57]

Stunned by the killings in Iraq that abruptly ended the Arab Union, Hussein called the murder of his cousin Feisal, "one of the heaviest blows I have thus far faced."[58] In his autobiography Hussein wrote that Nasser was responsible for the brutal overthrow of the Hashemites in Iraq. According to the grief-stricken king, the Egyptian leader wanted to dominate the Arab world and was envious of the Arab Union. "Moreover, I believe that he was astute enough to know that other Arab States would compare unfavorably what he had done with what we had done."[59]

Meeting with the British and American charges d'affaires in Amman on July 16, the king explained that he had information that a coup to topple his regime was planned for the following day. Hussein requested immediate military assistance from both London and Washington. British Prime Minister Harold Macmillan had already consulted Washington and had worked out an arrangement providing for the dispatch of British troops. Her Majesty's

Government (HMG) quickly responded to the king's request.[60] Nasser lashed out against the king. Radio Cairo continued to broadcast Egypt's strong objections to the return of British troops to Jordan. As a result of these broadcasts, which immediately reached the Jordanian street, Jordanian security men confiscated radios located in coffeehouses and arrested listeners.[61]

From Whitehall's perspective, Glubb's dismissal and the Suez crisis were no longer relevant. The British Ministry of Defense informed its commander-in-chief in the Mediterranean that the immediate task of his force was to secure the Amman airport and protect King Hussein and his government. "This is an operation in a friendly country at the invitation of and in support of a friendly Government."[62] In addition, the British asked Israel for permission to fly men and supplies to Jordan through Israeli airspace and proceeded to do so before receiving a reply. After checking with Washington, Israel agreed to London's request on the condition that no British soldier participate in any border conflict that might develop between Israel and Jordan. Prime Minister Harold Macmillan said that he planned to apologize for flying over Israeli territory but that London had not wanted to lose any time before moving toward Amman to insure the king's safety.[63]

After meeting with President Eisenhower on July 18, British Foreign Secretary Selwyn Lloyd reported to the Foreign Office that he had put forward London's request that Washington send troops to Jordan, even if only a small force. President Eisenhower explained that at present it would be difficult to convince Congress to agree. However, according to the president, in the event that serious fighting erupted in Jordan both London and Washington would unite to deal with the problem.[64]

Writing to Prime Minister Macmillan on July 18, President Eisenhower underlined that unfortunately the West had failed to counter Nasser's propaganda. He also repeated his support for Great Britain's decision to send troops to Jordan.[65] The following day Prime Minister Macmillan wrote to his secretary of state that despite the horror of the Iraqi revolution, the men now in control of Iraq might not be committed to Nasser but to Iraqi nationalism.[66] Both Washington and London agreed that King Hussein ought not to dispatch troops to Iraq.[67]

Although Washington did not send American forces to Jordan, as British troops entered the Hashemite Kingdom, the United States also became militarily involved in the Middle East. At the request of the Lebanese government, which also feared a take-over by radical elements, American troops were sent to Beirut. Lebanon's President Camille Chamoun had been delighted with the Eisenhower Doctrine and had worked to keep Lebanon allied with the West. Now he enjoyed the benefits of an American military presence.[68]

Despite the security provided by the British, King Hussein continued to press for American troops. At the same time, after the arrival of a British force of two thousand men, Prime Minister Samir al Rifai urged Great Britain to increase the number of British troops in Amman.[69] On July 23, Queen Zein called on British Ambassador Johnston and added her support to her son's request for additional forces. She advised that if more British soldiers arrived, their number should remain secret in order to provide the false impression that the total count on the ground was greater than it really was.[70]

Although the United States continued its refusal to send American soldiers to Jordan, Washington agreed to assist the British operation in every other possible way. London wanted to maintain Jordanian morale and continued to assure Amman that despite serious difficulties, the Hashemite Kingdom had the ability to maintain control.[71] Jordanian Prime Minister Samir al Rifai told British Ambassador Johnston that if British troops had arrived even a day or two later it might have been impossible to save the Hashemite Kingdom.[72]

Secretary of State Dulles met with Prime Minister Macmillan and other British officials on July 27. Dulles stated that if Jordan disintegrated, Israel would likely seize the West Bank, which could result in an Arab-Israeli war with a very dangerous chain reaction internationally. Dulles underlined that American action in Lebanon and British action in Jordan sent the Soviet Union the important message that London and Washington were prepared to protect their friends. Macmillan told Dulles that he considered it essential to obtain UN safeguards for both Amman and Beirut prior to the departure of American troops from Lebanon and British troops from Jordan. Dulles disagreed. According to the American secretary of state:

> Nothing could cancel out the fact that we had achieved our main objectives which were, not so much to preserve Jordan and the Lebanon, as to show that our friends did not call on us for help in

vain, to demonstrate to the Soviets that we could move quickly if we wished to and to show Nasser that he could not always assume that his plots could succeed without a reaction by us.[73]

At the beginning of August Whitehall decided that it was indeed necessary to increase the number of British soldiers serving in Jordan. Israeli Prime Minister David Ben Gurion had earlier urged the British to avoid flights over Israeli territory. The foreign office now asked London's ambassador to Israel to meet as soon as possible with Prime Minister Ben Gurion and explain that HMG was in the process of establishing a supply line through Aqaba.[74] Great Britain was committed to the king and Whitehall considered the worst-case scenario. The foreign office sent instructions to its embassy in Amman explaining that in the event of a coup against Hussein, British forces were not to intervene except to protect the king and other members of his family and government.[75]

Fortunately, the crisis passed quickly. On October 4 the British finalized plans for the withdrawal of their troops. But not all Jordanian factions were pleased with London's time table. Ambassador Johnston reported to Whitehall that the Bedouin faction wanted British troops to stay. King Hussein, however, was comfortable with British plans and even made arrangements to take a vacation after the British departure. He intended to fly to Rome and from their drive to Switzerland.[76] British forces completed their withdrawal from Jordan on November 2, 1958. With the permission of UAR authorities, British troops were flown from Amman over Syria en route to Cyprus.[77]

Clearly, King Hussein was occupied with grave problems, but he was an energetic young man who wanted a social life. Hence, although it was unusual for junior diplomats to become part of a ruler's social circle, King Hussein chose to socialize with others in his age group. As a result, in 1958, while on their first overseas assignment, Second Secretary at the American Embassy in Amman, Robert Keeley and his wife Louise, were invited to participate in the king's leisure activities, which included Scottish dancing and go-cart racing. As members of the king's set the Keeleys traveled in Hussein's helicopter to Southern Jordan for picnics, played canasta and charades. A lot of outings were arranged by telephone. Concerned that their phones might be tapped, the young diplomats used a code word for the king, "buffalo."

On one occasion the Keeleys invited the king to their house for dinner. He accepted the invitation. However, since he had been the target of several assassination attempts, including attempts to poison him, Hussein provided the food. Always on guard, the king discreetly carried a weapon, and at no time stood in front of a window.[78]

Although Hussein found time for pleasure, the burden of his position was ever present. In March 1959, the king made his first visit to the United States, a grand tour from coast to coast. He met with President Eisenhower, who emphasized U.S. concern with the spread of communism in the Middle East.[79] Eisenhower told Hussein that he understood that the Arabs were worried about Israel, but Eisenhower insisted that communist imperialism was the primary danger to the Middle East. The president assured Hussein that he recognized Jordan was also engaged in the struggle, that both Washington and Amman were fighting the same battle. The king told the president that Jordan needed his help. Two Arab Legion regiments still had out-dated equipment, while neighboring Arab States had "Joseph Stalin tanks." After his meeting with the king, Eisenhower considered the question of arms for Jordan. The Defense Department already had plans to ship twelve tanks to Amman. However, the Jordanians wanted more. They considered twelve tanks an insufficient number.[80]

Hussein continued to be concerned about Jordan's military and wished to obtain more tanks and additional airplanes. In April 1960, he wrote to Prime Minister Macmillan explaining his request for new equipment. He complained that London was not fulfilling his needs. Jordan's air force was using airplanes, which would soon be too old to fly. The king complained that, indeed, he was already apprehensive about their air-worthiness.[81]

The king's worries increased. On August 29, 1960, two time bombs exploded, killing Hussein's good friend, Prime Minister Hazza Majali, and ten others—among them the Under-Secretary of Foreign Affairs. It appeared that pro-Nasser activists were behind the murders. The king noted with pride that despite the shock of these deaths, within a few hours he had formed a new government with his Chief of Diwan, Bahjat al-Talhouni, serving as prime minister.[82]

Despite constant concerns about a possible assassination attempt, Hussein continued to participate in social activities and married for the second time in 1961. He met his second wife during a gathering at Shuneh, near the Dead Sea. She was the daughter of Lieutenant Colonel Walker P. Gardiner, who was attached to the British Military Mission in Amman. In 1955, at age nineteen, he had married his Hashemite cousin, Dina Abdul Hamid Al Aun, who had earned an MA degree in English Literature from Cambridge University and was a few years older than the king. Dina gave birth to a daughter, Aliya. Soon after the birth of her daughter, Dina asked a visiting British journalist if he thought that Hussein and the Jordanian people were disappointed that she had not produced an heir. The embarrassed reporter replied that every child was a blessing.[83]

Hussein's first marriage had only lasted for eighteen months. Prior to the king's marriage to twenty-year-old Toni Avril Gardiner, fearing that the king's choice of a Western bride might offend some Arabs, British Ambassador John Henniker-Major attempted to persuade the king not to marry an English woman.[84] The king ignored the ambassador's advice. Toni Gardiner converted to Islam, and the king selected a new name for his bride, Muna al Hussein, meaning "Hussein's wish." At a press conference before the wedding, the king was asked if he had considered that marrying an English women likely increased the danger to his life. Hussein replied, "I have never been afraid of anything. I have my belief in God, my belief in myself and my belief in my people."[85]

King Hussein did, of course, continue his attempts to maintain good relations with his brother Arab states. However, after the newly independent Amirate of Kuwait was threatened by Iraq in 1961, British Ambassador to Jordan Henniker-Major noted that Jordanians had no sympathy for wealthy Gulf Arabs. According to Henniker-Major, "Of moral indignation at the threat to a small and independent country, there was hardly a trace."[86] Despite the absence of warmth between Jordanians and Kuwaitis, relations between the Hashemites and the ruling Al-Sabah family remained sound. In February 1962, the Jordanian Military Academy accepted fifteen officers from Kuwait into its training program. The Kuwaiti government had decided to send their future military leaders to Amman because Jordan appeared to offer suitable training for Arabic speakers with limited military experience. An American charge d'affaires in Amman, Dayton Mak, noted that as a result, perhaps the wealthy oil state would provide more financial assistance to the needy Hashemite Kingdom.[87]

Tension among Arab countries remained high until the end of 1963, when Egyptian leader Nasser called for a summit meeting of Arab leaders. Nasser had a new agenda, a program to unite all of the Arab states, regardless of ideological or political differences. Relations between King Hussein and President Nasser slowly improved. But Hussein had to pay a substantial price, which would later haunt him. He agreed to accept formation of the Palestine Liberation Organization (PLO) and the Palestine Liberation Army (PLA). He also accepted Egyptian leadership in issues dealing with inter-Arab relations as well as the formation of a United Arab Command under an Egyptian commander.[88]

Israel, of course, remained the common enemy of all of the Arab states and Palestinian raids from Jordanian territory into Israel continued. Although both London and Washington had assured Israel that King Hussein was trying to prevent *fedayeen* from crossing into Israel, on November 13, 1966, Israel launched a massive operation to strike at the West Bank village of Samu.[89] According to Israel's future minister of defense, General Moshe Dayan, Samu (located near Mount Hebron) was a base for saboteurs. Hence, the raid was a response to Arab mines, which the previous day had killed Israeli soldiers patrolling the Israeli-Jordanian border.[90]

Israeli troops confronted the Jordanian army at Samu, resulting in numerous casualties and the Israeli destruction of a large number of homes, a school, and a Mosque. Although initially, the Israelis had intended a quick action, their attack developed into a pitched battle. Unfortunately, the Samu raid undermined the king, who appeared unable to protect his people. Israel's ambassador to the UN, Abba Eban, acknowledged to U.S. Ambassador Arthur Goldberg that the raid on Samu had been a serious mistake.[91] Inflamed by their losses and their animosity toward Israel, West Bank Palestinians reacted with riots directed against Hussein.[92]

Simultaneously, Syria, Egypt, and the PLO maligned Hussein, claiming that he was an agent of Israel. From Cairo a PLO broadcast called on Jordan's army to rebel against Hashemite rule. Shouting slogans denouncing the king, residents from nearby refugee camps entered Ramallah demanding arms. Hundreds were arrested. Nevertheless, riots also erupted in Jerusalem. The army fired at the troublemakers, wounding approximately forty people. Unrest spread to Hebron and Nablus. Throughout the West Bank, photographs of the king were torn down and destroyed.[93]

Washington sympathized with the king and censured Israel for its attack on Samu. Then at the UN Security Council the United States voted to condemn the raid. Late in the evening of December 10, the king summoned U.S. Ambassador Findley Burns to his Homar residence, where the two met for an hour. At this juncture Hussein's representative, Major General Amer Khammash, the Chief of Staff of Jordan's Armed Forces, had been in Washington for a week seeking arms. As yet, Khammash had no American commitment. Burns had never before seen the king so upset or so obviously under pressure. With tears in his eyes, he told Burns that discontent on the West Bank was increasing rapidly. Hussein claimed that the serious divisions between the two banks of his kingdom had ruined his dreams. He even expressed concern that the army was losing confidence in him. The king remarked that enemies, both within and outside his country, surrounded him. These enemies, including Syria, were sending terrorists and arms into Jordan. The king warned that time was running out for him; he needed immediate American support.[94]

Acting Secretary of State Nicholas Katzenbach informed President Lyndon Johnson that he had discussed American aid to Jordan with Israeli Foreign Minister Abba Eban. The Israeli candidly admitted that his country had as much of a stake in preserving the Hashemite Kingdom as Washington did.[95] President Johnson privately assured the king of American commitment to his kingdom's security, and the United States airlifted $4.7 million of military supplies into Jordan in December 1966.[96]

Hussein's government ordered the closure of Jerusalem's PLO office on January 3, 1967, and immediately arrested its staff members. Soon after, Amman informed the Arab League that since the overthrow of the king was now a PLO objective, Jordan had withdrawn its recognition of that organization.[97] Egypt joined in the protest against Hussein, claiming that rather than inviting Iraqi and Saudi troops to protect the West Bank, he had abandoned the region to Israeli assault. Then in a speech on February 22, 1967, Nasser— "punning on the Arabic word for king (*'abil*)—called Hussein the "whore (*'abir*) of Jordan."[98]

CHAPTER 2

MANAGING DEFEAT

As animosity between Hussein and Nasser grew, raids into Israel continued—some from Jordanian territory and others from Syria. On May 16, 1967, apparently responding to a Soviet message that Israel was preparing for war against Syria, Nasser asked the United Nations (UN) to remove the international forces that had been stationed in the Sinai near the Israeli-Egyptian border since 1957. Unfortunately, UN Secretary General U Thant did not stall but quickly ordered the UN troops to depart. As a result, Israel began to mobilize its forces.[1] After moving his troops into the Sinai and occupying Sharm al-Shaikh, on May 22 Nasser announced an embargo on Israeli shipping: "It was obvious to all that this was a *casus belli*."[2]

Suddenly, Egyptian-Jordanian relations improved. Calling Israel the enemy of all Arabs, on May 30, 1967, King Hussein traveled to Cairo to sign a Defense Pact with Egypt.[3] Chief of the royal court, Wasfi al-Tall, had begged Hussein not to become involved. The king insisted that he had no choice. He did not wish to be branded as a traitor to the Arab cause.[4] When the king returned home from Cairo, *The Palestine News*, published in Jordanian-controlled Jerusalem, proclaimed: "The heart of the Arab Nation pumps faster than the pen can record, the head spins webs of triumphant possibility beyond the competence of the fastest computer, the soul of the Arab Nation soars high into regions of ecstasy unknown to the most advanced rocketeers."[5]

Israel's minister of foreign affairs, Abba Eban, referred to the king's trip to Cairo as the final step that ensured the inevitability of war. Prior to Hussein's meeting with Nasser, Israeli military plans had clearly provided for leaving Jordan out of the conflict: "Hussein had now thoughtlessly renounced this immunity."[6] The king's cousin, commander of a tank brigade, Zaid bin Shaker, stated that the king had to go to war with Israel or confront civil war at home. However, according to Hussein's biographer Peter Snow, the king's decision was based on emotions: "For Hussein, it was not just a matter of expediency, it was a claim on his honour."[7] Later, Secretary of State Dean Rusk referred to Jordan's decision to go to war as "one of the sadder moments" of the crisis.[8]

In her memoirs the king's widow, Queen Noor, who married Hussein in 1978, wrote that the 1967 war was the king's "greatest sorrow." When Hussein discussed that war with her, he had tears in his eyes. Like his grandfather, Abdullah, who had gone to war against Israel in 1948, Hussein recognized that the Arab armies could not prevail against the better-equipped and better-trained Israeli army. According to Noor, both her husband and his grandfather had understood that the solution to the conflict had to be political rather than military.[9]

Although, of course, the king's move distressed Israelis, it pleased his own people, especially the Palestinians. Thousands of Jordanians marched through the streets of Jerusalem carrying photographs of both King Hussein and President Nasser. The crowd shouted slogans, including, "Palestine is Arab."[10] On June 1 an editorial in the *Palestine News* expressed pleasure at the signing of the agreement between the king and the president of the United Arab Republic, but the editor warned, "this is the beginning not the end of a struggle to the death with the vermin of Tel Aviv."[11] Now claiming, "we are brethren in Jihad" the king requested that the inhabitants of Jordan put aside their differences and prepare for battle.[12] Later, reporter Mohammad Jeelani wrote that the king's words inspired those who longed to see Jaffa, Haifa, and Nazareth in addition to the remaining Occupied Territory, which for more than nineteen years had been controlled by Israel.[13]

On the morning of June 5, 1967, the Israeli air force hit Egyptian airfields in the Sinai. However, Israel had no desire to attack Jordan and requested that the head of the UN Truce Supervisory Organization, General Odd Bull, persuade Hussein to stay out of the war. King Hussein answered the request with artillery shells fired into Israeli agricultural settlements and long-range guns fired into the coastal strip, hitting the areas near the population centers of Tel Aviv, Petah Tikva, Nathanya, and Lod. At the same time, from East Jerusalem the Jordanians fired into Jewish West Jerusalem. After the shelling began, U.S. Consul General to Jerusalem, Evan Wilson, phoned his Tel Aviv Embassy to report that a projectile had hit 150 feet from his office.[14] As the shells continued to fall, West Jerusalem's mayor, Teddy Kollek, who had arrived in his office wearing a white shirt, returned home to change into a darker color, so that he would not be an easy target.[15]

Together with their Egyptian and Syrian brothers, the Jordanians shared in the misery of defeat. British Ambassador to Israel Michael Hadow explained that the Israelis had wished to avoid the war. Jordan had a different perspective: "To King Hussein it was some sort of gallant and romantic game."[16] According to Israeli scholar Moshe Zak, King Hussein's decision to participate in the war so enraged Israel that on the first day of hostilities, its planes bombed King Hussein's palace.[17]

West Bank residents did not know how to react. At the beginning of the Six-Day War, Palestinian Ziad Abu Ziad, a Jordanian civil servant, was sitting in his East Jerusalem office. A twenty-seven-year-old lawyer who had been trained in Damascus, Abu-Ziad served as supervisor of immigration and passports. Confused about what action to take, he asked the Jordanian governor. The governor had no instructions. Abu Ziad and the other members of his staff scattered. Public transportation had stopped. Abu Ziad walked to his home six kilometers away and hid with his relatives. Many neighbors had fled to the mountains and others had crossed to the East Bank. Afterward, it was very difficult for those who had crossed the Jordan River to return home.[18]

In London, on June 5, Israel's ambassador, Aharon Remez, had called on a pro-Israel cabinet minister, Richard Crossman. Crossman inquired about Israeli intentions toward Jordan. Remez replied that Israel intended to occupy the triangle and the Samarian hills but not the entire West Bank. Remez explained that his country did not wish to increase its Arab population by six hundred thousand. Ambassador Remez assured Crossman that Israel supported the survival of King Hussein. The Israeli asked Crossman to send a message to the king warning him not to commit all of his troops to battle against Israel. According to Remez, Jordan might need its forces to defend the Hashemite Kingdom against Nasser.[19]

Despite Remez's earlier assurance, Israel occupied the entire West Bank and East Jerusalem. In addition, the Jewish State controlled the Syrian Golan Heights and the Egyptian Sinai. King Hussein was broken hearted. Speaking on Amman radio he said, "My brothers, I seem to belong to a family, which, according to the will of Allah, must suffer and make sacrifices for its country without end. Our calamity is greater than anyone could have imagined. But whatever its size, we must not let it weaken our resolve to regain what we have lost."[20]

A future British ambassador to Jordan, Glen Balfour-Paul, later wrote that no Arab leader, regardless of his distaste for the Palestinians and the Palestine Liberation Organization (PLO), would ever accept the loss of Arab Jerusalem or the West Bank: "This millstone is inexorably round their necks, and therefore round the world's."[21] All Muslims mourned the loss of Jerusalem.

The immediate shock of defeat was especially traumatic for residents of the now Israeli-occupied West Bank. However, although Hashemite rule had ended, Jordanian civil servants on the West Bank, including Abu Ziad, did not have to worry about finding new jobs. King Hussein declared that all of his civil servants would continue to receive their salaries. Initially, Abu Ziad assumed that the West Bank would quickly be returned to Jordan. He was certain that the Israelis would rapidly withdraw. The Palestinians on the West Bank waited impatiently for international initiatives, for UN action.[22]

At the end of June the British embassy in Amman reported to London that the king still did not accept that the Palestine problem had no military solution. He now wanted new military equipment and at the same time a diplomatic victory, the return of some portion of his lost territory: "He may well judge that alignment with Nasser and the Russians offers him the best prospects of obtaining these objectives."[23] Although the Jordanian public was disillusioned with Nasser, Radio Jordan broadcast programs that echoed those originating in Cairo and Damascus—frequent messages that called Israel, Great Britain, and the United States enemies of the Arab peoples. Even the music broadcast was exclusively Egyptian.[24]

Nevertheless, the Jordanian monarch was most anxious for American assistance and at the end of June, after addressing the UN General Assembly, the king traveled to Washington, DC, to meet with President Lyndon B. Johnson. Prior to his arrival, presidential adviser Walt Rostow suggested that the president point out to the king that before the June war Washington had tried unsuccessfully to prevent him from signing a pact with Nasser and accepting an Egyptian commander. Rostow suggested that the president underline that now he was unable to convince Israel to withdraw from the West Bank, "unless there are serious things that you are prepared to do in return." Rostow also advised the president to say, "Do not rely on any outside force to solve this problem for you;

neither the United Nations General Assembly, nor the UAR [United Arab Republic], nor the Russians, nor the Americans."[25]

After discussions in Washington, the King traveled to England. Before his arrival, on June 30, Israeli Ambassador Aharon Remez and his aide Yeshayahu Anug called on Foreign Secretary George Brown. According to the Israeli ambassador, during the recent war Israel had captured Jordanian orders "dated 25 or 26 May which called for the massacre of all inhabitants in areas to be occupied by Jordanian forces." Israel intended to publish these documents. However, Ambassador Remez was not certain that King Hussein was aware of the orders, which compared unfavorably with those captured from Egypt. The Israeli ambassador told Foreign Secretary Brown that Israel had no objection to Great Britain raising the issue of these orders during the king's upcoming visit.[26] Meanwhile, the British embassy in Amman recommended that in discussions with the king the Foreign Office emphasize the obvious: Israel had decisively defeated the Arab armies. No available evidence suggested that a future battle would provide a different result: "There is therefore no future in pursuing the will o' the wisp of a grand alliance supported by Russian arms."[27]

Arriving in England on July 1, the king spoke to the press at the airport. Reporters questioned Hussein about what was known as the "big lie," the accusation popular in the Arab world that the United States and Great Britain had militarily intervened on Israel's side during the Six-Day War. The king "was satisfactorily categorical in saying that he did not now believe that there had been any physical intervention."[28] At the same time, from Tel Aviv the British embassy reported that the Israeli government was considering the possibility that rather than reunification with Jordan, the Palestinians on the West Bank might prefer an entity of their own. This Palestinian entity would be the link between Israel and East Bank Jordan that might enable King Hussein, if not to come to a deal with Israel, then at least to come to a deal with the Palestinian entity.[29] From Tel Aviv, British Ambassador Michael Hadow emphasized the importance of American influence in Israel. He said that it was wise for London to keep in step with Washington and not permit the Arabs to exploit any possible differences between the two. Ambassador Hadow reported that Israeli opinion doubted that King Hussein would be ousted. However, if he was removed Tel Aviv would probably press for a Palestinian State on the West Bank.[30] Meanwhile, the Foreign Office speculated that if Jordan moved away from the other Arab States and made a separate peace with Israel, such a peace "would finish Hussein." Most likely he would be assassinated.

The king met with Prime Minister Harold Wilson and Foreign Secretary George Brown at 10 Downing Street on July 3. Prior to that meeting a brief prepared for the prime minister and the secretary of state emphasized that Great Britain had attempted to avert the Six-Day War. "The fact is that President Nasser engaged in the most dangerous kind of brinkmanship in pursuit of a diplomatic success for himself, which ended by bringing disaster on the Arabs. It is others who have paid the price of his irresponsibility. We hope that His Majesty now recognizes our sincerity in what we are trying to do. In particular, we are glad to hear that he gives no credence to the lies that were spread about our intervening in the fighting."[31] During his discussions with British officials, the king "strongly repudiated the allegation that Jordanian troops had orders to massacre Israelis in areas they occupied." At the same time after saying that the Israeli allegation was false, "he qualified this with the words as far as I am aware."[32]

On July 6 the British ambassador to the United States was invited to visit the under-secretary of state for political affairs, Eugene Rostow. The ambassador reported that the American under-secretary was "at his woolliest"—that it was difficult to evaluate if he was simply thinking aloud or if he was presenting the State Department's position. Rostow recognized that King Hussein would have to work diligently to maintain his position within a truncated Jordan but claimed that the king was the main source of hope for a settlement. The State Department official also noted that he had just lunched with the visiting governor of the Bank of Israel, David Horowitz, who said that the Israelis were trying to persuade the Jordanians to reopen their banks located in the occupied West Bank. Horowitz also confided to Under-Secretary Rostow that he was attempting to convince the Israeli government to buy the Sinai Peninsular. The idea of Israel buying the Sinai Peninsular led a British official to quip, "no doubt the Louisiana and Alaskan precedents were fresh in his mind on arrival in the United States!"[33]

No Arab state was prepared to negotiate with Israel. Meeting at the end of August, the leaders of the Arab world adopted the Khartoum Resolution on September 1, 1967. They agreed to say "no" to peace with Israel, "no" to recognition of Israel, and "no" to negotiations with Israel. In return for accepting the Khartoum Resolution, King Hussein was promised aid from his oil-rich Arab neighbors.[34]

While the Arabs lamented their lost territories, Israel celebrated its victory. For the first time since 1948 Jews had access to their East Jerusalem holy sites. Despite the 1949 Jordanian-Israeli armistice, which had guaranteed Jews passage to their religious shrines, prior to Israel's military victory, Jordanian authorities had ignored the armistice provision and denied entry to Jews.[35] Now the triumphant Israelis had no inclination to return their newly acquired territories.

For Jordan and the Muslim world, the Israeli conquest of the Temple Mount in East Jerusalem—holy to both Jews and Muslims— was among the most painful aspects of defeat. Jews considered the Temple Mount to be the site of their ancient temple that had been destroyed by the Romans in 70 CE. Muslims considered the site to be the location where the Prophet Mohammad ascended to heaven. Cognizant of the site's significance to all Muslims, on his first visit to the holy spot, General Dayan ordered removal of the Israeli flag, which victorious troops had placed over the Dome of the Rock. Dayan also declared the scared site off limits to Israeli soldiers. Although Israel annexed the old city, on June 17, 1967, Dayan returned the Temple Mount to Muslim control.[36] While Dayan's gesture irritated some Jews it did not at all satisfy Muslim opinion.

Israelis respected both Muslim and Christian holy sites, but at the same time, continued to offend the Arab population by how they chose to commemorate their 1967 victory. In April 1968, the U.S. embassy in Amman sent the State Department a message from the Jordanian government protesting Israel's plans to celebrate its independence day with a military parade, which would move through the occupied section of Jerusalem. Amman considered the planned parade a serious provocation and pointed out that although the armistice agreement ending the Six-Day War prohibited entry of heavy military equipment into Jerusalem, Israel intended to use such equipment in the parade.[37] Nevertheless, the Israeli government ignored protests and the parade took place. Jordanian complaints against Israel's presence in Jerusalem continued. On May 1, Under-Secretary of State Eugene Rostow met with one of Israel's victorious generals, now ambassador to the United States, Yitzhak Rabin. The State Department had learned that on May 26 Israel would celebrate Jerusalem Reunification Day. Rostow told Rabin that Washington was concerned that the Israeli celebration would cause a violent Arab reaction.[38]

Determined to keep all of Jerusalem, Israel ignored American complaints. American officials in Jerusalem continued to document Arab unhappiness. Arabs living in Jerusalem remained united in their desire for an end to Israeli occupation. After the *Knesset* (parliament) passed a law, which made residents of Arab Jerusalem residents of Israel, these Arabs protested. East Jerusalem's Arabs asked to be treated according to the Geneva Convention, as persons living under occupation; they did not wish to become residents of Israel.[39]

Washington's special envoy to the Middle East, former Governor of Pennsylvania William Warren Scranton, visited Amman in early December 1968. The king told Scranton that despite his previous problems with President Nasser, the two were now working closely together and he was convinced that Nasser wanted an end to the conflict. Although the king admitted that he was uncomfortable with Iraqi troops remaining in his country and with the presence of armed *fedayeen*, Hussein appeared confident that he would be able to maintain control.[40] At the end of December the U.S. ambassador again raised the question of Iraqi forces stationed in Jordan. Hussein insisted that he was carefully watching them: "We are penetrating them instead of having them penetrate us." Unfortunately, however, the *fedayeen* remained a source of concern. In addition, Hussein was unhappy to learn that Israel would soon receive new warplanes. Shortly before U.S. Ambassador Harrison M. Symmes met with the king, Washington announced conclusion of an agreement to sell Phantom jets to Israel. Hussein was certain the agreement would have a negative impact on the Middle East.[41]

Prior to leaving office on December 25, President Johnson sent a farewell letter to the king. Johnson wrote, "I reaffirm my great admiration for your wise leadership, gallantry and courage which have been so severely tried over the past months. I wish you success in your determination to bring peace, justice and prosperity to your people."[42]

A State Department memorandum, written at the beginning of 1969, set out Washington's commitment to Amman. In the previous fifteen years the United States had provided one-half billion dollars and had assured the Hashemites of support for the integrity of their kingdom. According to diplomat Talcott Seelye, during the Six-Day War Jordan lost more than any other Arab state. Seeyle erroneously predicted that if a peace agreement was not concluded within a year, it was unlikely that the present regime would survive. Seelye pointed to the cycle of *fedayeen* raids, which led to Israeli reprisals and claimed that the *fedayeen* were so popular that Jordan could not risk a total clampdown on their activities. However, Seelye noted that the king had the advantage of a loyal army and that his Bedouin troops would support him. Washington had agreed to re-equip the Jordanian military and would deliver approximately $100 million worth of equipment within the next three years. However, Washington had agreed to that arms package only after the king threatened to turn to Moscow, the arrangement left "sour taste with Jordanians." In addition, the United States refused to provide Jordan with some of the weapons it requested, including 155mm artillery guns.[43]

Hussein was not satisfied. According to the king, Washington did not sufficiently restrain Israel. An April 1969 State Department memorandum, prepared in anticipation of an official visit by Hussein to Washington, stated that since the 1967 war the king had been extremely disappointed with American Middle East policy. Moving Washington away from Israel appeared impossible.[44]

The unhappy king continued to claim that the United States had done little for him and that Washington had given Israel priority attention to the direct detriment of Amman. At the same time, in the spring of 1969, the king appeared prepared to consider some concessions to Israel but was unwilling to give Israel the right to retain troops on the West Bank or along the Jordan River. According to the State Department, the king hoped that Washington would bail Jordan out of its unfortunate situation by convincing Israel "to lower the price."[45]

Nevertheless, prior to Hussein's visit to Washington, the State Department assured President Nixon that "Hussein, in the best Arab tradition, will be above all conscious of his guest-host relationship with you and it will be uppermost in his mind to preserve a calm and courteous atmosphere during your talks, no matter what differences appear to arise or what contentious issues are discussed."[46]

Jordan's prime minister warned, in July 1969, that the more radical groups among the *fedayeen* appeared to be increasing their influence. He doubted that his government would be able to stop their activity against Israel. Ambassador Symmes now talked to the king about the continuing attacks on Israel from Jordanian territory. Hussein said that he understood the seriousness of the situation and was determined to control the *fedayeen*, but as he had previously explained, in order to do so he needed more time and additional military equipment.[47]

State Department intelligence memorandum predicted a possible showdown between the Jordanian army and the *fedayeen*.[48] In the summer of 1969 the Fifth National Conference of the General Union of Palestinian Students was held in Amman, the first such conference since the Six-Day War. Approximately 150 delegates attended. One goal of the conference was to unify the various *fedayeen* organizations under the Palestine Armed Struggle Command. The highlight of the conference was the appearance of Fatah leader Yasser Arafat, who was greeted with great enthusiasm. Arafat's reception clearly emphasized that he was the foremost leader of the Palestinian resistance movement.[49]

American officials closely monitored the political situation in Jordan. At the beginning of August, an American team advised the State Department that Washington should airlift the automatic rifles that the king had requested as soon as possible. Clearly, the *fedayeen* were a danger to his regime. The team reported that its members were confident that regardless of how other Arab countries viewed the *fedayeen*, Hussein would work hard to check them. The king was in the midst of a recruiting campaign to enlarge his military; salaries for recruits were increased and opportunities for promotion expanded.[50] *Fedayeen* anger could not easily be contained. Washington's support for Israel was a spur to action. During August, the Palestinians began to direct their activities against the U.S. embassy in Amman. Approximately two thousand demonstrators, mostly young men, gathered around the embassy. Stones broke one window before Bedouin troops fired into the air.[51]

Further inflaming Arab emotions, on August 21, 1969, a fire broke out in Jerusalem's Al-Aqsa Mosque. The fire, which burned for more than three hours, severely damaged the southern part of the ceiling, the twelfth century pulpit, and the walls. Amman sent a telegram to the UN Security Council, saying, "a new Israeli grave act of lawlessness which has shaken the conscience of mankind was committed against Al-Aqsa Mosque, one of the holiest places of Islam. The Jordan Government holds the Israeli authorities responsible for this horrible crime."[52] An Australian tourist had started the fire. He was tried in an Israeli court and found insane. However, despite the clear evidence against the perpetrator, legal proceedings did nothing to calm Arab emotions. According to the British consul in Jerusalem, John Lewen, who had previously referred to the Israeli unification of Jerusalem as the *anschluss*, the Arabs continued to consider the Israelis responsible. The fire served to increase Arab resentment against Israel further and became an additional factor in the on-going political warfare.[53]

Lack of progress toward a settlement of the Arab-Israeli conflict depressed the king. British Secretary of State Goronwy Roberts met with King Hussein on October 1. According to Hussein, the strategic balance was in Israel's favor and would likely remain so in the future. Discussing the foreign troops still stationed in his country, Hussein claimed that he was not worried about the presence of Iraqi forces but was concerned about the growing numbers of *Saiqa* members arriving from Syria. *Saiqa* (thunderbolt), a guerrilla unit primary composed of Palestinian volunteers from the Syrian Army, was politically aligned with the Syrian Baath Party, but served under the PLO.[54]

During his visit, Secretary of State Roberts asked Hussein about the status of the Soviet offer to provide aid to Jordan. The king replied that the Soviets had not renewed their offer, which had been made more than a year before. However, in the event that neither the British nor the Americans were willing to provide the weapons he needed, the shrewd king again warned that he would have to accept Soviet arms.[55]

A month after his conversation with the British secretary of state, dressed in military uniform, the king spoke to his National Assembly. Of course, the king wanted to reach out to his people, to maintain the support he had, but he also wished to attract dissatisfied elements, those who might be losing confidence in the monarchy. As Hussein began to speak, his audience was reserved. However, as the king praised the *fedayeen* and criticized Washington, the audience responded positively, even enthusiastically. The U.S. embassy in Amman noted the king's criticism of Washington but stated that he had earlier made the same critical remarks in private. Now for the first time, he was publicly finding fault.[56] Ambassador Symmes reported to Washington that given Hussein's mood, the State Department should avoid pushing him toward the Soviets. Symmes cautioned that it would be a mistake to jeopardize the king's commitment to a peaceful settlement. Hence, it was prudent to avoid doing anything that might irritate him.[57]

Also cognizant of the king's difficult position, British officials attempted to avoid distressing him. Reminiscing about his experiences in Jerusalem, retired British diplomat John Snodgrass—who served as British consul general from autumn 1970 until early 1974—noted that the British consulate in Jerusalem maintained two offices: one in Arab East Jerusalem, the other in Jewish West Jerusalem. According to Snodgrass, as the basis for the official British presence in Jerusalem, London held onto the *Corpus Separatum*, which had been set up for the Jerusalem-Bethlehem area. However, the *Corpus Separatum* was rejected by Israel, which considered a unified Jerusalem to be its eternal capital. Hence, the Israeli government tried to encourage all embassies to move from Tel Aviv to Jerusalem, but at the same time, did not attempt to argue against the legality of foreign consulates remaining in Jerusalem. The British considered it important that the Americans maintained their consulate general there, because as long as the Americans did, the Israelis would be unlikely to close them all down.[58]

Prior to the Six-Day War, Great Britain had loaned the East Jerusalem municipality funds for the construction of roads adjacent to its consulate general in Sheikh Jarrah. After losing control of Jerusalem, Amman stopped paying the installments due on that loan.[59] The British government still wished to be repaid and considered asking Israel to assume responsibility for the Jordanian debt. However, the political problems involved in requesting repayment were especially delicate. London did not recognize Israel's right to extend its jurisdiction to East Jerusalem, except as an occupying power. Therefore, if Great Britain asked Israel to repay the loan, Tel Aviv would likely publicize the British request. Jordan would be offended and Great Britain's standing in the Arab world would be damaged.[60]

Intending to show American support for the king, in the spring of 1970 Washington scheduled a visit to Amman for Under-Secretary of State Joseph Sisco. However, on April 15 students in Jordan gathered to protest Sisco's upcoming visit. At the same time, *fedayeen* groups called for a general strike and emphasized their wishes by threatening storekeepers who did not voluntarily shut their doors. Approximately eight hundred demonstrators congregated at the embassy shouting anti-American slogans, including "SISCO GO HOME."

About forty to fifty boys swarmed around the chancery building, breaking what windows they could, and destroying air conditioning units and other appurtenances. Upon reaching the parking lot, they smashed four embassy vehicles with stones and cement blocks, and set fire to them. They broke into unbarred General Services Officers (GSO) buildings, smashed up desks and typewriters, and scattered files.[61]

A Jordanian army captain told Ambassador Symmes that the *fedayeen* wanted the embassy's American flag removed. The ambassador refused. After uprooting the embassy garden, demonstrators tore down the flag and replaced it with a Palestinian flag. Those who had taken the American flag cut it into small pieces: "You could buy a piece of the American flag down in the *souk*." Demonstrators also burned the books located in the American Cultural Center. The fire was so strong that the library's iron shelves melted.[62]

On the second day of the demonstration, Ambassador Symmes, who had earlier tried unsuccessfully to reach the foreign minister, the prime minister, and the king, finally was able to contact Jordanian officials. Symmes asked if the Jordanian government planned to permit continuation of anti-American protests. The foreign minister explained that the previous evening he had met with *fedayeen* leaders, who promised that the demonstrations would remain peaceful. American officials lacked confidence in that promise. Ambassador Symmes stated that it might not be prudent for Under-Secretary of State Sisco to visit Jordan.[63] King Hussein insisted that despite the anti-American demonstrations, Sisco would be safe in the Hashemite Kingdom. He strongly objected to the ambassador's suggestion that Sisco's visit be postponed.[64]

In Washington, Acting Assistant Secretary Roger P. Davies expressed concern to Jordanian Ambassador Abd al-Hamid Sharaf. A relative of King Hussein, the young Jordanian ambassador had graduated from the American University in Beirut (AUB) and after his appointment in Washington had entered Georgetown University's doctoral program in political science, where he planned to write his thesis on the Jarring peace mission. Swedish Ambassador Gunnar Jarring had been appointed by the UN Secretary General to broker an Arab-Israeli peace and in early 1968 had arrived in the Middle East.[65] Ambassador Sharaf agreed with Secretary Davies that American concern was justified but also expressed the wish that despite the demonstrations, Under-Secretary of State Sisco, then in Israel, not cancel his planned visit to Jordan.[66] But American diplomats in Amman continued to have misgivings. Before Sisco had an opportunity to cross the Allenby Bridge into Jordan, Ambassador Symmes advised him to defer his scheduled stop in Amman.[67] The political counselor at the U.S. embassy, Morris Draper, transmitted the message to Hussein. The king was offended. He claimed that he had not had a fair hearing from Ambassador Symmes. Draper explains, "It was bad."[68]

Later, in the day, however, it seemed that cancellation of Sisco's visit had been unnecessary. The Jordanian capital appeared to be almost back to normal; shops opened and while large numbers of *fedayeen* remained on the street, most congregated around their headquarters.[69] Disappointed that Sisco had opted out the king expelled the U.S. ambassador.[70] This action annoyed Washington but did not placate the *fedayeen*. According to American Middle East military expert Norvell De Atkine, Hussein's expulsion of Ambassador Symmes was an unsuccessful attempt to appease the increasingly strident demands of the Palestinian militants in Jordan.[71] But perhaps it was also an attempt to restore his wounded honor.

Arab passions were further enraged by Israel's decision to hold its Independence Day military parade in Jerusalem once again. On May 2, 1970, the UN Security Council passed a resolution expressing disapproval of the Israeli decision. The British government was now concerned that Arab States would continue emotional discussion in the Security Council, interfering with any chance the Jarring Mission had of arranging a peace agreement. London wished to point out to King Hussein that their common objective was progress through the Jarring Mission. Hence, endless Security Council discussion was unwise.[72]

At the same time, Under-Secretary Sisco's failure to stop in Jordan remained an issue. During a meeting in Washington with Sisco on May 14, advisor to the king, Zaid al-Rifai—now acting as His Majesty's personal emissary—again expressed disappointment that Sisco had not stopped in Jordan. Al-Rifai—who had studied at Harvard University, where he had been a student of President Nixon's national security adviser, Henry Kissinger—expressed regret about the damage demonstrators in Jordan had done to the American Cultural Center and to the U.S. embassy. Al-Rifai explained that his government had not been prepared for the violence and had not expected the crowd to become so volatile.[73]

Amman asked Washington to quickly appoint a new ambassador to replace the recalled Symmes. Al-Rifai understood that the State Department was concerned that perhaps King Hussein had lost his hold on Jordan, that the *fedayeen* had become "a state within a state," and that the loyalty of the Jordanian Army was in doubt. Al-Rifai, attempted to reassure Sisco that the king remained firmly in control. Turning to the relationship between the Jordanian ruler and Nasser, the king's adviser insisted that the Egyptian leader relied on Hussexin. According to al-Rifai, "Nasser needs Hussein more than Hussein needs Nasser. If Nasser departed the scene, the UAR could continue to exist and conceivably the situation might 'even improve'. On the other hand, if Hussein departed the scene, the consequences beyond Jordan's borders would be serious. The effects on Saudi Arabia and Kuwait would be adverse."[74]

Turning to the general Arab view of Washington, al-Rifai expressed sorrow that neither Jordan nor the rest of the Arab world had confidence in the United States. He complained that despite the risk involved, King Hussein had pursued a pro-American policy but had received little in return. Now, continued the king's adviser, American assistance to Israel made the Jordanian position very difficult: "It is impossible to stress enough the emotional impact in the Arab world of the bombing of Arab cities and the killing of Arabs by U.S.-supplied Phantoms, about which the Arabs are incapable of doing anything." Al-Rifai also complained about Israeli control of American policy, claiming that Israel dictated and Washington obeyed.[75]

Two days before his May 14 meeting with Under-Secretary Sisco, the State Department had informed al-Rifai that Washington would approve an arms package for Jordan. The king's adviser had immediately sent details of the package to Hussein. The Jordanian monarch was unhappy with the scheduled delivery dates and the absence of some earlier requested items. After hurried consultations, Sisco was now able to tell al-Rifai that within one calendar year, Washington would deliver all of the major items that Jordan had requested.[76]

Meanwhile, *fedayeen* in Jordan continued attacks on Israel. With Iraqi guns participating, on June 3 they launched shells into the city of Tiberias. The attack on Tiberias was in retaliation for a prior Israeli attack on Ibrid. Earlier, the attack on Ibrid had been in retaliation for a *fedayeen* attack on Beit Shean. Through the U.S. embassy, King Hussein asked Israel to refrain from striking in order to provide some breathing space for him. According to Israeli Foreign Minister Abba Eban, the king spoke harshly against the *fedayeen*. He assured Tel Aviv that if the *fedayeen* established positions that enabled them to shoot Katusha rockets at Eilat, the Dead Sea works, or Beit Shean, and, if he was unable to stop them by other means his army would not take action against them. Foreign Minister Eban told the British ambassador to Israel that Israel welcomed any possible effort on London's part to support this arrangement. Eban asked that the information he had transmitted be treated as confidential. The U.S. embassy in Tel Aviv provided the British with a similar account and also requested that the information remain confidential.[77]

Pointing out that previous Israeli reprisals had increased support for the *fedayeen*, the British embassy in Amman welcomed the understanding between Israel and the king. At the same time, British officials cautioned that a large number of the men in the lower ranks of the Jordanian army were Palestinians and were likely to be reluctant to shoot *fedayeen* who might well be members of their own family. Hence, Israel ought not to expect too much from Hussein.[78]

While Israel was the *fedayeen*'s primary target, some groups were also dedicated to the elimination of the Hashemites. Then on June 9, as the king traveled toward Amman from his summer villa in Suweilih, *fedayeen* fired at his motorcade. The king escaped unharmed. Spokesmen for the PLO (the central Palestinian guerrilla organization) denied that their members had attempted to assassinate the Jordanian ruler. These sources claimed that PLO members had fired at the king's motorcade simple to prevent Hussein from reaching Amman.[79]

Clashes between the *fedayeen* and the Jordanian army continued. On June 11 the *fedayeen* demanded that the king dismiss the Army's commander-in-chief—his uncle Sharif Nassir—and several high-ranking officers loyal to the Hashemite monarchy, including General Zaid Bin Shakir. American officials in Amman reported that these dismissals would weaken the king, but that it appeared that neither side had yet decided on a final showdown.[80] Whitehall, told its ambassador in Tel Aviv to express the hope that the Israeli government not take any sort of action that might exacerbate the crisis.[81]

King Hussein and his government were in danger. So too were Westerners in Jordan. In early June George Habbash, the "swaggering leader" of the radical Popular Front for the Liberation of Palestine (PFLP), a Christian Arab doctor, held forty hostages in two hotels. These hostages included American, British, and German citizens.[82] As a result of *fedayeen* activity, American officials in Amman found it increasingly difficult to communicate effectively with Jordanian officials.[83] Washington requested that its Middle East posts press all of their contacts to ask for the release of the hostages. The State Department wanted its embassy in Beirut to contact local intellectuals, including AUB professor Walid al-Khalidi, who was reported to have direct connections with Habbash.[84] Uncertainty about the future of Jordan led to Washington's growing concern for the safety of an estimated four hundred Americans in the Hashemite Kingdom: "The *fedayeen* have broken into a certain number of American houses, are reported to have raped the wives of two official Americans, have apparently assaulted two American officials, and have stolen property.

In these circumstances, we have been trying to find ways with our embassy in Amman to effect an immediate evacuation of Americans."[85]

In addition, the Nixon White House considered how to respond if King Hussein requested American military intervention, especially under circumstances where the *fedayeen* were receiving active military support from Iraq and Syria.[86] Then a report broadcast from Jordan claimed that the king had agreed to the *fedayeen* demand that he dismiss his uncle, Sharif Nassir, and other high-ranking officers.[87] Washington asked its officials in Amman to estimate the probable effects of the removal of these men.[88] Meanwhile, *Newsweek* erroneously reported that the Jordanian ruler had given up.[89]

King Hussein had no intention of relinquishing control. Dedicated to the survival of his kingdom, he personally took command of his army. American officials in Amman considered it likely that with assistance from the International Red Cross (IRC) and the UN it would be possible to rescue Americans and other foreigners. Unfortunately, permission from the *fedayeen* was also necessary.[90] While Washington planned for the evacuation of foreigners from Jordan, Cairo Fatah Radio claimed that King Hussein had not gone far enough, that dismissal of his officers was only the beginning. Fatah demanded that the king renounce his commitment to a Middle East political settlement.[91] Watching the situation in Jordan with concern, Israeli officials viewed the resignations of Sharif Nassir and General Zaid Bin Shakir as a serious blow to King Hussein, but Tel Aviv anticipated that Hussein would not give in to those who opposed him, that he would continue to maintain control.[92]

What appeared to have been the dismissal of his officers did not indicate their complete withdrawal from the military. On June 14 General Bin Shakir attended the funeral of his sister wearing full military dress. The diplomatic community speculated that the two ousted generals would continue to maintain close contact with the king. However, PFLP members spread the word that their assassination squads would be sent against Sharif Nassir and Zaid Bin Shakir if the two did not quickly leave the country.[93]

Israeli Prime Minister Golda Meir now instructed that no public comment on conditions in Jordan be made. During a June 11, 1970, television interview, Israeli General Ezer Weizman appeared prepared to address the situation when "he was faded out." One Israeli official stated that Israel was exercising restraint in both action and speech. Tel Aviv was concerned that the dismissal of the two commanders indicated that perhaps in the event of a showdown the king might lose. In addition, Israel was distressed by Habbash's success at the expense of Arafat. According to an Israeli diplomat, Arafat was far more reasonable than Habbash. The PLO leader "had wanted to calm things down."[94] The British embassy in Tel Aviv told London that the Israelis were closely monitoring events in Jordan, and that the king had sufficient strength to prevail. However, British officials in Tel Aviv were not convinced. They now suggested the possibility of an Arafat regime.[95]

As the crisis continued, a group of American hostages held at Amman's Intercontinental Hotel were released. Before their release a *fedayeen* leader told the hostages, "You are no more important than our people—you are expendable." Once in London those released discussed their experience with U.S. Ambassador Walter Annenberg. They praised Foreign Service official Robert Pelletreau, "whose cool dignity in dealing with the *fedayeen* was both effective and [a] source of pride for all Americans involved."[96]

Speaking to a *New York Times* correspondent on June 14, Arafat stated that Fatah now controlled Amman. After Arafat spoke, one of his officials told the same reporter that Fatah had investigated the alleged June 11 rape of two American women. Although he provided no details, he said that two men had been arrested and executed for the crime.[97] The following day conditions in Amman appeared to improve. The price of food, which had dramatically increased during the crisis, started to descend; a general clean up began; and some previously stolen vehicles were returned to their owners. However, tension remained high. Local Jordanians employed at the U.S. embassy lived in fear. The ambassador's driver, George Razzouk, was so frightened that he placed his two children in the home of friends and moved into the chancery.[98]

Obviously, the crisis was not over. No permanent agreement between the *fedayeen* and King Hussein's government had yet been reached. American officials stated that it was naive to consider the possibility that the PLO might take action against the PFLP or any other extremist group. Rumors of Jordanian army movements continued to circulate. American officials in Amman reported that although Jordanians remained friendly, and often apologetic about the crisis, most were uncomfortable about any contact with Americans, especially on the telephone, which they assumed was often tapped. On June 21, Arafat warned Arab rulers meeting in Libya about new anti-Arab conspiracies formulated by the U.S. Central Intelligence Agency. In Amman, the Pakistani ambassador ordered all Pakistani women and children out of the country by June 24 and told his American colleague that during a future conflict with the *fedayeen* the Jordanian army had only a 50-50 chance of prevailing.[99]

Defeated by Israel in 1967, three years later the king was once again faced with a formidable enemy, the *fedayeen*. He was confident, but concerned. Unfortunately, Arab nations were unwilling to help him. At this juncture it was not even certain that he would be able to maintain the loyalty of his East Bank core.

CHAPTER 3

WHITE SEPTEMBER

Some notable Jordanians continued to accuse King Hussein of cooperating with the United States and conspiring against their revolution. His critics included the president of Jordan's senate, tribal leaders, numerous mayors, leaders of professional organizations, and labor unions. Chief of the Royal Court Zaid al-Rifai called the situation precarious. He underlined the significance of the increased number of critics who were true Jordanians, indicating that they were not Palestinians.[1]

At the end of June 1970, Secretary of State William Rogers announced the appointment of a new U.S. Ambassador to Jordan, L. Dean Brown. Following his arrival in Amman, Ambassador Brown traveled through the city in an armored personnel carrier. Explaining that he did not wish to upset American policy by becoming a hostage, Ambassador Brown carried a pistol.[2] The new U.S. ambassador inspired confidence. Head of the embassy's political section, Hume Horan, later called Brown "one of the great officers of my, or any generation." According to Horan, the new ambassador was direct and irreverent, an outstanding leader: "With Amman in turmoil, we needed a boss who made us feel we were safe with him."[3]

Washington then agreed to undertake a fresh initiative to end the Arab-Israel conflict—the Rogers' Plan, which included the principle of land for peace. Given his precarious situation, King Hussein was unwilling to commit himself to the new American peace proposal until it was clear how Nasser would react. Shortly after Nasser agreed to the plan on July 26, the king expressed his approval. In a cable to the Egyptian leader, Hussein wrote, "What you accept, we accept, and what you reject, we reject."[4]

Violence in Jordan continued. At the end of June, American officer Norvell De Atkine, who had been studying at the American University in Beirut (AUB), was sent to Amman to replace assistant army attaché Major Bob Perry, who had been murdered by Palestinian gunmen in the presence of his wife and children. Upon arriving at Amman airport, De Atkine noted that there were two competing visa control checkpoints—one manned by Jordanian authorities, the other by Palestine Liberation Organization (PLO) representatives. On the city's streets De Atkine observed several different *fedayeen* factions driving Toyota trucks with machine guns mounted on them.[5]

For the few American diplomats remaining in Amman, celebrating the Fourth of July holiday was stressful. The members of the embassy staff who had not been evacuated now received hardship pay, reserved for the most dangerous posts, including Saigon. These officials dispensed with speeches and fireworks. Instead, behind the high walls of the ambassador's residence they held a cookout.[6]

In early July, yet another agreement was worked out between Jordan's government and the PLO Central Committee, an agreement signed by Chairman Yasser Arafat, who was designated as the sole authority responsible for all *fedayeen* organizations. Hussein's government had dealt with the *fedayeen* as if they constituted a sovereign entity. The understanding also spelled out the principle that the sovereignty of Jordan's government would be preserved. However, according to Zaid al-Rifai, "The agreement is nothing: implementation is everything." The reaction of the Popular Front for the Liberation of Palestine (PFLP) was also unknown.[7]

The agreement did not end agitation in Jordan. King Hussein remained uneasy and was especially concerned about Iraqi army maneuvers. The Jordanian ruler feared that the *fedayeen* and Iraqi forces were conspiring against him because he had followed Nasser's lead and accepted American peace proposals.[8] Once again the king wanted to purchase arms. He wrote a letter to British Prime Minister Harold Wilson, providing the history of his lengthy arms negotiations with Washington. After a year of protracted discussions the United States had finally agreed to supply some arms to Amman. However, Jordan had additional requirements and the Saudi king was now willing to provide £15 million for the Jordanian armed forces. Hussein insisted on 100 Centurion Mark 9 tanks and 105mm ammunition for them. The king wrote, "We feel that this deal, plus many others, which we hope to raise funds for from our Arab sister states, might depend on a satisfactory agreement regarding the items mentioned above. I am confident that your Excellency will spare no effort to assist us in this matter for the mutual benefit of our two countries."[9] Then on August 29 Hussein delivered a speech to his nation during which he administered a "verbal spanking" to the *fedayeen*. Following the king's speech, *fedayeen* fired on army headquarters. American observers noted that the Jordanian government appeared calm and did not overreact, but both sides still remained tense.[10]

King Hussein escaped yet another assassination attempt early on September 1. Following the unsuccessful attempt on the king's life, the Hashemite government received an ultimatum from Iraq, threatening to intervene in Jordan if the king did not immediately end all military action against the *fedayeen*. Baghdad Radio accused Jordanian forces of shelling refugee camps; the accusation was not true. Although the State Department realized that there were limits to how much pressure the Soviet Union could apply on the unreasonable Iraqi Baathist government, Washington asked the U.S. ambassador to the Soviet Union to inform the Kremlin that the United States would appreciate a Soviet effort to influence Baghdad not to intervene in Jordan. Washington also wanted Cairo to understand the gravity of the situation and asked that the United Arab Republic (UAR) do whatever possible to help.[11]

American officials in London discussed their concerns with Foreign Office officials, who were also very disturbed by events in the Hashemite Kingdom. Jordan had asked for a Four-Power statement in support of the Hashemite Kingdom, but according to the acting head of the Near East Department, Richard Evans, a Four-Power statement was unlikely because Iraq was aiding the *fedayeen* and the Soviets would be unwilling to blame the Iraqis. Hence, Evans considered the Jordanian request for a Four-Power statement to be a non-starter.[12] Then on September 3, the king established a privy council. Some observers claimed that Hussein would use the council as yet another line of defense in his efforts to resist pressure from his own right wing "to mop up *fedayeen* once and for all."[13]

Travel in Amman became extremely dangerous. American Political Counselor Morris Draper went out early one evening to contact an Arab friend in the Amman area close to the refugee camps. Driving his car, which had diplomatic license plates, Draper was halted at a *fedayeen* roadblock. The *fedayeen*, members of George Habbash's PFLP, took Draper captive. Before his kidnapping, Draper had been stopped by other *fedayeen* groups: "Not just once, seven, eight, ten, twelve times! I was use[d] to talking my way through." According to Draper, who spoke fluent Arabic, he was treated well. Most of his captors had never spoken to an American before. They had an austere life in a slum area of one hundred thousand people, without banquets or feasts. "Some of the young men liked to throw their Kalashnikovs around. They were continually playing with the trigger guards and so forth, shoving shells into the chambers. They just couldn't stop fondling their weapons."[14]

King Hussein arranged for Draper's freedom. The released American political counselor was taken to see the king and left Jordan immediately afterward. Draper recalled that during his tenure in Amman, Palestinians clearly outnumbered East bankers. Although the power of the Palestinians had increased, the army had kept its Jordanian roots—at least in the officer corps—and King Hussein had not lost the loyalty of his Jordanian tribesmen. Draper stated that the army had pushed the king that the officers wanted Hussein to crack down on the *fedayeen*.[15]

Members of the PFLP began what was to become their most spectacular coup on September 6, when they tried to hijack an El Al airplane. El Al's crew foiled their hijacking attempt, however. One of the hijackers, Nicaraguan Patrick Arguello, was killed; the other, twenty-six-year-old Palestinian Leila Khaled—an experienced hijacker who had earlier participated in the August 1969 hijacking of a TWA flight—was arrested after the El Al plane landed in London. However, on the same day as the attempted El Al hijacking, the PFLP successfully hijacked a TWA aircraft, which was ordered to land in Jordan on a desert strip known as Dawson's Field. The TWA plane was soon joined by a Swissair aircraft and later a British plane.[16]

King Hussein was unable to do anything at all. Bragging about the international aircraft forced to land in the Jordanian desert forty miles northeast of Amman, one guerilla claimed that the desert was a good airport: "We will fill it with planes if Allah is willing."[17] After both the Swissair and TWA jets were standing in the desert, the hijackers established a command post between the aircraft and planted a Palestinian flag. The guerillas warned that they would blow up the planes, along with their passengers, unless their demands were met—demands that included the release of their comrades who had been arrested during several earlier unsuccessful hijacking attempts.[18]

In Washington, Talcott Seeyle, who had been in charge of the State Department's Jordanian desk since the summer of 1968, was appointed to lead a task force to deal with the problem of the three hijacked planes. Washington's policy was not to give in to blackmail. According to Seeyle, "So often the knee-jerk reaction of the White House was to flex military muscles. I pointed out look, you have American hostages here." There was no easy way out; "it was pretty dicey!"[19]

In a televised address to his nation on September 6, the king admitted that since the June 1967 war, his government had neglected internal affairs and now assured the *fedayeen* that he would not attempt to destroy them under any circumstances. At the same time, the king asked the Arab League to work out a solution, to set up a committee to deal with disputes between the *fedayeen* and his government.[20] On September 8 yet another cease-fire was arranged, one that appeared to give equal status both to the Jordanian government and to the *fedayeen*. However, American diplomats in Amman assumed that fighting would erupt again.[21] After the cease-fire was declared, the U.S. embassy received a phone call from a man who identified himself as a *fedayeen* spokesman. He urged that the Bedouin guarding the embassy be ordered to refrain from firing their weapons, because if they did so, the *fedayeen* would attack the embassy. When informed of the *fedayeen* warning, the commander of the Bedouin guards promised to exercise caution.[22]

In Washington, British Ambassador John Freeman called on Assistant Secretary Joseph Sisco to review the situation in Jordan. Great Britain was discreetly advising non-essential personnel to leave the Hashemite Kingdom, and officials were in the midst of discussing evacuation contingencies with the International Red Cross (IRC). Sisco said that forty American officials remained in Jordan and that Washington had also studied evacuation plans. Then requesting that the information be held closely between their two governments, Sisco told the British ambassador that he personally believed that if the point was reached where the safety of the hijacked hostages depended on Israeli release of some Palestinian prisoners, then Israel would agree to their release.[23]

Sisco also observed that each crisis further weakened the king; in the previous month Hussein's actions had been vacillating. The American official stated, "We were very confident in several past crises that if King used will and resolve, he had full support of Jordan army and military outcome in event of confrontation would be favorable. We are less sure today, although we still hold to judgment if Hussein exercised his will and resolve military outcome would be successful."[24]

Washington did not want to intervene in Jordan. Therefore, the State Department hesitated to offer advice. Sisco noted that the pattern of numerous inconclusive confrontations between the king's government and the *fedayeen* had further complicated the Arab-Israeli peace effort. The Israelis then ask the relevant question: with whom do they make peace?[25]

On September 10 the U.S. embassy in Amman reported to Washington that the Red Cross had provided assurance that all of the hostages were in good condition—both those still detained on the planes and those who had been allowed to leave for Amman. The passengers now in Amman were housed in a hotel and a representative of the Red Cross was attempting to obtain the release of women and children.[26] Finally, on September 14 a majority of the passengers were released, but the PFLP retained fifty-six men. The Red Crescent reported that these men were held in various locations in southern Amman.[27]

Not even Yasser Arafat was able to deal with the PFLP. While in the midst of discussions with the IRC about the three airplanes at Dawson's Field, Arafat was informed that the planes had just been blown up. Although some hostages still remained in PFLP hands, the PLO Central Committee expelled the PFLP. Arafat underlined that the PLO Central Committee would adopt a firm stand against any PFLP action that it deemed prejudiced the safety and security of the Palestinian revolution.[28]

During a telephone conference on September 16, Permanent Under-Secretary of State at the Foreign and Commonwealth Office Sir Denis Greenhill, Assistant Secretary of State Joseph Sisco, and National Security Adviser Henry Kissinger discussed Israel's resistance to the *fedayeen* demand that Tel Aviv release Palestinians held in Israeli prisons. As yet, the PFLP had not provided a list of those they wanted released. Frustrated, Sisco mused, "how in the hell are we going to influence the Israelis" when the *fedayeen* did not provide information about either the number of prisoners or which prisoners they wished to exchange.

Sir Denis Greenhill did not accept Sisco's position and insisted that Israel ought to agree in principle to the release of the prisoners. The British under-secretary expressed the hope that somehow or other the king would successfully emerge from the crisis. Jordanian troops had surrounded Amman, and according to Sisco, the king was not going to force the issue.[29] The following day, Sisco spoke to Greenhill again. They discussed several possible ways to gain the release of the hostages, including a plan that asked for the exchange of all of the hostages excluding the Israelis. Greenhill was distressed to learn that the three Israeli hostages—and there were only three—held dual citizenship; they were American citizens as well as Israeli citizens. Disappointed, the British official now suggested another possibility: that the Germans, Swiss, and British exchange the prisoners for those hostages who were their nationals. "The final stage is that we should agree amongst our-selves that nobody would mutually reproach the other if each person did the best they could for their own people." Sisco told his British col-league to take into account that such a scenario would greatly offend Americans, so "be very sure your Ministers understand that." Greenhill insisted that, indeed, Whitehall understood but expressed anger that Israel was unwilling to exchange prisoners for hostages. The British diplomat expressed frustration that Israeli Prime Minister Golda Meir "won't lift a bloody finger and put any contribution to a bargain and our people get killed."[30]

Four days earlier, Israeli Foreign Minister Eban had responded to a message from Whitehall saying that he saw no reason for Israel to make concessions to terrorists.[31] At approximately midnight on September 19, Sir Denis Greenhill told the Soviet ambassador that Syrian tanks had crossed the Jordanian border and fired on Jordanian positions. The British under-secretary of state also spoke to Kissinger. He asked if there was any shift in Prime Minister Meir's position on releasing Arab prisoners held in Israel. Kissinger replied that Israel's position had not changed.[32]

While the British complained about Tel Aviv, the king expressed frustration with the BBC Arabic service, asserting that its broadcasts were extensively quoting *fedayeen* sources and thus doing more harm than Kol Israel radio (The Voice of Israel). King Hussein considered the BBC's emphasis on Palestinian sources to be sabotage and an impediment to the continuation of good relations between Great Britain and Jordan. The BBC explained that its staff sincerely wished to provide more balanced reporting and hoped that it would be possible to do so when the three BBC reporters in Amman were no longer restricted to the Intercontinental Hotel.[33]

Tension continued to escalate. On September 17 Nasser dispatched the chief of staff of the Egyptian army, Ahmed Sadiq, to Jordan to demand that the king cease activities against the *fedayeen*. Nasser claimed that such activities only served to strengthen Israel and the United States.[34] Ignoring the Egyptian command, Hussein replaced his cabinet with a military government. Although two-thirds of Jordan's population was Palestinian, the army, whose elite armored brigades were almost entirely Bedouin, began an assault on PLO bases in Amman. The Palestinians suffered heavy losses, including hundreds of civilian casualties.[35]

Secretary of State Rogers told Whitehall on September 21 that Washington was not considering military intervention and had not yet decided to evacuate American citizens from Jordan. However, in the event evacuation appeared necessary, the State Department wished to organize a joint Anglo-American effort. Secretary Rogers admitted that such an evacuation might very well be a fatal blow to what was left of the king's prestige. At the same time, he emphasized that Washington did not wish to announce publicly that it had no plans to intervene because such a declaration would comfort the Soviets, who were not doing enough to restrain their client, Syria.[36]

Whitehall discussed how the Israelis would react, whether or not Tel Aviv would intervene in Jordan. Concluding that Israel had no particular attachment to Hussein, London assumed that Tel Aviv would not become involved in an effort to save his kingdom. According to one British official, referring to the Israelis, "On the whole we thought they would be unlikely to intervene if a moderate Palestinian Regime, for instance led by Arafat, took over Jordan: they could do business with such a Regime."[37]

Concerned about the safety of expatriates residing in the Hashemite Kingdom, the British anxiously discussed how to proceed with the evacuation of Britons and citizens of other friendly nations. By September 21 it appeared that it might not be possible to take off safely from Amman airport. The British listed the possible alternatives, including obtaining safe conduct from both the *fedayeen* and the Israeli government, which would permit departure from Jordan via the Allenby Bridge. London also considered requesting a Jordanian military escort to conduct evacuees to the port of Aqaba.[38]

While the British were discussing possible evacuation routes, the king sent an urgent message to President Nixon and informed the British embassy in Amman that following a massive Syrian invasion, the situation was rapidly deteriorating.[39] Meeting at the White House with a member of Kissinger's staff at 2AM on September 21, Sir Denis

Greenhill said that the king had urgently requested that Great Britain inform Tel Aviv that he wanted the Israeli air force to strike the Syrian troops now, inside his territory. However, London preferred that Washington pass the king's message to Tel Aviv. According to Greenhill, "We think that it is important to handle the matter this way since you are closest to the Israelis and will be able to influence them on whether or not to act upon the King's request."[40]

During a conversation with Whitehall on September 22, 1970, British officials in Amman reported that the courageous king appeared to be tired and discouraged, and might decide to abdicate. Speculating on what might take place if Hussein abdicated, British officials suggested the possibility of a military junta using the king's brother Prince Hassan as a figurehead. Finally, if the king either abdicated or was assassinated it seemed likely that Jordan would disintegrate.[41]

Whitehall prepared a message for Prime Minister Edward Heath to send to President Nasser, a note that expressed admiration for the Egyptian leader's opposition to the hijacking of aircraft. The message also stated that the British, Swiss, and German governments had agreed that in return for an exchange of all the hostages, they would free Leila Khaled together with the body of her dead companion and the other six people whose release was sought.[42] Ambassador Phillips in Amman had earlier told London that Leila was considered an important symbol of Palestine resistance and that she was a folk heroine.[43] According to Cabinet member, Margaret Thatcher, who referred to Prime Minister Edward Heath as Ted: "Ted resisted any British involvement on the King's side and was certain that we were right to negotiate with the PFLP. Though it went against the grain to release Khaled, in the end the deal was made."[44]

Although Damascus denied that the Syrian military was involved in Jordan, Israeli sources reported increased Syrian activity in the area of Irbid, where Syria had deployed two armored brigades and two armored regiments. If the Syrians decided to do so, they could quickly reach the outskirts of Amman. So too could the Iraqi troops now active inside the Hashemite Kingdom. Despite reports of Syrian and Iraqi strength, Amman claimed that the Jordanian air force had already interfered with Syrian movements and was able to continue intercepting enemy troops.[45]

As the crisis continued, the evacuation of foreign nationals became a matter of growing concern. Given Great Britain's long experience in Jordan, the German government asked London to include German nationals among the evacuees. On September 23 the British embassy in Amman confirmed that its officials were in touch with German officials, but that on that day they had been unable to include any German citizens. While evacuations proceeded, King Hussein asked the permanent members of the Security Council to use their influence to stop the invasion of his country.[46]

The Red Cross arranged to fly emergency supplies to Jordan, and Whitehall requested that the two aircraft scheduled to bring in the supplies be used to evacuate mothers and children.[47] Although the Red Cross agreed, when the planes departed Amman, many passengers were members of the press. The prime minister was distressed to learn that reporters left before women and children.[48] Despite the rush to leave by some journalists, other journalists continued efforts to enter Jordan. A British official in Beirut complained that on the morning of September 24 twenty-four journalists attempted to board an aircraft bound for Amman. British authorities refused to take the reporters: "This was not only because of the conduct of the rats yesterday, but also because in seeking clearance we had informed the Syrians that these were humanitarian flights."[49]

On September 23 one of Yasser Arafat's deputies, Abu Ayyad—who had earlier been captured by troops loyal to the Jordanian ruler—together with King Hussein, broadcast a statement that called for a cease-fire.[50] Meanwhile, as the evacuation of foreigners proceeded, conditions in Amman deteriorated. The British ambassador reported that conditions in the city were appalling; many sick and wounded were lying in the streets. The director general of the British Red Cross explained to British officials that he had only limited influence with the International Committee of the Red Cross (ICRC). He suggested that the ICRC defer operations until after establishing contacts with the *fedayeen* and receiving some sort of assurance that they would refrain from harming Red Cross personnel.[51]

As the violence continued, the Greek government asked Washington to assist in the evacuation of its citizens from Amman. The State Department was willing to provide seats on American chartered aircraft but was unable to contact members of Jordan's Greek community. As a result, the Americans requested that the British embassy in Amman notify the Greek community that its members were welcome to take the available empty seats during the ongoing American airlift.[52]

Despite the growing danger, King Hussein remained resolute. After the fighting began, he had discovered that some of those close to him had helped his enemies. Hussein's personal driver served as a major in Fatah and his cook too was ranked among the *fedayeen*. Nevertheless, the king continued to express confidence in the future of the Hashemite Kingdom.[53]

Appearing on television on September 24, Prime Minister Heath said that British officials in Jordan had been unable to contact eleven of their citizens but would continue efforts to reach them. All other Britons who had wished to leave Jordan had been evacuated: "There are some—and I pay tribute to them—who are determined to stay there and carry on with their jobs, including many personnel at the embassy—and they've done a magnificent bit of work during these past few weeks."[54] Among the numerous Britons who delayed departure was Michael Adams. At home in Great Britain his wife assumed that he had a good reason for remaining in Amman, but she wished to learn that reason. A British official in Jordan explained that Michael Adams had prepared the list of those who were to be evacuated and placed himself at the bottom.[55]

During the battle for Amman more than one hundred reporters from various news organizations were guests at the Intercontinental Hotel, where they enjoyed "front-line accommodations." From their windows they viewed the fighting and took care to avoid stray bullets. Michael Adams took charge of a committee to run the hotel. Adams, who had been a prisoner of war in Germany during World War II, used his experience to organize the guests. International correspondents now swept the lobby, cleaned toilets, and carried out trash.[56]

After a week of constant fighting the *fedayeen* agreed to a cease-fire, which under pressure from Arab States, the king reluctantly accepted. Undoubtedly, Hussein had prevailed. However, the Jordanian army had not yet finished the task of removing all of the *fedayeen*. Groups of *fedayeen* remained in control of certain sections of Amman and of several northern towns, including Ibrid.[57] The king and Palestinian leader Arafat met in Cairo on September 27. With Nasser's blessing, King Hussein and Yasser Arafat signed a cease-fire. The following day President Nasser suffered a massive heart attack and died.[58] According to a British diplomat serving in Jordan,

> Even in normal circumstances it would perhaps be a little early to assess the effect of the recent events in Jordan on the people of the West Bank. Arab emotions tend to be highly volatile, and just as they were cooling down after the agreement between King Hussein and Yasir Arafat, they were raised to even greater heights by the sudden death of President Nasser who was largely responsible for achieving the agreement, and who died on the day of the Moslem feast celebrating Mohammed's ascension into Heaven.[59]

The crisis was not over. On the evening of October 2 U.S. Ambassador Brown stood on the terrace of Hummar Palace with former Prime Minister Wasfi al-Tall. Pointing across the valley toward the Gilead Hills, al-Tall said that within the last twenty-four hours a large number of Iraqi soldiers and Iraqi supported *fedayeen* had moved into the area.[60] At the request of Washington, Israel now sent reinforcements to the Syrian border. The king later declared that "the Syrians had been given a very bloody nose."[61] As a result, the Syrians went home, and although Iraqi troops remained in Jordan, many of the Palestinian fighters were forced out of the country. Hussein retained control.[62] Reports of the number of casualties varied. Some reporters estimated that twenty thousand had been killed. According to King Hussein, however, the number of casualties was approximately two thousand. He insisted that journalists got the number wrong because during the conflict between his army and the *fedayeen*, reporters in Amman had been confined to the Intercontinental Hotel.[63]

From President Nixon's National Security Adviser Henry Kissinger's perspective, "The forces of moderation in the Middle East had been preserved. The King had prevailed by his own courage and decisiveness. Yet these would have been in vain but for his friendship with the United States. The Soviets had backed off, raising by another notch the growing Arab disenchantment with Moscow."[64] Palestinian leaders had made a crucial error. They had not understood the Arab Legion's attachment to the king or the cultural importance of his Sharifan descent. Most of the Bedouin who fought for Hussein were uneducated and unable to read Palestinian pamphlets. According to historian Fouad Ajami, "For them the fight was between the king—their chieftain, their financial provider, a man who claims descent from the Prophet—and atheistic troublemakers, townsmen with alien and offensive ways."[65]

U.S. Ambassador to Tunisia John Calhoun had a different viewpoint. He understood that from the perspective of King Hussein no *fedayeen* group appeared reasonable. However, the Tunisian government claimed that Arafat and Fatah now represented the best bet for moderate Arabs. Arafat was not devoted to a foreign ideology; he was not a communist, a Baathist, or a Maoist. Ambassador Calhoun warned that moderate Arabs were increasingly turning to the Soviet Union because Washington was so closely identified with Israel and ignored the aspirations and even the very existence of the Palestinians. The Tunisian government now requested that Washington establish direct contact with Arafat and his Fatah movement.[66]

Following Jordan's successful rout of the *fedayeen* and the demise of Nasser, rumors circulated that Washington visualized creation of a Palestinian state on the West Bank. Ambassador Brown visited King Hussein to reassure him that these rumors were false. Brown stated that the United States wanted a strong viable Hashemite Kingdom. Insisting that his people would never accept a Palestinian state that included major chunks of Jordanian territory, the king told Brown that he had dismissed these rumors.[67]

In the Israeli-occupied West Bank, powerful anti-Hashemite, and anti–East Bank feelings, which had lain dormant since 1948, were ready to explode. After King Hussein's expulsion of the *fedayeen*, Palestinians under Israeli control denounced the Hashemites, blaming King Hussein's grandfather for the plight of the Palestinians, who had fled their homes in 1948. King Hussein's grandfather, Abdullah, was accused of having called on Arab residents of Jaffa and Haifa to evacuate their neighborhoods and of having relinquished Ramleh and Lydda without a battle. As for King Hussein's sins, according to prevalent West Bank opinion, before 1967 he had favored those on the East Bank. Then in 1967, he had failed to defeat Israel. Finally, in September 1970 he had attempted to liquidate the *fedayeen*.[68]

Acting British Consul General in Jerusalem C. W. Woodrow considered Arab emotions volatile and speculated about whether or not the emotional climate of the moment would have a lasting effect. He suggested that if the king made the appropriate speeches about the liberation of Palestine, the present tide of hostile emotions might diminish. However, Woodrow stated that Palestine was now on the political map and the king would have to keep his promise that after liberation of the West Bank and East Jerusalem, the population of those areas would decide their own destiny. Woodrow claimed that the most important result of events in Jordan was an increase in Palestinian nationalism.[69]

In early November, Great Britain's minister of state for foreign and commonwealth affairs, Joseph Godber, met in Jerusalem with Israel's deputy prime minister, Yigal Allon. The Israeli asked Godber how he viewed the possibility that Israel might successfully pursue a Jordan-first policy. Minister of State Godber replied that independently entering negotiations with Israel would put the king in a very dangerous position. Hence, it was unlikely that Hussein would agree to such a policy.[70]

During his visit to Jerusalem, Godber also had a conversation with the director of Israeli military intelligence, General Aharon Yariv. Godber asked if the king's success against the *fedayeen* had strengthened his position. General Yariv pointed out that although damaged, the *fedayeen* had not been destroyed and that they still had funds. The Israeli general doubted that PLO leader Arafat could come to terms with King Hussein and expressed certainty that the *fedayeen* would not support a deal that offered only autonomy. Nevertheless, according to Yariv, Nasser's death had benefited the king. However, direct negotiations between Israel and Jordan were still a long way off, because such negotiations would "damn the King with other Arabs."[71]

Still anxious about the future of his kingdom, King Hussein wanted to visit Washington to press for increased American support. At the beginning of November, Jordan's recently appointed prime minister, Wasfi al-Tall, insisted that the ruler delay travel until the situation at home was stable. Al-Tall informed the U.S. ambassador that if the king traveled to Washington, he would be providing ammunition to his opponents throughout the Arab world.[72] According to a October 13, 1970, agreement, reached between the Jordanian government and the *fedayeen*, the transition period ended at midnight on November 9. As the hour approached, Amman was tense. Residents had stockpiled food; and although on the morning of the ninth schools, government offices, and stores were open, and joint police-*fedayeen* units patrolled the streets, most residents remained at home.[73]

Quickly, the Nixon Administration tried to buttress the king further. In a message to Congress on November 18, asking for additional foreign aid—including $30 million for the Hashemite Kingdom,—President Nixon praised Jordan's recent activities against the *fedayeen*. He explained that Jordan, which had formerly paid for its own military equipment, did not have funds to meet its new defense burden and had asked for American assistance.[74]

Economic aid to Jordan was a priority, but of course, an end to the Arab-Israeli conflict was Washington's goal. A State Department memorandum to President Nixon explained that although the Jordanian army had been successful, King Hussein's survival depended upon rapid progress toward a negotiated Arab-Israeli settlement, which would return the Israeli-occupied West Bank to the Hashemite Kingdom. Warning that the *fedayeen* who had been driven out of Jordan might recover from this set back and once again threaten the king, the memorandum pointed to reports that Arafat continued to mobilize Arab support for a Palestinian entity. The entity suggested would comprise Gaza, the West Bank, and parts of the East Bank, creating a Palestinian State that would severely reduce the Hashemite Kingdom. Hence, the king had to build up his military, but, unfortunately, his country was poor, and he lacked the necessary funds.[75]

Prior to leaving Jordan for his long anticipated visit to Washington, the king also arranged to schedule meetings in Riyadh, Cairo, London, Paris, and Bonn. In addition, after completing all of his official business, he hoped to return to London once more to spend some time with his wife and children, who had been living outside his kingdom since the crisis intensified.[76] In early December, the king stopped in London. Prime Minister Edward Heath expressed his appreciation for the cooperation Great Britain received from the Jordanian government during the recent hijackings. King Hussein assured Prime Minister Heath that although his country continued to face serious problems, the situation had improved. At the same time, the king stressed the necessity of movement by the UN-sponsored Jarring Mission.[77] When Heath turned to the issue of Iraqi troops still stationed in Jordan, the king explained that one of the reasons Baghdad did not withdraw its forces was that the al-Bakir government was reluctant to have these troops back in Iraq. The king said that his relations with the regime in Baghdad were poor and that he considered it possible that the present unpopular Iraqi government would be toppled.[78]

Accompanied by both his ambassador to the United States, Adul Hamid Sharaf, and Zaid al-Rifai, who now served as ambassador to Great Britain, on December 8 King Hussein called at the White House. Hussein met with President Nixon, Assistant to the President for National Security Affairs Kissinger, Assistant Secretary for Near Eastern and South Asian Affairs Sisco, and Ambassador to Jordan Brown.[79] Prior to the king's meeting with the president, Ambassador Brown informed Washington that he had heard from the French ambassador to Jordan, who had gleefully reported that the king feared Washington favored establishment of a Palestinian entity—one that would harm Jordan's interests. Ambassador Brown suggested that the king "thinks enough people are already ganging up on him without adding USG to list."[80] President Nixon told the ruler that a strong Jordan was an essential factor in bringing about a resolution to the Middle East conflict and that Jordan's survival depended on the survival of the king.[81]

During discussions with President Nixon, the king explained that the new Egyptian leader, Anwar Sadat, was under even greater pressure than his predecessor Nasser. President Sadat wanted Security Council Resolution 242—the resolution that called for Israeli withdrawal from the occupied territories and Arab recognition of Israel—implemented. He also wanted guarantees for the future security of the region. The king said that the Egyptians had already approached the Soviets about the possibility of guarantees, which might be worked out by the Americans and Soviets together, or possibly by the Four-Powers.[82]

While in Washington, King Hussein expressed his lack of confidence in the Jarring Mission, which he predicted would fail. Jarring was faced with the difficult task of bringing the two sides together, but the only way to resolve the conflict was to impose a solution. President Nixon also doubted that Jarring would prevail. Secretary Sisco had pointed out that Jarring had no divisions to back him, and the president added that Jarring had "no more than the pope—maybe less." Nevertheless, President Nixon insisted that imposing a solution was only possible if all the parties involved were prepared to accept such a solution. Clearly, this was not the case at that time.[83]

Then President Nixon claimed that the survival of King Hussein was both a recent miracle and key to resolving the conflict. Contributing to the discussion Ambassador Sharaf turned to the question of Israeli withdrawal from occupied Jordanian territories. He stated that the Arabs had accepted Israel as a State and that now Israel had to withdraw from those territories. His colleague, Ambassador al-Rifai, interjected that Jordan had paid the price of defeat in 1967, but that peace too had a price. Israel had to leave Arab territories. Calling the Jordanian government the most responsible government in the area, President Nixon declared that the Hashemite Kingdom had earned the right to survive.[84]

At a State Department luncheon in his honor on December 9, King Hussein referred to his army as his regime's principal support and stated that given the potential threats from Syria and Iraq, it was vital for him to obtain military equipment quickly. The king also pointed out that the *fedayeen* carried Kalashnikovs. Therefore, the Jordanians needed M16 rifles. Secretary of State Rogers explained that the Nixon administration had to take into account two serious stumbling blocks: the problem of delivery and the absence of funds. Nevertheless, Washington wished to be as cooperative as possible.[85]

During the luncheon the king discussed his perception of the Egyptian position on Israel. According to Hussein, Egypt had accepted Israel's right to live in peace in the context of UN Security Council Resolution 242. However, the king was convinced that without active third-party involvement, a peace settlement was impossible. Secretary Rogers emphasized that Security Council Resolution 242 consisted of principles that had to be negotiated. These principles were not automatically operative. Rogers stated that Resolution 242 was written to be imprecise in order to achieve agreement and with the expectation that the negotiating process would result in further refinements. The king stated that Israel appeared to be preparing to remain inside the occupied territories and seemed to be advocating the creation of a Palestinian state on the West Bank.[86]

After King Hussein's visit, Deputy Assistant Secretary Alfred L. Atherton briefed the British embassy's First Secretary Ramsay Melhuish. Atherton explained that American officials had emphasized to the king that rumors suggesting that the United States now favored a Palestinian entity were false. Washington did not want to undermine the king or limit his role as spokesman for either bank of the Jordan.[87]

Both in Amman and in Washington King Hussein's visit with American officials was considered successful. The Americans had pointed out that funding for the supply of military equipment the ruler wanted necessitated congressional approval. Before Hussein left Washington, however, the State Department told him that given his difficult situation, the United States would attempt quickly to deliver the arms he required, including fourteen M60 tanks and sixteen thousand M16 rifles. In addition, Atherton informed the king that Washington might find it possible to provide him with $5 million from existing funds. However, the Nixon Administration had not yet worked out how to obtain the necessary congressional approval.[88]

The traveling monarch was in Paris on December 15, where he again discussed his doubts about Jarring. King Hussein told the British ambassador that he did not consider Jarring the right man for the job. According to the King, "Jarring was not of the same calibre as Hammarskjold had been, in that his reactions were very much those of a civil servant; he would only do what he was told to and inspired little confidence in the people with whom he had to deal."[89]

Three days later, lunching at London's Chatham House, British diplomat Philip Adams had a brief conversation with Israeli Foreign Minister Eban. The two discussed Jordanian Ambassador Zaid al-Rifai. Eban said that he had encountered al-Rifai several times at meetings that "never took place." Eban also told Adams that on one such occasion Hussein brought an uncle, who Adams assumed indicated Sharif Nassir. Apparently, the uncle owned a boat (normally used to smuggle hashish), which brought the Jordanians to their secret meeting with the

Israelis—a meeting that the British assumed took place on the water, in the Gulf of Aqaba.[90]

Reports of secret Israeli-Jordanian contacts persisted. At the end of December, the British embassy in Tel Aviv reported that the Israeli press was speculating about the possibility that General Dayan had recently held a secret meeting with King Hussein. These reports suggested that Israel would not embarrass King Hussein's government by entering Jordanian territory in pursuit of suspected terrorists.[91] The Jordanian government, of course, was most anxious to keep Israeli-Jordanian contacts secret, and in November 1970 the Jordanian embassy in London issued a statement claiming, "Certain reports have been circulating in the British Press and Television about alleged meetings which took place between His Majesty King Hussein and some Israeli officials. The Embassy would like to deny categorically these reports which are completely unfounded and no more than mere fabrication."[92]

At the same time, the Jordanian government continued to be concerned that *fedayeen* attacks on Israel from Jordan would result in Israeli retaliation. Despite Jordanian efforts to prevent such strikes against Israel, Prince Hassan (the king's brother) feared that some would succeed. At the end of December, King Hussein's army was doing its utmost to extinguish the last sparks of organized *fedayeen* resistance. Meanwhile, the Jordanians continued to express concern that possible Israeli reprisals would once again bolster support for the *fedayeen*. Prince Hassan requested that both London and Washington press Israel to refrain from striking Jordanian territory.[93] Now Palestinian guerillas had regrouped and some had formed a *fedayeen* group called Black September. However, Jordanian East Bankers were pleased that the Hashemite army had prevailed and viewed September 1970 not as Black September but as White September.[94]

In his assessment of events in Jordan during 1970, British Ambassador John Phillips reported to London, "In Hashemite eyes the militant Palestinians are the first enemy, with Iraq and Syria not far behind. Israel remains in public the conventional devil but there are many in court and army circles who privately regard the Prince of Darkness, if not a gentleman, at least as a better friend than enemy."[95]

CHAPTER 4

THE MURDER OF WASFI al-TALL

At the end of 1970, King Hussein's loyal military maintained security throughout the kingdom, but the danger of a serious renewal of violence remained. During an afternoon stroll in Amman on December 18, security forces stopped British Ambassador John Phillips. Because it was a cold day and he had a toothache, Ambassador Phillips had covered his jaw with a *Kuffiyah*. As the ambassador passed a police post, a nervous security guard grabbed his arm. Speaking in Arabic the irate Englishman cursed the guard. Immediately, additional guards approached. Quickly the British ambassador removed his *Kuffiyah* and identified himself. After lavish apologies the security men explained that they had mistaken him for a *fedayeen* leader, whom they hoped to apprehend. Ambassador Phillips continued his stroll but soon after was again stopped at a newly established post close to the Jebel Amman water tower. As Phillips attempted to take his official identify card out of his pocket, security men seized his arms. Realizing their mistake this group apologized as well, stating that ambassadors did not walk; they traveled by car. The Jordanian soldiers explained that they were on the lookout for a Palestinian who resembled the ambassador. They showed Phillips a picture of a chubby man with a *Kuffiyah* wrapped around his jaw. The man in the photograph was Popular Front for the Liberation of Palestine (PFLP) leader George Habbash. Phillips had met Habbash before in Aden and insisted that except for their build they did not look alike.[1]

Earlier, on October 28, Prime Minister Wasfi al-Tall had addressed the National Assembly, where he pledged that Jordan would observe the Cairo and Amman agreements with the Palestine Liberation Organization (PLO). At the same time, he emphasized the importance of law and order. In addition, he called for the elimination of corruption. Prime Minister al-Tall also stated that "The government looks upon the proposed Palestinian State, which has been talked about, as in fact a blow to the sacred meaning of unity and a step toward the liquidation of the Palestinian cause. The Government will work with all its might to foil this plot."[2]

Soon after, al-Tall attended a party hosted by an Egyptian embassy official. The Egyptian referred to al-Tall's attitude as "moderate and restrained." However, a Jordanian physician attending the party declared that it was indeed odd that the plan suggesting a Palestinian State on the West Bank had been vetoed. If under the terms of United Nations (UN) Resolution 242 Israel returned the West Bank to King Hussein, there would not be a Palestinian State.[3]

At the end of January 1971, a British official in Amman met with Palestinian leader Kamal Adwan, a member of the "inner nine" secretariat of the Central Committee of the Palestine National Congress (PNC). Prior to the September 1970 clash between the king and the *fedayeen*, Adwan had been certain that some factions in the Jordanian army would turn against the king and that the *fedayeen* would emerge victorious. Now Adwan complained that Prime Minister al-Tall continued to oppose the *fedayeen* and that the Jordanian government refused to recognize identity documents issued by the PNC. Adwan said that it appeared the king erroneously assumed that he could recover the West Bank without *fedayeen* assistance. Discussing plans for the future, Adwan claimed that the *fedayeen* would go underground. When asked if an underground regime would be used against Jordan or against Israel, Adwan replied that the *fedayeen* would continue activities against Jordan, because without a secure base to return to, it would be useless to attack Israel.[4]

Visiting London in January 1971, the king met with Defense Secretary Lord Carrington. Before the meeting, Lord Carrington received a Foreign Office memorandum explaining why Great Britain wished to maintain good relations with King Hussein:

> We support him because he is a moderate and pro-western Arab leader and because, if his regime were overthrown, it could seriously jeopardise what prospects there are of arriving at a durable settlement of the Arab-Israel conflict: one of the major aims of our foreign policy.

But, despite the recent successes of the Government forces against the *fedayeen*, the threat posed to the regime, internally by the Palestinians remains; and, externally, several Arab states make no secret of their hostility.

The king continued his efforts to obtain military equipment and was especially interested in 105mm ammunition and Hawker Hunters. Whitehall wanted to assure Hussein that Great Britain was doing its very best for him.[5]

During his meeting with Lord Carrington on January 19, the frustrated king expressed unhappiness with British efforts to assist him. He needed more. However, the besieged king did not have the luxury of allowing his emotions to control his head. On January 21, regaining his composure before leaving London to return home, the king expressed his appreciation for all that the Foreign Office was attempting to do for Jordan.[6]

King Hussein's brother, Crown Prince Hassan, also visited Whitehall in February. His visit was considered a special occasion because it was his first visit since he had been appointed Heir Apparent in April 1965. Throughout discussions with Prime Minister Edward Heath, Prince Hassan claimed that his brother's government "had an open mind, and whatever political autonomy the Palestinians wanted they could have."[7]

Soon after his meetings in London, Prince Hassan traveled to Washington. Preparing a brief biography of the prince, a State Department official wrote that Hassan had made a good impression, in part because of his strong support for Wasfi al-Tall's efforts to suppress the *fedayeen*: "Burdened with a most unmilitary figure and bearing, the Crown Prince, nonetheless, has worked very hard to cultivate the younger JAA officers with varying degrees of success."[8]

While in Washington, Prince Hassan did not meet with President Nixon but was received by Vice President Spiro Agnew. The king had recently been hospitalized in London. After expressing concern about Hussein's health, Agnew complimented Prince Hassan on how well he had handled affairs of State during his brother's absence.[9] In the course of his discussions with the vice president, Prince Hassan claimed that the king wanted the West Bank Palestinians to have complete freedom to determine their future. At the same time, Hassan stated that during the previous September's conflict with the *fedayeen*, the king had clearly prevailed. Hassan emphasized that the

Jordanian nation was resilient and could now negotiate with Israel from a position of strength. Vice President Agnew agreed that Jordan ought to play an important role in the region. The prince then turned to the subject of Egypt. Although Anwar Sadat had replaced the late President Nasser, Amman was concerned about the continuation of Soviet influence. Prince Hassan also noted that Iraq remained a difficulty. Iraqi troops had withdrawn from the Hashemite Kingdom, but Baghdad's intentions toward Jordan were not clear. Finally, the prince addressed what was the major theme of his visit: Jordan's economic difficulties. The oil-rich Arab states had been cowed by the radical Arab states into cutting their subsidies to the Hashemite Kingdom. For example, the Kuwaitis calculated that they "had given a little to 'Arabism' in order to keep a lot of it away from their door." Jordan desperately needed economic aid. Agnew expressed understanding and sympathy but cautioned that the congress, rather than the executive branch, controlled the American purse.[10]

Accompanied by Ambassador Sharaf, the crown prince also met with Assistant Secretary Sisco. Prince Hassan emphasized Jordan's continued commitment to a peace settlement. He again referred to his brother's ability to put down the *fedayeen* the previous September and once more requested both military and financial assistance. Playing the Cold War card, Prince Hassan stated that, supported by the Soviet Union, extremist elements in the Middle East had attempted to cloak themselves in the question of Palestine, but their real intention was to destroy Jordan. Hassan also claimed that last September's movement of Syrian troops into the Hashemite Kingdom had been approved by Moscow, which wanted a direct route from the Mediterranean to the Red Sea. Hence, Jordan and the United States shared two major interests: solving the Arab-Israeli conflict and evicting the Soviets from the Middle East region.[11]

Sisco indicated that Washington was prepared to consider a request for increased aid to Amman. In addition, the American official advised that Jordan exercise patience in response to Israel's recent unsatisfactory reply to Jarring, a reply that frankly the U.S. government had considered inadequate. Hassan underlined that Jordan wished for a peaceful solution. At the same time, the Hashemite Kingdom envisaged return of the West Bank to King Hussein. The king's brother also stated that Jerusalem was important to Jordanians, to all Arabs, and to all Muslims. Therefore, Jordan protested the continued "Israelization" of the holy city. Referring to the Palestinians,

Hassan underlined that they had every right to choose their own future but only after the end of Israel's occupation. Hassan warned that it would be unwise to pander to the ambitions of persons, parties, or movements that had previously tried to take advantage of the aspirations of the Palestinian people.[12]

According to the Hashemite prince, Israel wanted a bribe to make peace—not Jordan! His country merely needed help to establish economic viability. Jordan asked only that some of the assistance allocated for Vietnam be diverted to the Hashemite Kingdom as a stopgap measure to compensate for the funds that both Kuwait and Libya had earlier promised, but now, after Hussein had defeated the *fedayeen*, were too cowardly to provide.[13]

At an earlier meeting the governor of Jordan's Central Bank had emphasized to State Department officials that despite a great many spending cuts, the deficit would climb to 26 million Jordanian dollars. Jordan had continued efforts to secure a loan from Kuwait, but the Emirate had frozen funds for the Hashemite Kingdom. The Kuwaiti government did not respond to Jordan's economic crisis, because a large number of Palestinians were residents of Kuwait. Hence, when the king moved against the *fedayeen*, Kuwait did not wish to be associated with Jordan. Kuwaiti reluctance to provide economic assistance to Amman not only affected Jordanians but also harmed Palestinians, who composed half of the Hashemite Kingdom's population. Jordan's Central Bank governor wanted Washington to intercede with Kuwait as well as Saudi Arabia. It was, of course, wishful thinking to assume that American pressure would convince Jordan's wealthy Arab brothers to be more generous.[14]

During his meeting with Prince Hassan and his entourage, Assistant Secretary Sisco turned to the subject of Egypt's new leadership. Sisco asked his Jordanian guests for their assessment of Anwar Sadat and whether it was possible that Egypt might seek a separate peace agreement with Israel. Ambassador Sharaf immediately claimed that an Egyptian-Israeli agreement was impossible without American assistance. Prince Hassan stated that it would always be difficult to trust Cairo, and the West ought not to embark on a "love affair" with Egypt in the false hope that it would be possible to eliminate Soviet influence. Hassan considered it "naive" to assume that the Soviets could be removed simply because Egypt now wanted peace with Israel.[15]

Sisco also addressed the present situation of the *fedayeen*. Prince Hassan replied that the most important *fedayeen* weapon was propaganda in the Western press. Ambassador Sharaf immediately interrupted explaining that Hassan was referring to the guerrilla movement and not to the sad plight of the Palestinian people. Prince Hassan then proceeded with his remarks, claiming that various groups within the *fedayeen* were arguing among themselves, and some groups were having difficulty obtaining funds. Jordan had no intention of again permitting *fedayeen* bases in the Hashemite Kingdom; hence, they would have to locate elsewhere.[16]

Soon after Prince Hassan's visit to Washington, rumors about Prime Minister al-Tall circulated in Amman: some suggested that the king would soon replace him, others that al-Tall had decided to resign. Zaid al-Rifai told British Ambassador Phillips that the king was worried about the possibility that Egypt was seriously considering a separate peace with Israel. Therefore, Hussein wished to visit Cairo and appeal to President Sadat, "perhaps invoking Nasser's ghost." However, Prime Minister al-Tall advised the king not to go to Egypt without him. So it seemed likely that although al-Tall was plainly persona non grata in Cairo, he might resign if the king traveled to Egypt alone.[17]

Attending a dinner party in Amman on March 18, the British ambassador had a private conversation with Ambassador al-Rifai. Al-Rifai was annoyed that Whitehall had not yet responded to a Jordanian request to permit the kingdom's national carrier, Alia Airlines, to fly Boeing 707 flights into London. He complained that Great Britain was taking a "hell of a long time" to make the decision. According to the British Ambassador to Jordan John Phillips, "Zaid has been thoroughly spoiled by the king for years and when thwarted is more prone to tantrums than he used to be when I knew him years ago." Phillips reported that al-Rifai, who had attended Harvard University, spent most of the evening with the U.S. ambassador.[18]

At this juncture, the American Deputy Chief of Mission William H. Brubeck reported to Washington from Amman that the British continued to be very sympathetic toward the king and appeared willing to provide additional support. According to one British diplomat after meeting with King Hussein in London, former Prime Minister Sir Alec Douglas-Home said, "I want to help this fella." At the same time, it appeared unlikely that London would provide economic aid.[19] Soon after, inspired by Brubeck's cable, the State Department instructed the U.S. embassy in London to suggest that Whitehall do more for Jordan.[20]

Meanwhile, the Christian hierarchy in Amman turned British attention to how Israel controlled Jerusalem. Christian leaders blamed Israeli occupation for the departure of Christians from the holy city. In the middle of March, the Greek Orthodox Archbishop, the Roman Catholic Bishop, and the Latin Archbishop called on British Ambassador Phillips, who reported that "This unlikely alliance of, in normal times, mutually backbiting prelates, could only herald either a resumption of the Crusades or a protest about recent Israeli building activity in Jerusalem, and it was of course on the latter account that my visitors had composed their feuds and come to see me."[21] Greek Orthodox Archbishop Diodorus claimed that it was not the Russians, but the Israelis who were "the devils" of the present era. After listening to the complaints of his visitors, Ambassador Phillips stated that anxiety over Jerusalem's status was widely shared.[22]

Jordanian officials were concerned about conditions inside the holy city, but the kingdom's security was their primary focus. Security within the Hashemite Kingdom improved to such an extent that in April the king and his brother decided to mingle with the population. While visiting a trade school near the Al Hussein refugee camp, the king socialized and danced the *debke* with students. During a picnic among the ruins of Jerash, the king greeted local subjects who expressed their loyalty to him.[23] At this juncture King Hussein was looking forward to the upcoming visit of Secretary of State Rogers. American sources claimed that the king feared that he was being left out of the ongoing peace efforts and had been worried since the Egyptians accepted a cease-fire proposal in the summer of 1970. Earlier King Hussein had claimed that settlement with Israel was possible only if Jordan had a strong relationship with Nasser. After the Six-Day War the king had devoted considerable effort to cementing ties with the Egyptian leader. However, following Nasser's death, relations between Egypt and Jordan had deteriorated.[24]

The king remained unhappy with the position of Anwar Sadat. Nasser's successor had initially objected to Hussein's appointment of Prime Minister al-Tall. Jordanians also complained that Sadat permitted the resumption of *fedayeen* broadcasts from Cairo.[25] Ignoring the king's objections, President Sadat continued to assist the *fedayeen*.

Syrian President Hafez al-Assad joined the Egyptian leader. Supported by Syria, Palestinians called for the dismissal of Prime Minister al-Tall and continued to clash with the Jordanian military. The *fedayeen* blew up an oil refinery pipeline and planted mines on roads in the vicinity of the Jordan Valley along the cease-fire line with Israel. According to the PLO newspaper *Fatah*, published in Damascus, the PLO wanted al-Tall removed from office, and until he was replaced, would refuse to sign a new agreement with the Hashemite Kingdom.[26]

Ambassador Phillips reported to London that the situation remained tense, partially because the PLO no longer controlled its younger commanders. At the same time, the Egyptian government encouraged *fedayeen* extremism and opposed al-Tall. Cairo wanted to emphasize to the Arab World that Egypt did not condone the liquidation of the *fedayeen*. Phillips claimed that Sadat was wrong to assume that King Hussein wanted to destroy the *fedayeen*. According to Phillips, the king simply wanted to control them—a desire that the British ambassador considered completely reasonable. Ambassador Phillips also stated that encouraged by the Saudi ambassador, contacts between the Jordanian government and the PLO quietly continued. At the same time, however, the *fedayeen* still received ammunition, mostly smuggled into Jordan from Syria. They also continued to receive funds from Kuwait and other Gulf States.[27]

Committed to the rule of law and unmoved by demands that he dismiss al-Tall, on April 6 King Hussein ordered the *fedayeen* to remove their weapons from his capital within two days. If they did not comply, he warned that the results would be cruel.[28] A representative of a group called "Jebel Taj Fedayeen" stated that the recent agreement between the Jordanian government and the Palestinian Central Committee had no force insofar as local *fedayeen* were concerned. They would not relinquish their heavy weapons nor would they leave Amman. These Palestinians feared that if they left the capital, the Jordanian army would mistreat the remaining Palestinian residents.[29]

Unmoved by reports that Kuwait would not resume financial assistance to Jordan without President Sadat's consent, the king stood firm. Leading Jordanians now surmised that Cairo's consent would not be forthcoming until Prime Minister al-Tall resigned.[30] Nevertheless, the king showed no indication that he was prepared to dismiss his prime minister.

Despite these difficulties, there was reason to celebrate when, on April 26, 1971, Jordan marked the fiftieth anniversary of the establishment of the Hashemite Kingdom with a military display at the King Hussein Sports Stadium. The event did not go smoothly; "it seemed as though the whole population of Amman decided when they got up in the morning to go along to the Stadium to enjoy their first carnival in years." The multitude attempting to reach the event was so large that the approach was blocked. As a result, foreign dignitaries, including the British ambassador, were unable to force their way through the crowd and gain entry into the stadium. Nevertheless, a British observer wrote that the happy crowd indicated relief that the *fedayeen* had been removed and that the rainy season had passed. Hence, although Jordanian officials were embarrassed that their diplomatic guests did not fare well, they were delighted by evidence of overwhelming public support.[31] The British defense attaché in Amman, Colonel Harrison, reported that the pent-up tension of the past year, which had been caused by the militant *fedayeen* presence in Amman, was now history. However, Colonel Harrison emphasized that Jordan's problems remained unresolved.[32]

In May the king distributed a gramophone record to various Western governments, in which he denounced Israel's annexation of Jerusalem and asked those who believed in God to raise their voices "to save our common heritage." Hussein claimed that Jerusalem had always been the "city of peace" but was now becoming a city known for strife and hatred. A Foreign Office official stated that the king's tone was reasonable and that HMG sympathized: "It is clearly part of a routine publicity exercise, aimed at Western public opinion and intended to coincide with Easter, but in true Arab fashion missing it by more than three weeks."[33]

British Consul General in Jerusalem John Snodgrass emphasized that Israeli insistence on dominating Jerusalem was inconsistent with a true desire for peace.[34] However, in a later dispatch from Jerusalem, Snodgrass reminded the Foreign Office that from 1948 to 1967—during the nineteen years that Jordan ruled East Jerusalem—Jews had been denied access to their sacred Wailing Wall. Nevertheless, after Israel took the holy city, the Jewish State had upheld its guarantee that both Christians and Muslims would have access to their holy places. Of course, Muslims who were citizens of countries that had not established diplomatic relations with the Jewish State were excluded, but "the Israelis can claim with some justice that the obstacles are more on the Arab side than their own."[35]

Given the tension between Arabs and Israelis, diplomats serving in Jerusalem had a difficult task. According to Consul General Snodgrass,

> The Palestinian Arabs tended to regard us as a sort of shoulder to cry on and so we heard a lot about the alleged misdeeds of the Israeli administration. One lady we know from Nablus was beside herself with anxiety. Her son had been arrested. She came to see me. I expressed sympathy, but, said that I was afraid that it was entirely her problem. There was nothing I could do! She went out and said to the press that she had the support of the British Consulate. The Israelis complained to our Embassy about this.[36]

Diplomatic life in Amman also remained complex. Problems with *fedayeen* factions continued. On May 16, 1971, the Jordanian ministry of foreign affairs presented the chiefs of mission of Arab countries with yet another note accusing Fatah of orchestrating a campaign against Jordan. The note stated that Fatah was involved in attempts to assassinate Jordanian officials and was trying to paralyze the Jordanian economy. Jordan requested that all Arab nations caution Fatah's leaders. Amman warned that if Fatah did not discontinue activities that harmed the Hashemite Kingdom, the government of Jordan would take severe action.[37]

King Hussein wrote to Prime Minister Wasfi al-Tall declaring, "He who is of our people, who loves this people, who has faith in our aim and works to achieve it, who marches on our path and does not lose his honour is one with us and we with him, but he who is ungrateful to our people and who betrays our path has no place in our ranks."[38] Prime Minister al-Tall replied, "We realize Your Majesty that the shadows of today are being cast by an extensive conspiracy against our nation and its sacred cause. These conspirators aim at us and attempt to impede and distort the march by stirring dust around us and inventing fabricated events about our country."[39]

According to the British embassy in Amman, the messages reflected growing Jordanian concern that although Israel now occupied the West Bank, that area might eventually become a "Palestine statelet." King Hussein adamantly objected; he still wanted the West Bank returned to the Hashemite Kingdom.[40] Although it appeared that the king and his prime minister were working in harmony, in

Amman Saudi Ambassador al-Kuhaimi doubted that al-Tall would remain in office much longer. Al-Kuhaimi told U.S. Ambassador Brown that King Hussein often changed ministers: "They all have their day and the longer they are in power the closer that day comes." The Saudi suggested that if indeed the *fedayeen* threat decreased, the king might decide to replace al-Tall, but now the Jordanian ruler refused to give into threats.[41]

At a reception to celebrate Queen Elizabeth's birthday, Prime Minister al-Tall told British diplomat John Champion that his government intended to move the *fedayeen* residing in the Jerash-Ajloun area away from populated villages.[42] Champion assumed that the purpose of the move would be to permit Jordanian authorities to secure both the main North-South road through Jerash and the Jerash-Ajloun road. Together, Hussein and al-Tall continued efforts both to protect the throne and to retrieve Jordan's lost territory. Insisting that the ongoing construction projects that Israel had undertaken in Jerusalem must stop, the king declared that the only acceptable settlement to the conflict was a complete Israeli withdrawal from the West Bank and Jerusalem.[43] At the same time, opposition to Wasfi al-Tall increased. British diplomats in Amman suggested to London that he ought to resign: "He has proved an effective and necessary purge, but what Jordan needs now is a nourishing diet. Restoration of some Arab financial aid and better relations with the UAR are unlikely so long as he remains."[44] On June 18 Ambassador Phillips reported that although al-Tall was now a liability to Jordan, he remained self-assured, and the king appeared to have maintained his confidence in him.[45]

Supported by the Egyptian ambassador to Jordan, a whispering campaign against al-Tall gained momentum. Rumors circulated that he worked for the CIA and that he was an enemy of Egypt. In addition, his opponents pointed out that neither Kuwait nor Libya would provide much needed funds to Jordan until al-Tall left office. But the king continued to support his prime minister, and unlike his British counterpart, so too did the U.S. ambassador, who claimed that al-Tall still had work to do; he ought to liquidate the *fedayeen* who had not yet left Jordan.[46]

Intent on totally eliminating any *fedayeen* threat, on July 13 the king ordered his forces to move against the remaining *fedayeen*. PLO leader Yasser Arafat requested assistance from Syria and Iraq. Both countries ignored his pleas. Arafat now declared war on Jordan. The king responded by announcing the end of the Cairo Agreement.[47] During the course of the summer, al-Tall continued to clear the *fedayeen* from their bases in areas of Jerash and the Ajlun hills northwest of Amman. Reports circulated that *fedayeen* were crossing the Jordan River and surrendering to Israel. The Israelis allowed some of these men to speak to the press: "The press has naturally taken the opportunity to draw the moral of the willingness of the *fedayeen* to throw themselves on the mercy of Israel in preference to that of the Jordan government. It has also not concealed its satisfaction over the extent to which the power of the *fedayeen* has now been broken and over the demoralised state in which most of them crossed into Israel."[48]

By the end of July, the Jordanian army had cleared *fedayeen* from their bases in Jerash and the Ajlun hills. In addition to the 80 fighters who entered Israel, approximately 2,000 *fedayeen* were captured and 200 were killed. As for Jordanian casualties, the official number was 120 dead and wounded. However, unofficially the figure was approximately 200, according to American diplomats in Cairo. Finally, the *fedayeen* no longer posed a threat to Jordan. Before resuming their activities, they would be screened to insure that their future actions would be directed against Israel and not against the Hashemite Kingdom. Jordanians were elated. However, their Arab neighbors were distressed. Iraq closed it border with Jordan and demanded that the Arab League expel the kingdom. In addition, Egypt, Libya, Sudan, and Syria condemned King Hussein.[49] Under pressure from his Arab brothers, President Sadat was unable to ignore the Palestinians. The Egyptian media produced vivid portraits of the Jordanian massacre of the *fedayeen* and claimed that Israelis and Jordanians were working together to liquidate Palestinian resistance. At the same time, the Egyptian newspaper *Al-Ahram* underlined American economic support for Jordan and blamed Washington for King Hussein's action against the *fedayeen*.[50]

British Ambassador Phillips claimed that King Hussein indeed supported the Palestinians but that he had limits and was intent on safeguarding his own country. The *fedayeen* movement wanted more than Palestine "under its multi-coloured sunshade." Most of its members planned to overthrow the king, and that goal appeared to be a priority. As a result, the king considered the *fedayeen* a greater danger to him than to Israel.[51] At this juncture, Jordanian intelligence received indications that Palestinian factions planned to kidnap Jordanian diplomats and members of their families. It appeared that those serving in the Jordanian embassy in Washington and the Jordanian delegation to the UN were in the greatest danger.[52]

Egyptian President Sadat continued to fuel anti-Hussein sentiment, claiming that the king wanted to acquire American arms—including M60 tanks—in order to use them against Syria. Disturbed by the Egyptian leader's accusations, Amman denied them, stating that the Jordanian army was trained for one purpose: the liberation of Arab lands. Prime Minister al-Tall announced that Jordan would continue to support Arab sister states, including Syria.[53]

Not only was the king unable to work out a solution with Israel, he continued to be unable to reach an understanding with neighboring Arab States. Speaking to Ambassador Brown in early September, the king was gloomy. He feared that Jordan would become isolated and pointed to the possibility that Egypt might cut off access to the Jordanian airline, Alia; he feared that as a result all Middle Eastern air carriers might refuse to fly to Jordan. The king also worried that Saudi King Faisal's efforts to mediate the dispute between the *fedayeen* and the Hashemite Kingdom might not achieve positive results. Although he feared that the *fedayeen* would send delegates to Jidda to sabotage efforts to achieve peace in the Hashemite Kingdom, the king decided to send his representatives to meet with King Faisal. Hussein assured Ambassador Brown that under no circumstances would he accept an Arab military team to supervise a new agreement with the *fedayeen*. The U.S. ambassador encouraged the king telling him "to stick to his guns." According to Brown, in the almost twelve months that he had been in Jordan, much had improved, and he assured the king that if Jordan became temporarily isolated from the Arab states, Amman could rely on its good friends in the West—friends who wanted stability in his kingdom.[54]

While the king worked to drive the last *fedayeen* from his country, the UN continued efforts to seek a solution to the Arab-Israeli conflict. Supported by both London and Washington, on September 25, 1971, the Security Council passed Resolution 298. This resolution deplored the failure of Israel to respect previous resolutions concerning measures and actions that affected the status of Jerusalem. Resolution 298 stated that all actions taken by Israel to change the status of the city of Jerusalem—including expropriation of land and properties, transfer of populations, and legislation aimed at the incorporation of the occupied section—were invalid.[55] Prime Minister al-Tall sent a letter to Ambassador Phillips thanking Great Britain for supporting the resolution.[56]

Evaluating the situation, in November 1971 Great Britain's Country Director for Jordan Robert J. Allen agreed that King Hussein continued to have the final say in the kingdom. On the other hand, Allen emphasized that the Jordanian army had substantial influence in decision making. Allen stated that although Wasfi al-Tall was a civilian, he had been appointed prime minister precisely because he was in agreement with the army's position. Despite the havoc the *fedayeen* had caused and the suffering they had inflicted on British subjects, in November Ambassador Phillips expressed sympathy for these fighters. Although claiming that he did not wish to see them return to Amman, he stated that "In concept the movement was noble. In practice it was sometimes heroic. That it foundered on excesses and rivalries and the fission-fusion-fission process which seem inseparable from Arab affairs does not detract from the tragedy."[57]

Two weeks after Ambassador Phillips expressed compassion for the *fedayeen*, Prime Minister al-Tall went to Cairo to attend a meeting of Arab leaders. As al-Tall walked toward the Sheraton Hotel on November 28, 1971, Palestinian gunmen, who were based in Lebanon, waited for him.[58] When al-Tall entered the hotel, he was shot at close range. One of the murderers licked al-Tall's blood as it gushed from his wounds and dripped onto the marble floor. Screaming, al-Tall's wife rushed into the lobby calling her husband's assassins "Arabs—sons of dogs!" A Jordanian officer knelt down next to the slain prime minister and kissed his forehead.[59]

Following al-Tall's murder, American officials feared that attempts to assassinate moderate Arab leaders might continue. Meanwhile, King Hussein appointed one of his senior officials, Ahmad al-Lawzi, to succeed al-Tall. One analysis suggested that the appointment of al-Lawzi provided "continuity if not strength."[60] The king asked his new prime minister to retain al-Tall's ministers and to follow his predecessor's policies.[61]

Black flags flew throughout Amman. On November 29 Jordanian radio broadcast eulogies and funeral chants as al-Tall was buried in the royal cemetery, the first person not in the royal family ever to be buried there. Dressed in military uniform, as supreme commander of the armed forces, King Hussein, led the state funeral.[62] A large, grief-stricken crowd gathered: "Rhythmic chants cursing Egypt and demanding revenge alternated with more traditional ones praising the prime minister and the king." The Egyptian delegation attending the funeral was provided with Jordanian military security. Those protecting the Egyptians had a difficult task and resorted to their fists and gun butts to keep their charges safe.[63]

Following al-Tall's funeral, Egyptian journalist Mohammad Haikal wrote an article in *Al Ahram*, stating that after Black September, the late Jordanian prime minister's visit to Cairo for meetings of the Arab Defense Council was an unnecessary provocation. However, according to Haikal, Egyptian security was lax and ought to have been better. Haikal cautioned that it was unwise for Palestinians to consider al-Tall's assassination a victory.[64]

Opening a session of his parliament on December 1, King Hussein paid tribute to his murdered minister, declared the unity of both banks of the Jordan River, and called for the liberation of the Sinai, Gaza, and the Golan. Although he emphasized the unity of the Jordanian East Bank and the Israeli occupied West Bank, he stated that after liberation of the occupied territories, Palestinians had the right to self-determination.[65] Commenting on the king's speech, Ambassador Brown suggested that the ruler was attempting "to keep lid on" in order to discourage "East Bank hotheads" from seeking revenge against Palestinians. After leaving parliament, the king stood in an open car and was cheered by a small group of civilians, who had been kept fifty yards away from the entrance, and "there was no tape recorded applause played from a land rover as last year."[66]

The *Baghdad Observer* published an article referring to the late al-Tall as a traitor and reported that the Iraqi bar association would send three lawyers to Cairo to defend the accused assassins.[67] At the same time, the Cairo press reported that one of the accused, Mohammad Kamil Salama, claimed that in the past fifteen months, the Palestinians had suffered at least twenty thousand casualties at Jordanian hands. He insisted that Jordanians had raped and tortured Palestinians. Salama stated that Wasfi al-Tall had topped the list of those responsible for crimes against Palestinians. The four accused appeared to be delighted with what they had done and from prison continued to repeat that these were the happiest days of their lives. At least fifteen Egyptian lawyers volunteered to defend them. One attorney demanded the release of the defendants on the grounds that they had acted in defense of the Palestinians. As the popularity of the four defendants soared, Egyptian security officials warned the British embassy in Cairo that the PFLP might try to kidnap a foreign diplomat to keep as a hostage in order to obtain the release of al-Tall's killers.[68]

Soon after, responding to a condolence message from President Richard Nixon, King Hussein referred to his late prime minister as his "closest friend," who had paid an extremely high price for his devotion. King Hussein assured President Nixon that Jordan had successfully weathered the crisis and was united. Then the king pleaded for American financial assistance, saying that never before had Jordan needed financial aid to the extent that it needed such aid at that time.[69] In order to underline the dire situation in his kingdom, the king, who had his back to the wall, claimed he might have to "go on a *Ghazou*" (a raid against neighbors to loot). King Hussein understood that the president had to work with Congress and now asked that he intervene to save Jordan.[70]

Excerpts from King Hussein's plea for help were published in journalist Jack Anderson's December 20, 1971, *Washington Post* column. Jordan's Ambassador Sharaf called on Deputy Assistant Secretary Alfred L. Atherton to express unhappiness that private correspondence between the king and the president had been leaked to the press. Claiming that Jordan's enemies would exploit the leak, Sharaf asked that its source be located. Atherton told the Jordanian ambassador that the matter was already under investigation, and that the White House was distressed by the incident and expressed its deepest regrets.[71] In Amman, Ambassador Brown expressed his dismay to the Palace.[72]

Whitehall quickly speculated that a Jordanian raid against Kuwait might be a possibility. During the Khartoum Conference, which followed the Six-Day War, the Kuwaitis had promised aid to the Hashemite Kingdom but had failed to deliver what was needed.[73] However, after considering the matter, British diplomats in Washington told the State Department that the king was likely speaking symbolically, emphasizing his country's difficult economic situation.[74] The king personally confirmed this interpretation in a conversation with Ambassador Phillips. The ambassador asked if the king planned to raid Damascus, "an enterprise which might yield a booty of Baathists but little cash and less credit, or maybe as an alternative the capture by the royal guards' armored division of the Kuwaiti oilfield." According to Phillips, the king appeared to be embarrassed but grinned and explained that his intention had been to convey Jordan's desperate economic condition. King Hussein also explained that the Kuwaitis were not helpful; indeed, they were openly hostile.[75]

Jordanian newspapers carried an official statement from the Royal Court on December 22, blaming the kingdom's enemies for the leak of Hussein's message to Washington. According to the statement, the enemies of Jordan wanted to embarrass the kingdom, undermine it both politically and economically. In addition, these enemies persisted in their efforts to destroy the unity of the Jordanian people.[76]

Concerned about the unstable situation of the Hashemite Kingdom, and the leak of the text of the king's letter to President Nixon, the State Department underlined the importance of providing a concrete boost to the king's morale by immediately providing Jordan with $10 million.[77] Responding to the king's letter, President Nixon reminded Hussein that he had earlier acknowledged the White House's legislative problems. Because of these difficulties, Washington had to delay financial assistance to several friendly countries. Nevertheless, President Nixon told the king that an additional $10 million was now immediately available to Jordan. President Nixon assured the king that the United States was aware of "the urgency of this matter" and would soon communicate with Jordanian officials about it.[78]

Al-Tall's murder in Egypt was yet another indication of King Hussein's precarious position. Nevertheless, the king was not alone. His friends did not abandon him. Both Washington and London remained prepared to help maintain the stability of the Hashemite Kingdom.

CHAPTER 5

SEEKING STABILITY

On December 15, 1971, in London's Kensington neighborhood, just weeks after the assassination of Prime Minister al-Tall, an unsuccessful attempt was made on the life of Jordan's ambassador to Great Britain, Zaid al-Rifai. At the scene the would-be assassin left a Black September calling card.[1] Fortunately, al-Rifai escaped with only a gunshot wound to his hand.[2] King Hussein referred to the attack on his ambassador, for which Fatah in Beirut claimed responsibility, as an attack on "Arab honor, manliness, and ethics."[3]

Speaking to Jordan's parliament at the end of December, Prime Minister al-Lawzi stated that his government would reform the country's administration. The prime minister was in the midst of preparing a three-year development plan, which he hoped would increase employment opportunities in the kingdom, stabilize prices, and distribute wealth more evenly. Al-Lawzi wished to complete the program championed by the late Prime Minister al-Tall; during his tenure, al-Tall had fired many incompetent civil servants and transferred others. The martyred prime minister had also insisted that foreign ministry officials pass examinations and—"horror of horrors" had prohibited the drinking of coffee during office hours.[4]

Reviewing the events of 1971 from his embassy in Amman, Ambassador Phillips underlined that the king had completed the eradication of the *fedayeen*, and that if Hussein's regime was to survive, he had no alternative than to destroy the extremist Palestinian organizations that publicly proclaimed that the destruction of the Hashemite State was an essential first step in their program to recover Palestine.[5] Earlier, West Bank Arabs had expressed joy after the assassination of al-Tall. According to Consul General Snodgrass, "To an even greater extent than those across the River, they feel [they are] Palestinians first and Jordanians second." Snodgrass claimed that resentment against the Hashemite regime was all-encompassing. The Palestinians blamed Jordan for the surrender of Jerusalem. Snodgrass speculated that if King Hussein was assassinated, the Palestinians would once again attempt to seize power.[6]

On the fortieth day after al-Tall's assassination, January 10, 1972, a memorial ceremony took place at Amman's Palace of Culture. The weather was chilly. King Hussein, who was wearing a light suit, caught a cold and was indisposed for a few days. The similarly clad British ambassador "staved off possible pneumonia with stimulants and a hot bath." The king decreed that a stamp be issued in memory of his slain minister, and that a square or street in every Jordanian community be renamed in al-Tall's honor. In addition to planting trees and endowing scholarships in his memory, the king ordered that the 99 Royal Armored Brigade henceforth be called the 99 Martyr al-Tall Brigade.[7]

Apprehensive about the safety of Jordanian diplomats serving in the United States, Ambassador Brown now requested that Washington provide protection for Jordan's ambassador to the United States. According to U.S. law, the Jordanian guards protecting Ambassador Sharaf were not permitted to carry guns. Emphasizing that in Amman the Jordanian government provided ample armed guards at both the U.S. embassy and at his residence, Ambassador Brown urged that the State Department provide his counterpart with the same level of security that the Hashemite Kingdom provided him.[8] The State Department assured Ambassador Brown that he had been misinformed. Ambassador Sharaf had been provided with twenty-four-hour protection. In addition, two plainclothes detectives followed the Jordanian ambassador's car, whenever he wished to have them available.[9]

In February 1972, four men were tried in Cairo for the assassination of the late al-Tall. Although the four claimed they had indeed murdered al-Tall, the official medical report stated that the bullets that killed the Jordanian prime minister had not come from the guns belonging to the accused. The defense attorney asked for the immediate release of the defendants. Subsequently, the director of Cairo's Palestine Liberation Organization (PLO) office, Jamal Sourani, said that if the accused were tried, he would demand the trial of the three Arab leaders who had referred to al-Tall as a traitor—Egypt's Anwar Sadat, Libya's Muammar Qadhaafi, and Algeria's Houari Boumedienne. American officials in Cairo speculated that perhaps Qadhaafi was pressing Cairo to release the accused or perhaps Egypt wanted to move closer to the Palestinians in order to exert more influence over them. Meanwhile, most Egyptians were unconcerned about the case and its contradictions; the issues were "quietly smothered in [the] embrace of Egyptian doublethink and inertia."[10]

The four accused were released on bail. Recalling that after al-Tall's murder President Sadat had promised to punish the perpetrators, on March 1 the Jordanian government issued a statement referring to their release as a disgrace. Meanwhile, al-Tall's younger brother claimed that the release of the murderers was not a major concern; Jordan's primary goal was to strike at those leaders who had sent the assassins.[11] From Cairo, the U.S. embassy reported to Washington that although the Jordanian embassy had no concrete proof, its officials insisted that Qadhaafi was the most important factor in the release of al-Tall's killers.[12] Jordanians had earlier predicted that the assassins would go free. Now in the streets of Amman news of the release of the four accused was greeted with apathy.[13] The *fedayeen* had earlier been driven from the Hashemite Kingdom, but clearly those loyal to the king had to remain defensive.

Wishing to attract moderate Palestinian support, in March 1972 the king announced that after recovery of the West Bank, he planned to provide autonomy to the Palestinians in order to give them a voice in their future.[14] On March 15, without any reference to Israel, the king stated that he intended to establish a United Arab Kingdom composed of two regions: the East Bank of the Jordan River and the West Bank of the Jordan River. Amman would be the capital and retain control of foreign affairs, defense, and finance. East Jerusalem would serve as the seat of the Palestinian regional government. The kingdom would retain its National Assembly, but each region would have its own elected governor and its own House of Deputies. According to Whitehall, the plan acknowledged the concept of a separate Palestinian entity and, therefore, was a major development.[15]

However, King Hussein's proposal immediately generated hostility. Egypt, Libya, Syria, Iraq, Algeria, and the *fedayeen* all opposed the plan. They claimed that the king was working together with the United States and Israel to the detriment of the Palestinians. British

Prime Minister Edward Heath had been informed of the plan before it was publicly announced. A message from Heath to the king stated, "I am sure Your Majesty would not wish the British government to come out, at least at this early stage, with a public declaration of support for your proposals. Such a declaration might be *widely misunderstood in the Arab world and jeopardise their chance of gaining acceptance.*"[16]

Israeli Prime Minister Golda Meir did not hesitate to state her opinion of the king's plan. Speaking to the *Knesset*, Prime Minister Meir claimed that the plan did not promote peace, that without Israeli agreement there could be no settlement. Hence, Israel would continue to improve her security.[17] Meir underlined that the king's proposal had not called for peace on terms acceptable to Israel. She called the king's proposal, "pretentious, one-sided, and sterile."[18] According to the Israeli prime minister, Israel was prepared to negotiate with Jordan without prior conditions. However, the statement by Hussein negated the cause of peace and created obstacles on the road toward its attainment.[19]

Shortly after King Hussein announced his plan, British official Anthony Parsons lunched with a member of the Palestine National Assembly, who declared that the king had no right to make decisions for the Palestinians. In accordance with the United Nations (UN) charter, the PLO wanted self-determination. Parsons suggested that the PLO refrain from denouncing the king's proposal because on the West Bank coexistence between Israelis and Palestinians was expanding. West Bank Palestinians had no positive alternative; King Hussein's proposals might provide such an alternative.[20]

Following a meeting of its Executive Committee, the PLO issued a statement rejecting the king's planned federation of both banks of the Jordan. Then on March 17 Fatah designated all those who wished to cooperate with the king as traitors. In addition, Fatah called for the elimination of the Hashemite dynasty.[21] The following day the Presidential Council of the Confederation of Arab Republics announced its rejection of King Hussein's plan, claiming that the plan was part of an imperialist, Zionist plot to liquidate the Palestinian movement. The council also criticized the plan as an effort to interfere with Arab solidarity, which was a united front against Israel.[22] Even the Kuwaiti parliament condemned the king. Yet, despite public Kuwaiti reaction, there was some evidence that the ruling al-Sabah family sympathized with the Jordanian ruler. At the end of February, Kuwait's foreign minister explained to the Jordanian ambassador that privately the royal family favored renewal of the subsidy to Jordan, which had been eliminated after the king's expulsion of the *fedayeen*. However, fearing opposition in the National Assembly and Kuwait's large Palestinian population, the al-Sabah family was unwilling to speak out publicly in favor of assisting the Hashemite Kingdom. In Kuwait, U.S. Ambassador William Stoltzfus discussed the issue with Jordanian Ambassador Dhuqan al-Hindawi. The Jordanian insisted that the al-Sabah claim that resistance to subsidy renewal to Jordan was so great that it posed a threat to the government of Kuwait was total nonsense. He believed it was simply an excuse to neglect Jordan. The U.S. ambassador assured his Jordanian colleague that he would do what he could to encourage Kuwait to renew its subsidy.[23]

Then speaking to a Cairo meeting of the Palestine National Council, an organization formed by various *fedayeen* groups, President Sadat announced the end of Egyptian-Jordanian relations. According to the Egyptian leader, "[We] will fight from house to house if necessary and pay the price in blood if need be."[24] Jordan had no advance warning of Cairo's intentions. After the announcement, the Hashemite government deported a number of Egyptians and ordered a staff reduction at the Egyptian embassy. Jordanian officials claimed that the Sadat government was simply attempting to please the *fedayeen*, who were now meeting in Cairo.[25]

At this juncture, the State Department prepared for a visit from King Hussein; it would be his third visit to President Nixon in three years. A State Department memorandum for Secretary of State William Rogers suggested that President Nixon reaffirm American support for a settlement based on Security Council Resolution 242. Secretary of State Rogers told Nixon that Washington's objective was to ensure that Hussein concluded his visit reassured that the White House attached importance to the U.S.-Jordanian connection and to the continuation of a stable, moderate Hashemite Kingdom under his leadership. However, the question of a political settlement was difficult. According to the Secretary of State, Israel strongly opposed encouraging Jordan to look for the settlement terms the king desired: the return of his occupied territory. "We now know much more clearly than before that a settlement along these lines is unacceptable to Israel; their position on territorial questions has hardened. I believe the best thing is to be frank with Hussein about the realities of the situation."[26]

The king's visit to Washington did not result in an American commitment to Hussein's plan. According to London, "There is little the American administration can do during a presidential election year." At the end of April, London noted that Hussein had hoped to travel to Moscow to discuss his plan for a United Arab Kingdom. However, it appeared unlikely that the Soviets would issue an invitation. Whitehall explained that if the Soviets received the Jordanian monarch they would risk straining their relations with their Arab allies—Egypt, Syria, and Iraq—a risk that Moscow was unlikely to take.[27]

King Hussein's estrangement from the Arab world was so great that, from a British perspective, it again appeared possible that Israel and Jordan might successfully engage in dialogue. Of course, an interim Israeli-Jordanian settlement would enrage the Palestinians and the Egyptians. Hence, the best possible plan appeared to be an interim Egyptian-Israeli agreement, which could quickly be followed by a Jordanian-Israeli agreement.[28] According to British Ambassador Phillips, most Arabs believed that the king had "already sold his soul to the Israelis."[29]

Obviously, the king's planned federation was out of reach. At the same time, it appeared essential that the king maintain some sort of contact with Israel. British official Michael Shea noted that if the ruler stood on his balcony in front of a row of microphones and declared that he was engaged in dialogue with Israel, he would be killed. However, secret conversations between Israel and Jordan were essential: "The King will remain in the bad odour he is in already, but so what?"[30]

King Hussein had ruled Jordan for twenty years and that anniversary was celebrated on May 2, 1972. Assessing the king's career, a British official claimed that Jordan was the "most stable" of the Arab monarchies. However, there was no respite for the king. In addition to the Palestine question and his relations with the Arab world, the king had several annoying family problems. One of his cousins, Sharif Ghazi Rakan, smuggled both hashish and gold to London aboard the Jordanian airline Alia, and British authorities at Heathrow Airport found the illegal goods. In addition, while traveling to Bermuda with two friends, the king's brother, Prince Mohammed, tried to board a British plane while carrying weapons.

Finally, it seemed that additional fuel had been added to the Palestinian-Jordanian conflict. A rumor circulated that the head of Jordan's Information Office, Moussa Kailani, went to the office of Foreign Minister Abdullah Salah, a Palestinian loyal to the king, and beat him up. A British official speculated that if the reports of an altercation were indeed true, it would increase the king's difficulties with the Palestinians.[31]

Fedayeen activity against Jordanian targets continued. In May the targets were Jordanian trucks hauling phosphates to Beirut. Inside the Lebanese-Syrian border, two trucks were ambushed and both drivers killed. Amman blamed Beirut for failing to provide adequate protection.[32]

In the middle of May, the king's political advisor, Zaid al-Rifai, sent the White House the king's views on a final peace settlement. According to Hussein, the starting point for negotiations had to be the June 4, 1967, line between Israel and Jordan: "There can never be a lasting peace in the Middle East if a solution is based on the outright annexation of Arab territory." In addition, King Hussein insisted that Jerusalem should never be divided again. However, the Arab sector of the city had to be returned to Jordanian sovereignty.[33]

British officials claimed that the king and his advisers assumed that after the November 1972 presidential election, the Americans would introduce a new plan to resolve the Arab-Israeli conflict. No Jordanian official expected that Washington could convince the Israelis to compromise: "In effect, we distinguish what the King hopes, from that which he expects."[34] However, at the end of June, King Hussein had a brief respite, a three-day visit from a brother Arab ruler, the Sultan of Oman, Qaboos bin Said. The sultan laid a wreath at the tomb of King Abdullah, and at a Saturday-evening banquet, the two rulers exchanged medals.[35]

Efforts to achieve agreement with Israel continued to be a Jordanian priority; secret contacts between the two states were ongoing. In July, senior political adviser to the king, al-Rifai, wrote to Henry Kissinger to report details of a June 29 meeting. The Jordanian emphasized that Israel insisted on keeping most of the occupied territory and did not appear to be concerned that the price of continued occupation would be a state of perpetual war. Al-Rifai concluded that only Washington could exert pressure on Israel. The Jordanian official claimed that time was running out, and that if no breakthrough was achieved, another Arab-Israeli war was inevitable.

Amman explained to Tel Aviv that the Hashemite Kingdom would not take part in a new round of hostilities, as long as there was the smallest glimmer of hope for the establishment of a permanent peace.[36]

Washington was pleased with Hussein's efforts to find a solution to the conflict. In August, Assistant Secretary of State Sisco told Ambassador Brown that relations between Washington and Amman have never been better than they were now. However, Sisco warned that if in the next several months Jordan attempted to involve the Security Council in the issue of Jerusalem, serious difficulties might arise.[37] Meeting with the king on August 15, Ambassador Brown bluntly explained the United States' position. The king had received a considerable number of visitors from Jerusalem and the West Bank, who petitioned him to stop Israeli infringement on Arab Jerusalem. Nevertheless, Hussein agreed that despite his distress at Israeli behavior, he would "put the *kibash*" on any Jordanian attempt to encourage debate about Jerusalem in the Security Council.[38]

During a visit to the United States in early August, al-Rifai asked to meet with President Nixon's security adviser, Henry Kissinger. Amman was convinced that Washington was in a singular position to persuade Tel Aviv to finally settle the conflict. At the same time, the Jordanian understood well that until after the fall elections, the United States would not be in a position to press the issue.[39] At the end of August the king told Ambassador Brown that he was preparing the groundwork for peace with Israel, and that prior to the end of the year, he hoped to take concrete steps toward that goal. He had already broached the subject with some trusted West Bank leaders and had explained to them that compromise was necessary. Those he approached had agreed to support him. Reporting to Washington, Ambassador Brown cautioned, "This is all pretty vague. I don't think we should start jumping in the air and clapping our hands."[40]

Then during the September 1972 Olympic games in Munich, Palestinian terrorists (members of Black September) attacked the Israeli Olympic team, taking hostages. Later at the airport, during a show-down between the German police and the terrorists, eleven hostages were killed. In a message to German Chancellor Willy Brandt, King Hussein declared that the attack on the Israeli team was a terrible crime perpetrated by "sick minds who are opposed to humanity, the Palestinian people, and Jordan and opposed to Arabism, its traditions, and its cause."[41]

Neighboring Arab leaders did not join King Hussein's public condemnation of the Munich massacre. Expression of sympathy for Israel or any indication of cooperation with what the Arab States called the "Zionist Entity" was dangerous. Complaining that the bridges over the Jordan River, which linked the East Bank with the Israeli-occupied West Bank, encouraged coexistence between the Hashemite Kingdom and the Zionist entity, at the end of the summer, Egypt demanded that the Arab League States pressure Jordan to close these bridges. West Bank Palestinians were extremely distressed at such a possibility. West Bank mayors joined forces to send a memorandum to the Arab League in support of traffic between both banks of the Jordan River.[42] Hussein had secretly encouraged the mayors to engage in vigorous protests. According to Court Minister Hamad Toukan, under no circumstances would the king agree to close the bridges.[43]

During a visit to New York in September, Jordanian Foreign Minister Salah Abu Zaid told Assistant Secretary of State Sisco that in an effort to reduce *fedayeen* influence, the king was trying to keep up West Bank spirits. Sisco assured the Jordanian minister that the United States would continue to support Amman. He also expressed Washington's appreciation of King Hussein's courage, emphasizing the impact that the king's statement on the Munich massacre had throughout the United States. Foreign Minister Abu Zaid turned to the plight of the one million Jordanians under Israeli occupation and suggested that Washington might press Israel to cease activities— including the construction of Jewish settlements, which were changing the nature of the occupied territories. According to the foreign minister, Israelis claimed that they were improving the economy of the territories, but "prosperity in [an] area [that] Israelis talk about is [a] dagger in [the] back of [the] Jordanian economy."[44]

Moreover, there was concern that Israel was planning to extend the municipality of Jerusalem to include some West Bank villages. Arab leaders stated that the proposed extension would include Bethany and Abu Dis as well as the Jericho highway. In addition, Amman feared that Israel intended to establish Jewish settlements between Jerusalem and Jericho. Mayor Teddy Kollek's assistant on Arab affairs, Yehoshua Palmon, stated that the extension of Jerusalem's boundaries would assist the neighboring villages, providing them with water and other services.[45] Palmon added that since the murder of the Israeli athletes in Munich, West Bank Arabs had been more reluctant to cooperate with Israeli authorities. Local Arabs were not worried about their personal safety but rather family interests in nearby Arab countries. Hence, they wished to keep a low profile.[46]

Speaking to the Lower House of Jordan's parliament on September 14, Prime Minister al-Lawzi emphasized that the government considered security and sovereignty its top priorities. No compromise would be made on these issues. According to the prime minister, both Jordan's military and police force would be strengthened. He again stated Jordan's commitment to recovering its lost territory. He claimed that reports of any sort of settlement between Jordan and Israel were nonsense. Al-Lawzi insisted that Jordan was working diligently to restore relations with other Arab states.[47] On the very day that the prime minister spoke to Parliament, Israel sent a message to the king asking for information about all suspected Palestinian commando sites in both Lebanon and Syria. As soon as possible Israel wanted specific landmarks and map coordinates.[48]

At this juncture, Jordanian authorities were in the midst of releasing imprisoned *fedayeen*, including female detainees. On September 18, 166 released prisoners chanted slogans wishing the king long life and prosperity. Soon afterward, the authorities announced that the sentences of five convicted *fedayeen* who had been condemned to death had been commuted and that they would instead serve prison terms, between five and fifteen years.[49]

But the king's life continued to be threatened. In September 1972, the Jordanian government foiled yet another attempted coup. After his arrest, the leader of the failed coup, Major Rafa' Mohammaed Hindawi, claimed that he was responding to Jordanian mistreatment of the *fedayeen*. However, because he was carrying a considerable amount of foreign currency, Jordanian authorities assumed that his motive was profit. Apparently, Libyan leader Qadhaafi, who had allocated £5 million sterling for a coup, employed Hindawi. British sources reported that supporting Qadhaafi, PLO leader Yasser Arafat had pressured Syria to keep its border with Jordan closed in order to facilitate the planned coup.[50] Learning about the foiled plot, Whitehall asked if the king wished to have the British expose Qadhaafi's role in the effort to eliminate him. At the same time, a Whitehall official commented that it was not Qadhaafi alone who was out to get the king. Both Syria and Egypt had engaged in plots against the Hashemite ruler. Referring to Qadhaafi, the official cautioned that, "our policy has been to try not to let ourselves be provoked, not to try to follow his twists and turns." Great Britain had benefited because its exports to Libya had increased, and Libya appeared to be Great Britain's largest market in the Arab world. Hence, it seemed prudent to allow the Jordanians "to play their own hand as they think best in the light of their own national interests."[51]

Given the escalation of anti-Hashemite sentiment in the Arab world, London expressed concern for the safety of King Hussein's children—two sons who attended British public schools. The British ambassador to Jordan advised King Hussein that Her Majesty's Government (HMG) would not accept responsibility for the children if they returned to Great Britain in the fall of 1972. The king was insulted and, naturally, very angry with HMG. Both boys, who had attended St. Edmund's in Surrey, spoke English as their native language and were good students. As a result, the king now wanted to send his two sons—Abdullah, age eleven, and Faysal, age nine— to an American prep school. Although he realized it was late to begin the search for the present semester, the king nevertheless requested Washington's assistance immediately to locate an appropriate school. An American official in Amman remarked that, of course, security was an issue, but he assumed that Washington could handle the issue better than London.[52] A team of three agents completed a security check of schools in Deerfield, Massachusetts, a quiet New England town with five hundred inhabitants situated in the foothills of the Berkshires.[53]

Although the term had already begun, the two princes were admitted to Eaglebrook and Bement schools in Deerfield, Massachusetts. Suitable security arrangements were worked out— arrangements that included a six-man team to provide twenty-four-hour coverage. Washington advised that no Jordanian security men be assigned to guard the two princes because, surely, Jordanians would attract attention. In view of the cost, which was approximately $150,000 a year, the State Department wanted the king to understand that such security arrangements would only be made for his children.[54]

As the king's children settled in Deerfield, the Greek Orthodox Prelate of East Jordan, Archbishop Diodoros, complained that efforts were being made to provoke an outbreak of Christian-Muslim violence in the Kerak region. Human waste had been smeared on a statue of the Virgin Mary and the altar of the Orthodox Cathedral had been vandalized. The Archbishop telephoned King Hussein and the ruler ordered an investigation. Security forces detained approximately eighty people. Meanwhile, Muslim notables in the Kerak region called on Archbishop Diodoros to express support for their Christian neighbors. Following the incidents at the cathedral, in a small village outside Kerak, human waste was found spread throughout a mosque.

The Archbishop concluded that Protestant missionaries acting as Zionist agents were responsible for the incident. According to the American Consul in Jerusalem, of course, Zionism was "the convenient bogeyman," but numerous local Christians insisted that the Muslim Brotherhood was responsible. However, the majority of East Bankers, both Muslim and Christian, claimed that the introduction of religious discrimination was a Palestinian innovation. The U.S. embassy in Amman reported that there had been several recent manifestations of discrimination against Christians, and lacking confidence in Crown Prince Hassan, many talked about leaving Jordan in the event something happened to King Hussein.[55]

Great Britain's new ambassador to the Hashemite Kingdom, Glen Balfour-Paul, however, had the utmost confidence that Prince Hassan was capable of resolving such tensions. Reporting to the Foreign Office, the British ambassador explained that while the king concentrated on external affairs and public relations, his talented brother focused on internal affairs, planning, and the economy. Prince Hassan so impressed Balfour-Paul that the British ambassador wrote, "At twenty-six his powers of intellectual concentration, though his ideas may not be original, are formidable, his jokes sophisticated, his English distinctly more fluent than mine."[56]

Retired U.S. Ambassador Roscoe Suddarth later recalled that he very much liked Prince Hassan, who was a genuine intellectual. The crown prince was interested in dialogue with a variety of groups and underlined the importance of reaching out to Jewish and Christian communities. Suddarth noted that the two Hashemite brothers were very different. While Hassan was especially interested in economic issues, the king's eyes glossed over if you attempted to discuss economics with him.[57]

At the beginning of October, Prince Hassan visited Washington and at the White House met with National Security Adviser Kissinger. Hassan told Kissinger that recent inconclusive Israeli strikes in Lebanon had provided an opportunity for the Soviets to increase their influence in both Syria and Iraq. Kissinger asked if the Israelis should strike again: "We are speaking privately here, of course." Prince Hassan did not directly answer Kissinger's question but said that the *fedayeen* were concentrated in Syria, and that both the Jordanians and the Lebanese wondered why they, and not Syria, got the brunt of Israel's attacks. Kissinger assured Hassan that Washington was extremely interested in the security of Jordan and admired the king: "You know, he has no business surviving all the things he's been through; you have to conclude that destiny has played a part in it."[58]

Fearing additional attempts by *fedayeen* and their supporters to topple the Hashemite regime, security authorities remained vigilant. On October 1 Jordanian police dismantled a car carrying fifty kilograms of TNT, wired to detonators. The car, which had crossed into Jordan from Syria, was parked in a busy traffic circle near the British embassy and two blocks away from the U.S. embassy.[59] The Jordanian government widely publicized the foiled plot in order to remind the public that the *fedayeen* remained a threat and to illustrate the efficiency of Jordanian security forces.[60] Several weeks after the incident at the same traffic circle, a young French woman working with the *fedayeen* was killed while attempting to arm a bomb. The Jordanian press claimed that the woman's target was unknown, but the government actually did know that her target had been the U.S. embassy. Ambassador Brown was concerned that if it became known that the woman intended to hit his embassy, the information would increase the danger of yet another such effort. Jordan's prime minister told American officials that details of the attempted attack would not be made public, and he requested that Washington assist Jordan to secure French collaboration with the investigation, because he was not confident that the French would be willing to cooperate with Amman.[61]

King Hussein moved forward with his plans for the future of his kingdom. He now turned his attention to the establishment of Jordan's Arab National Council (ANC). After elections for 240 members, on both the East and West Banks, the king appointed an additional 120 members, among them, ministers and East Bank district governors. On October 10 Hussein opened the first meeting of the ANC.[62] Not all Jordanians were pleased. Some expressed unhappiness with the king's appointments. Refusing to be discouraged,

Hussein articulated his vision that the ANU would provide continuity, and that it would assist in the survival of his dynasty and reinforce traditional social organization.[63]

Opening a new session of his parliament on November 1, the king denounced Israel's refusal to accept UN resolutions. He said that talk about a partial settlement was "nonsense." Reviewing the previous year, Hussein claimed that the most important achievement was establishment of the ANU, which represented the unity of both banks of the Jordan.[64]

Then on November 15 the *London Times* carried an article stating that an attempted military coup against the king had occurred ten days before. The story came from the Iraq News Agency, which obtained it from an even more unreliable source: the Voice of Palestine. The British embassy in Amman expressed irritation, claiming that no responsible journalist would give credence to such a story.[65]

Later that month, British officials visiting Jerusalem called on Assistant Director-General of Israel's Middle East Division Eliyahu Sasson. According to the British, Jordan was prepared to be the first Arab country to make a peace agreement with Israel. King Hussein, however, continued to emphasize that sovereignty over East Jerusalem had to be returned to him. Nevertheless, the British insisted that the Jordanians were flexible and wished for a total reconciliation. Sasson claimed that it would not be prudent for Jordan to become the first Arab country to negotiate with Israel, and that it would be best if Egypt went first. Sasson told his guests that the Arabs continued to live in a dream world in which they assumed that they could apply the principle of nonacquisition of territories by force to deny Israel a peace based on its new borders.[66]

Although, of course, how to recover his territory remained on the top of the king's agenda, in November an international conference was held in Amman to address economic issues. After the presentation of a proposed three-year development plan (orchestrated by Crown Prince Hassan) was introduced to the conference, Ambassador Balfour-Paul advocated more British economic support for Jordan. Balfour-Paul reminded London that only the Hashemites had the ability to prevent the *fedayeen* from returning to the Jordan Valley. According to the British ambassador, the Hashemites provided the only barrier to a Palestinian drift toward terrorism: "Lastly, and however, old-fashioned it may seem to restate it, this is the only

Arab regime in the Near East (the Lebanon excepted) explicitly committed to the Western cause and to the repulse of Communism. Were Jordan a reactionary tribal anachronism, its partisanship would be valueless. But it isn't."[67]

Jordan remained on guard against enemies of the regime, but suddenly, at the end of November, the king's personal life again became the focus of considerable international attention. King Hussein separated from his second wife, Muna, and provided her with a property settlement that included Hummar Palace in Jordan, a residence in London, and possibly an additional residence in Washington, DC. The king had decided to marry a member of a prominent Palestinian family, Alia Toukan. As had been the case with his marriage to an English bride, there was now opposition to his selection of a Palestinian bride. Ambassador Brown explained that many of those close to the king opposed the marriage. Some objected because they claimed the young woman had led "a rather free and easy Western-style life, which has not helped her reputation."[68]

While the king visited the home of his intended, the French ambassador ordered one of his employees to park near the Toukan house. Officials continued to gossip about the couple. Prince Hassan was reported to be against the marriage but did not confront his brother, claiming that he wished to remain loyal to the king even when His Majesty made mistakes. However, military leaders, including all of the most important generals, were against the marriage and did not hesitate to so inform the king. As a result of opposition from his senior military officers, the king postponed the wedding but did not cancel it. Jordanian officials expressed the hope that the marriage could be delayed long enough for the king to recover from his anger against those who opposed it, and that the king would reconsider his decision.[69]

King Hussein was not swayed and made arrangements to marry on December 24, 1972. Wedding plans were not announced in advance. Three days before the wedding, Ambassador Brown informed Washington that he had no information about when the official announcement would be made. Jordan's prime minister had not yet signed the required decree authorizing the wedding. He told friends that he did not want to bear the blame at some future time. But Brown predicted that the prime minister would eventually sign the necessary documents.[70]

As he had planned, the king married Alia Toukan on December 24, and the following morning a Royal Diwan announcement referred to his new bride as "Her Majesty." Hence, Alia was officially Queen Alia.[71] Ambassador Brown had assumed that the marriage would damage the king's image. However, he accepted that "there is not a damn thing [the United States] can do about it."[72]

British and American officials were not only interested in the king's wedding plans; they were also concerned about reports that the Jordanian ruler now considered himself strong enough to move ahead of other Arab governments and negotiate directly with Israel. The chief of the political section of the U.S. embassy in Tel Aviv, Walter Smith, disagreed with the British perception that the Israelis wished to encircle Jerusalem. Smith said that it was likely that Tel Aviv would be willing to leave an opening between the city's Jewish neighborhoods, which might, in favorable circumstances, return to Arab sovereignty.[73]

The U.S. embassy in Tel Aviv reported to Washington that throughout the country Israelis were discussing how their future relationship with Jordan would evolve. Most Israelis assumed that King Hussein would be unable to reach an agreement with Israel prior to an agreement between Tel Aviv and Cairo. However, a majority of Israelis wanted a treaty with Jordan and viewed Hussein as their best potential peace partner.[74] Prime Minister Meir told British Ambassador to Israel Bernard Ledwidge that King Hussein was the only realistic Arab leader and that Israel would agree to negotiate with Jordan if Hussein were willing to take the risk. Prime Minister Meir stated that the king would regain much of his lost territory but not all that he had ruled prior to the Six-Day War. Israel would not accept Jordanian troops returning to the West Bank of the Jordan River.[75]

Ambassador Ledwidge reported to London that the West Bank economy was improving because Israel was providing the Arabs with job opportunities that raised their standard of living but also created an interdependence, which Ledwidge suggested might be difficult to end if it continued to expand further. The ambassador noted that neither Prime Minister Meir nor King Hussein wanted two Arab states on Palestinian territory and he assumed that HMG agreed with that position. However, during a meeting with Abba Eban on December 11, a high-ranking British official suggested the possibility of an independent Palestinian State on the West Bank.[76]

British officials discussed a variety of scenarios. From the vantage point of the British embassy in Washington, the future of Jerusalem remained the most difficult of all problems. According to one British official, "it is really crying for the moon" to expect that an American administration would pressure Israel to make the kind of concessions over Jerusalem that appear necessary to enable King Hussein to negotiate a final settlement with Israel.[77]

Longing for Zion had inspired the dream of a Jewish State and had kept that dream alive for almost two thousand years. American Jews shared the Israeli-Jewish attachment to Jerusalem. In addition, non-Jewish Americans continued to be impressed with Israeli claims that when the Jordanians controlled Jerusalem, they refused Jews access to their holy sites. British diplomat John Moberly explained that there was no American Christian lobby promoting the internationalization of Jerusalem, which could possibly exert the sort of influence that the Jewish lobby possessed.[78]

In 1972, the British Air attaché in Amman, Group Captain JMA Parker, remarked that it had to be very difficult for the king to look out at Jerusalem's lights from the ridge at Homar that year. East Jerusalem "might as well be the moon for all the chance there is of regaining it." Parker also noted that Jordan now had an impressive air force. He reminded London that the Hashemite family was Jordan and that the army remained the real power in the country. Hussein continued to project the image of a solider king. Parker concluded that the king sought and received a strong emotional loyalty that was unique in the Arab world. Parker claimed that although Hussein's regime was a military dictatorship, it was efficient and reasonably free from corruption in a region where inefficiency and corruption were the norm.[79]

Ambassador Balfour-Paul agreed that Jordan's air force was efficient and its army competent, but he sadly noted that in 1972 the kingdom spent more on its military than the country's total revenue. In addition, the British ambassador praised Chief-of-Staff, Major General Zaid bin Shakir, and expressed confidence that the military remained completely loyal to the king. Balfour-Paul was pleased to note that although Jordan heavily depended on American military aid, the Hashemites would continue to purchase British equipment.[80]

Assessing Jordan's relationship with Great Britain, Ambassador Balfour-Paul reported,

Our own preoccupations are increasingly with Europe and our limping economy. Jordan's importance to us—perhaps even its special value in the context of peace in the Middle East—seems to be diminishing. Our problem is to make the gradual process of disengagement or normalisation as painless as possible. As the year closes the Jordanians certainly do not regard our showing in 1972 as satisfactory. As they see it we are failing to respond generously to their pleas for increased assistance in the field of civil and military development; we have been slow in measuring up to the terrorist threat in the United Kingdom and in providing for the protection of their representatives there—including the King's schoolboy children; there have been other lesser disappointments. "You are losing interest in us" is the bitter cry—even though there is more sadness in it than anger.[81]

After receiving Ambassador Balfour-Paul's report, Foreign Office official AGM Craig replied that regrettably both he and Balfour-Paul had been born too late. Yet they were not too young to feel a bit of nostalgia for "the (partly specious) glamour of Lawrence and the (partly admirable) naiveté of Glubb." According to Craig, "So we and Jordan, both, are having to adjust ourselves to the new climate. We join Europe and Jordan joins America."[82]

CHAPTER 6

MANAGING THE 1973 WAR

At the beginning of 1973, another Arab-Israeli war did not yet appear likely and diplomats in Jordan had the leisure to focus on the king's personal life. The U.S. embassy in Amman reported to the State Department that some conservative East Bankers remained unhappy with the king's chosen bride, Alia Toukan; at the same time, Palestinians in Jordan expressed their approval. As for the king's recently divorced second wife Muna, according to the embassy, she and her family had emerged with substantial dignity. The most sensitive aspect of the king's new family situation appeared to be his mother's refusal to receive his new bride. U.S. Ambassador Brown predicted that if Queen Alia gave birth to a son—a proper Arab heir— the queen's popularity would immediately increase.[1] In the spring the king wanted to plan a coronation ceremony for his bride. However, his mother continued to object to her new daughter-in-law. Among her complaints was that Alia, whose first language was English, spoke poor Arabic.[2] Gossip about the Toukan family continued. In August when the king appointed Alia's father, Bahaeddin Toukan, minister of court, the appointment was regarded "as a case of jobs for fathers-in-law." British Ambassador Balfour-Paul admitted that the new minister of court's relationship to Queen Alia was, of course, a factor, but Alia's father was an experienced diplomat and prior to his daughter's marriage had served as the Head of Jordan's delegation to the United Nations (UN) and as ambassador to Great Britain.[3]

But, of course, the king was occupied with more serious issues. How to regain his lost territory remained his obsession. British Ambassador to Israel Bernard Ledwidge still considered it possible for Israel and Jordan to work out an agreement before Egypt was willing to negotiate. According to Ledwidge, U.S. embassy officials in Tel Aviv agreed with his assessment. Of course, Ledwidge emphasized the often heard Tel Aviv mantra that the king had to be willing to accept the return of less than what he had lost and that Western nations would have to recognize Jerusalem as Israel's capital. Ledwidge warned that a demand to declare Jerusalem an international city would serve only to stiffen Israel's resolve and eliminate fruitful discussion.[4]

As the deadlock with Israel continued, so too did the king's financial problems. Commenting on Ambassador Balfour-Paul's annual review for 1972, Foreign Office official Michael Pike wrote that it was important to make it clear to Amman that Great Britain was unable to provide much additional financial aid. Of course, Great Britain would be willing to offer advice and technical assistance. According to Pike, during discussions with the Jordanians it was important to be honest and realistic. It was prudent to avoid giving the false impression that Great Britain would be able to do more.[5]

The king yet again tried to obtain assistance from Saudi Arabia. After returning home from a visit to Riyadh, Hussein told Balfour-Paul that the purpose of his visit had been to promote cooperation between the two governments. Reporting to Whitehall, Balfour-Paul wrote that this was "an old song, however, laudable; and on this occasion it may have served mainly to give decent clothing to a rather naked begging-visit." During his visit with the Saudis, King Hussein turned King Faisal's attention to the presence of terrorists in Saudi Arabia. The Jordanian ruler pointed out that the Saudis provided haven for a large number of well-known Arab terrorists, including one who had been involved in the Munich Massacre. King Hussein warned his host that, like the Hashemites, the Ibn Saud dynasty was also a target.[6] Ambassador Balfour-Paul once more reminded his government that despite the small size of the Hashemite Kingdom, King Hussein was the Arab leader most useful to the West and that it was in the interest of Great Britain to secure Jordan's survival.[7]

The Saudis were unwilling to assist the king. London, however, was prepared to review Jordan's military requirements. British officials studied the reports made by their defense and air attachés who concluded that the Jordanian army was the most effective in the Arab World. However, the army had several serious problems, including training, organization, and co-ordination among various branches.

After several successful encounters with both the Syrians and the *fedayeen*, the Jordanians appeared to become overconfident. In addition, British observers noted that segments of the Jordanian Army were not adequately prepared for battle.[8] As a result, despite Great Britain's financial constraints, the Defense Department now proposed that Her Majesty's Government (HMG) increase funding to Jordan.[9]

While preparing for a visit to Washington, DC, scheduled for February 1973, the king wished to restore diplomatic relations with both Syria and Egypt. Before his trip to the United States, the king wanted an opportunity to exchange views with Syrian President Assad and Egyptian President Sadat. Ambassador Brown was not optimistic. The U.S. ambassador suggested that there were two certainties in the Middle East: (1) no Arab nation would permit any other nation to speak for it; and (2) each was prepared at any instant to denounce the other.[10]

Prior to the king's arrival in the United States, the State Department became impatient with diplomat Zaid al-Rifai's numerous concerns about scheduling and hotel accommodations. Assistant Secretary Sisco told Ambassador Brown to inform al-Rifai "that he should keep his shirt on." He advised the U.S. ambassador to Jordan to underline that Washington too wanted the king's visit to be a success.[11] Meanwhile, Stewart Chase, headmaster at Eaglebrook, the Massachusetts school attended by the king's children, invited Hussein to visit the school during the annual winter carnival.[12] At the same time, the State Department made arrangements for the royal entourage to spend time in a Palm Beach Hotel, where the management had to cancel other reservations in order to clear space for their Jordanian guests.[13]

As Jordanian officials made plans for the king's travel abroad, the *fedayeen* continued their efforts to undermine him. Speaking in Cairo, at the end of January, Fatah leaders urged an increase in terrorist activity. Black September member, Salah Khalaf, encouraged his organization to engage in additional hijackings.[14] King Hussein was now informed that terrorists had recently settled in Canada and that there might be an attempt to assassinate him during his forthcoming visit to North America.[15]

While in the United States, King Hussein told *U.S. News and World Report* that he hoped Washington would show more interest in resolving the Arab-Israeli conflict. It once again appeared that

Hussein might now be serious about a separate peace with Israel. Of course, peacemaking between Jordan and Israel would have to include both what to do about the future of the Palestinians and the question of Jerusalem. The king wanted Washington to press Israel to change its position on Jerusalem, to agree to the return of what had been Arab Jerusalem. Clearly, it was unlikely that Israel would return the Old City and certainly would never willingly relinquish either the Jewish Quarter or the Western Wall. At the same time, the Jordanians continued to emphasize that the king would not accept an Israeli military presence along the Jordan River.[16]

During the king's visit to Washington, DC, the U.S. embassy in Tel Aviv sent the State Department its analysis of the Israeli attitude toward a peace agreement with Amman. It appeared that Israelis now accepted an Egypt-first policy and that despite the king's fine intentions, it was unlikely that any Arab country would agree to a peace treaty in the foreseeable future. The U.S. embassy reported that most Israelis were not in the mood to make a serious territorial compromise with Jordan. Hence, Washington had to decide if it should attempt to change Tel Aviv's perspective and whether or not it was essential for Israel and Egypt to make peace before Israel and Jordan did so.[17]

The king and his delegation met with Secretary of State William Rogers on February 6, 1973. Rogers underlined that negotiations were the only route to a settlement and pointed out that Washington had reached an agreement with Vietnam, that adversaries all over the world were able to sit down and talk. Secretary of State Rogers insisted that Middle East peace was unlikely unless the Arabs and the Israelis were prepared to negotiate. Of course, Hussein was ready to talk to Israel, but unfortunately, other Arab leaders were not, or—as in the case of Egyptian President Anwar Sadat—had set preconditions. Rogers insisted that if Washington had set preconditions before negotiating with the Soviets, no agreements would ever have been achieved. Jordanian Foreign Minister Salah Abu Zaid responded that the Israelis and not the Arabs had refused to negotiate without preconditions. Tel Aviv insisted on maintaining control of all Jerusalem, Sharm Al-Sheikh, and the Golan Heights. The secretary of state explained that Washington could not impose a solution. At the same time, Secretary Rogers assured the king that within the limit of American resources, the United States would assist Jordan.[18]

Emphasizing the importance of immediate action, Hussein warned that President Sadat had begun seriously to consider a new war. According to the king, Sadat assumed that if Egypt started a war, he would be able to maintain control of the situation, that the hostilities would be manageable. Hussein did not understand why the Egyptian leader expected "Israel to play the game of war with him in accordance with his own rules."[19] Two months earlier, when a reporter had asked Israeli Foreign Minister Abba Eban whether he anticipated that 1973 would be a year of negotiations or a year of war, the foreign minister had responded that Israel did not tremble whenever a neighboring country rattled a sword. Eban said that the Arab countries were not the only ones who had swords, and rattling swords did not necessarily indicate that they had any talent when using them.[20]

During Hussein's meeting with Rogers, with the king's permission, his finance minister, Saad Said, turned to the issue of Jerusalem and the West Bank, where Israel continued to build new settlements. The secretary of state admitted that the situation was difficult and emphasized that Washington did not support Israeli West Bank settlements. He admitted that American disapproval had not stopped the Israelis but suggested that it may have slowed down construction.[21]

Prior to the end of their meeting, Rogers remarked that Washington was delighted that the king had been able to eliminate the threat posed by the *fedayeen*. King Hussein assured Rogers that Jordan would not permit the return of the *fedayeen* and stated that at a recent Defense Council meeting in Cairo, he had insisted that Jordan would not allow *fedayeen* to enter its territory, nor would Jordan agree to place its army under any other command.[22]

After the king's visit, the British embassy's counselor in Washington, met with Deputy Assistant Secretary Alfred Atherton, Jr., at the State Department. Atherton explained that both in public and in private the king said that now was the time to move toward a peace settlement. He was prepared to negotiate and his attitude was conciliatory. At the same time, the king complained that Israel remained inflexible and, therefore, he made no new proposals that could be presented as forming the basis for new negotiations.[23] Hussein's analysis of Israel's position was confirmed by a message from the U.S. embassy in Tel Aviv to the State Department, which claimed that, at present, a peace settlement was unlikely. Jerusalem was the central issue. Before 1967 Israel would have been willing to settle for a divided Jerusalem. However, after capturing the Old City without a second thought, Israel had immediately united the city. American observers were convinced that Israel would tenaciously hold onto both West and East Jerusalem.[24]

In Amman, Ambassador Balfour-Paul was most interested in learning about the results of the king's visit to Washington, DC. After pumping the foreign minister, Balfour-Paul learned only that the Jordanians were happy with the warm reception that the king had received and with the promise of financial assistance. Balfour-Paul also discussed the king's visit with the American charge d'affaires who said that the president had "a soft spot" for King Hussein and that the Jewish lobby would not oppose increased aid to Jordan.[25]

British officials in Israel continued to express concern about ongoing Israeli seizure of land in East Jerusalem and on the West Bank. In January, once again Consul General Snodgrass expressed his discomfort at Israel's Jerusalem policy, noting that Israel wished to maintain control of the entire city: "She may or may not get away with this, but I can see no good reason why the West should deliberately choose the role of her accomplice."[26] Snodgrass also discussed Israeli activities with the mayors of Bethlehem and Beit Sahur. It appeared Israel was planning a settlement seventy square kilometers south of the Jerusalem-Jericho road. Snodgrass observed that construction had not yet started on the settlement, which would be called Ma'ale Adoumim, but that if Israel intended to build a town similar to the previously constructed Kiryat Araba, it would control the gateway to Jerusalem from Jericho and complete the encirclement of East Jerusalem. In addition, there was evidence of planning for other such projects in Israeli occupied territory. West Bank Arabs were gravely concerned that when the Israelis announced that they were taking over parcels of land for military exercises, they intended to keep the land and build Jewish settlements. General Dayan met with a group of West Bank notables to assure them that Israel would only seize land that had belonged to the Hashemite State or absentee property. In addition, Israel would buy land for a fair price from willing sellers or exchange land for another parcel of equal value. The notables were not reassured.[27]

Consul-General Snodgrass later noted that Israel's major expropriations of Arab land had taken place in East Jerusalem, within the extended boundaries of Jerusalem, which were arbitrarily drawn by the Israelis themselves. Some Israeli officials admitted that military necessity had not been the reason for the expropriation of Arab property.[28] The issue of Israeli confiscation remained an ongoing concern. Dispatches from Snodgrass reflected sympathy for Arab villagers and indignation at Israeli policy. The British diplomat recalled the Biblical story of Israel's King Ahab who seized the vineyard of his subject Naboth:

> Far be it from me to draw any parallels. But one thing which has not changed is the almost religious attachment to their land of the peasants of this area. The fields of the impoverished families of Askarya have been terraced and planted with vineyards for many generations. The families have already lost much, and if they now face eviction, for no other reason than that they form an inconvenient presence in an area scheduled—in our view surely illegally—for Jewish settlement, then Israel has a long way to go before she can be counted a humane and civilised country.[29]

Despite British sympathy for the king, at the beginning of 1973 relations between Jordan and HMG were strained. From Amman, the U.S. embassy informed the State Department that, according to Zaid al-Rifai, King Hussein had refused an invitation to visit London—information that British Ambassador to Jordan Glen Balfour-Paul had not discussed with his American colleague.[30] In February, Minister of State Lord Balniel prepared for a March visit to Amman. Despite strained relations, London assumed that as a result of his personal history, King Hussein was more comfortable with the British than with the Americans. At the same time, when providing background information to the minister of state, the Foreign Office noted that the king understood that the survival of his kingdom depended on American support.[31] Lord Balniel wished to assure both King Hussein and Prince Hassan that Great Britain would also help. Writing to the minister of overseas development, Lord Balniel asked for approval to offer the Jordanians £200,000 to re-equip their police force. The British minister also wanted authorization to suggest the possibility of increased British assistance.[32] Minister of Overseas Development Richard Wood replied that he would propose a substantial increase in aid to Jordan. During the previous four years, assistance to Jordan had averaged less than £1.5million annually. Wood wished to raise the figure to £2 million in 1973/74 and increase the figure to £2.5 million yearly during the subsequent three years. Wood explained that the British aid program depended on Jordan willingness to honor its scheduled previous loan repayments. An installment of £500,000 was due in April.[33]

Meeting in Amman with Crown Prince Hassan on March 13, Lord Balniel underlined that Great Britain wished to help Jordan. He explained that in addition to the earlier promised financial assistance for specific projects, Great Britain would provide £10 million for Jordan's three-year plan, funds earmarked for projects that both London and Amman approved. Prince Hassan was delighted. According to Hassan, he planned to work on urban renewal in the overcrowded areas of Amman and Zarka. The prince also thanked Lord Balniel for the British contribution to the establishment of a special branch of the Jordanian police department. Then Hassan discussed the contrast between the radical and conservative governments of the Middle East. He cautioned that investment in radical regimes would not pay dividends: "There was a silent Arab majority throughout the Arab World which looked back with nostalgia to a time when stability prevailed in the area."[34] Lord Balniel also met with King Hussein and presented a portion of the financial package that had been worked out. The king thanked his British guest and asked if it was possible to reschedule payment of the loan that was shortly due.[35]

After his visit to Amman, Lord Balniel told the Israeli Ambassador to Great Britain that, unlike President Sadat, King Hussein was actively ready to seek a solution to the conflict, but that the king could not move without Arab support. Sadly, the United States was not prepared to propose an initiative. Hence, it appeared that no progress would be made for at least three or four years while Washington continued to study the problem.[36]

Speaking to his own government, Lord Balniel reported that Jordanian officers had recently arrested seventeen terrorists who had entered Jordan with a plan to attack several targets, including the British, French, and German embassies. Lord Balniel suggested that the quality of civil intelligence between London and Amman be improved. The king was willing and closer cooperation could be a great benefit. Referring to the king's removal of his children from British schools and the attempted assassination in London of former Jordanian Ambassador Zaid al-Rifai, Lord Balniel said that the king had reservations about Great Britain's security services and suggested that security concerns might have been among the reasons that Hussein had not visited London the previous February.[37]

Soon after Lord Balniel's return to London, Ambassador Balfour-Paul met with the head of the Royal Diwan, Ahmad Toukan, who had earlier been secretly putting together ideas for how to arrange a settlement with Israel. Toukan explained that following the king's last visit to Washington, DC, he clearly understood that Israel was unwilling to withdraw from Jordanian territory. It now appeared that Jordan had to continue efforts seriously to work out an understanding with the other confrontation States, because it was impossible for Jordan to independently make peace. At the same time, Jordan would continue efforts unofficially to develop cooperation with Israel on practical matters.[38]

Later, speaking to Balfour-Paul, the king blamed Qadaafi for the failure of his efforts to achieve some measure of agreement with other Arab States on how to work toward a comprehensive settlement. Hussein was convinced that the deadlock would result in further radicalization and increased terrorism. He claimed that the *fedayeen* movement was growing more radical and Soviet influence was increasing. Then, responding to Israeli statements that the king was willing to make peace, Hussein replied, "Certainly I am—on acceptable terms; but they are not on offer."[39]

The king then took steps to strengthen the Lower House of his parliament. Measures were taken to fill vacant seats when circumstances prevented elections. Three West Bank seats were empty because members holding them had died. In addition, a fourth seat was also empty, because in 1970 its occupant had supported the *fedayeen*. Sitting members of Parliament were permitted to elect new representatives to fill these seats from among those who were registered electors in the vacant constituencies: "This form of election has been criticised already as being no more than 'appointment.' But the citizens of the East Bank are disfranchised too by the decision not to hold new elections until the West Bank returns to Jordan."[40]

Despite a vast number of problems, the question of Jerusalem never moved from center stage. In March the U.S. embassy in Amman had reported that Jordanian efforts to discredit Israel's policies in Jerusalem and on the West Bank had intensified.[41] Speaking to a group of visiting American Jews, Jerusalem's Mayor Kollek said that the local Arabs continued to view themselves as a conquered people. The mayor emphasized that Jerusalem's Arabs ought to control their own affairs, including their school system. According to Kollek, Arabs needed equal rights both as individuals and as members of an ethnic group. However, the mayor explained that, for the present, Arab autonomy was impossible; Arabs who agreed to cooperate in such a program would be regarded as traitors and those willing to stand for election to the Municipal Council would become likely targets for terrorists. In addition, Mayor Kollek criticized his own people, claiming, "We sometimes rub our victory in too much. The city is going to stay united. We don't have to say it six times a day—and we do."[42]

As Israel's annual Independence Day celebrations approached, the issue of the official parade again caused apprehension. According to London, a Dutch official said the Jordanians had requested that the Italian government attempt to convince Tel Aviv not to hold the annual parade in East Jerusalem. The Dutch decided that it would not be appropriate for a member of the European Economic Community to coordinate an approach to the Israeli government. However, if Amman asked the Hague to express disapproval of the parade route, the Dutch would do so. Whitehall continued to oppose a parade through occupied territory. According to Anthony Parsons, if the Jordanians took the matter to the UN Security Council, London would feel obliged to vote in favor of a resolution condemning Israel.[43]

During a visit to Israel, a British officer, Brigadier NT Bagnall, who was studying the Israeli army, was invited to attend the May parade. Since the Brigadier was on sabbatical, had no official position, and would not be in uniform, the British ambassador did not object to his attendance. The Foreign Office agreed that under the circumstances Bagnall had permission to watch the parade.[44] At the same time, London was firmly opposed to permitting any official British representation at the parade.[45] Two months earlier the Charge at the U.S. embassy in Tel Aviv, Owen Zurhellen, told his British colleagues that he doubted that American diplomats would be authorized to attend the parade: "He thinks that the State Department view will be that attendance in West Jerusalem would not seriously upset the Arabs; but neither would non-attendance seriously disturb the Israelis."[46]

Celebration of Israel's twenty-fifth anniversary took place on May 7, 1973. Although Jerusalem's Mayor Kollek had requested that the proposed military parade route pass only through Jewish neighborhoods, once again Tel Aviv insisted on a parade through both sections of the city. According to Consul General Snodgrass,

Indeed the mild international reaction to this year's parade could encourage the Israel government to make further unilateral moves to consolidate their hold on the whole of Jerusalem. If so, the outlook for peace would be even bleaker than it is. For whatever other compromise the Arab States may eventually make in negotiations with Israel, it is inconceivable, so long as Islam retains any of its present force, that they could agree to exclude any element of Arab sovereignty from the holy city.[47]

As it turned out, during the mayor's reception after the parade a strong *khamseen* (wind) swirled through the city. Snodgrass wrote, "Some see this as an omen of divine (as well as consular) displeasure, but I am inclined to think that if Jahweh had wished to punish his chosen people for violating the sanctity of Jerusalem the wind would have arisen a few hours earlier during the parade itself."[48] Immediately after the Israeli parade, Jordanian Permanent Representative to the UN Abdul Hamid Sharaf sent a letter to the UN secretary-general, protesting Israeli behavior. Ambassador Sharaf wrote that Israel continued to violate UN resolutions and that the parade was "a sharp reminder to the international community of the plight and agony of Jerusalem in Israeli captivity."[49] At the end of April, Ambassador Ledwidge had reported that he doubted the Israelis were seriously distressed at the Arab refusal to offer reasonable peace terms. According to Ledwidge, Israel would never agree to go back to its 1967 borders or permit a significant number of Arab refugees to return, "except under *force majeure.*"[50]

In Amman, some Jordanian officials again expressed concern that Sadat was seriously preparing for a new war against Israel. The Egyptian president had told Hussein not to participate in the next round. Some nervous Jordanians speculated about what the kingdom ought to do in the event of yet another war. If the Hashemites joined the hostilities, they might very well forfeit the East Bank and be left with nothing at all. On the other hand, if King Hussein refused to participate, the Jordanians might be condemned as traitors by their Arab brothers and used as a scapegoat for another Arab defeat. At the same time, although the kingdom was concerned about the dangers of war, Amman was also interested in restoring relations with its Arab neighbors, with the stipulation that no Arab State "propose or accept any purely bilateral settlements with Israel without prior consultation and agreement with the others."[51]

An election took place in Jordan in May, an election to fill the four vacant West Bank seats in the fifty-member Lower House of the Jordanian parliament. Prior to the election a law was drafted giving women the right to vote and the right to seek office. Although the king supported the measure, it did not pass. As a result, women were barred from participating.[52] Now King Hussein decided to change his government, which according to Ambassador Brown was a "do-nothing" government. Since the assassination of Prime Minister al-Tall, the government was composed of lackluster bureaucrats. The king wished to pursue reconciliation with the Arab World. He also wanted to improve the quality of life for every Jordanian. To achieve his goals he was prepared to appoint younger, more vigorous men. Brown predicted that the king would also make changes in the army, retiring some of the most senior officers.[53]

Hussein appointed Zaid al-Rifai to replace Prime Minister al-Lawzi. The appointment of the experienced al-Rifai made a positive impression on both Washington and London, but some of the new appointments surprised observers. Although his own education had been "minimal," former Head of the Intelligence Services Mudar Badran was appointed to the post of minister of education. Against the wishes of the head of his clan, and still in his twenties, Taher Nashaat al-Masri of Nablus was appointed minister of affairs for the occupied territories. According to a British official, Masri's appointment indicated that the government was not seriously interested in addressing complex West Bank problems.[54]

Upon taking office, the new government reaffirmed a ban on alcohol at official parties and banned titles—including "His Excellency"— and expense accounts for ministers. From a British perspective, the new government appeared business-like, concerned with everyday practical matters and anxious to generate a degree of popularity.[55] Discussing the new government in Amman, Assistant Secretary of State Sisco told Secretary of State Rogers that al-Rifai was far more talented than his predecessor Ahmad al-Lawzi. Sisco was confident that the new prime minister would continue to support close ties between Washington and Amman. However, Prime Minister al-Rifai, who was hated by *fedayeen* groups, would have difficulty restoring relations with the Arab World and convincing Kuwait once again to contribute funds to the Hashemite Kingdom. Al-Rifai was likely to have problems with Arab countries, because he represented both

Jordan's link with the United States and also Jordan's Open Bridges Policy with Israel.[56]

At the end of May, Beirut newspaper *L'Orient-Le-Jour* published the text of what it claimed was a secret message from King Hussein to his military officers. Hussein warned that the Arabs were not ready to confront Israel and if now they did so, defeat was inevitable. The king also underlined his desire to regain his lost territory. According to the message,

> Fedayeen have purposely worked to destroy Jordan and have poisoned inter-Arab relationships rather than serving as focus for efforts at unity. Fedayeen leaders personally profit from financial support given movement while stupidly allowing IDF to capture documents relating to operations in Israel. (Thus endangering lives of true patriots.) Arab armies are hampered more by inter-Arab political strife than by IDF. Consequently, Fedayeen will never be allowed to return to Jordan.[57]

Speaking to the Jordanian house of representatives on June 9, Prime Minister al-Rifai pointed to new difficulties facing his country: a serious drought and rising prices. Turning to the Palestine question, al-Rifai stated that in order to liberate Arab land, it was essential to obtain Arab cooperation. He called on the Arab League to unify the Arabs and promote joint action. From Amman, British diplomat Michael Tait reported to Whitehall that neither Cairo nor Damascus had responded positively to King Hussein's recent overtures.[58]

Following the installation of Jordan's new government, in June a group of 250 female journalists from 30 countries visited the West Bank city of Bethlehem, where the possibility of peace seemed a distant dream. Mayor Elias Freij, a Christian Arab, spoke to the group. He claimed that the present situation was "intolerable," that the peoples of the Middle East feared the possibility of yet another war. Mayor Freij emphasized that Palestinian Arabs wanted their right to self-determination "put into practical effect within the framework of our unity with Jordan." According to the mayor,

> Time is working against our interests. The establishment of Jewish settlements in the occupied areas endangers the existence of our people, provokes their feelings and will constitute an obstacle in the path of peace. Any procrastination and postponement of a settlement to

the Middle East problems could be prejudicial to the rights of all nations in this region.[59]

London too was skeptical about the possibility of a peace settlement. But from Jerusalem, Consul General Snodgrass presented some positive factors. He said that Israel so valued the lives of its citizens that the State would not accept the high casualty rate that the British army was prepared to accept in Northern Ireland. In addition, Snodgrass noted that although retired generals often entered politics, many appeared to be more dove-ish than civilian politicians.[60]

The king was planning a summer visit to London, and at the end of May Ambassador Balfour-Paul provided Whitehall with Hussein's perspective. Hussein considered a new round of hostilities inevitable and did not see any way that his country could avoid participating. Hence, the king included expansion of the Jordanian military among his priorities. Balfour-Paul noted that Jordan, a country existing on charity, spent far too much money on its army. The ambassador speculated that perhaps, the king considered the army a welfare program for the lower classes and hoped to use military expansion as a tool to wrangle additional funds from the United States. Concluding his dispatch, Balfour-Paul wrote that even with its shortcomings, the Hashemite Kingdom served British interests and deserved British support.[61]

Visiting England in the middle of July, once again the king expressed willingness to negotiate with Israel even before negotiations started between Cairo and Tel Aviv. Of course, Hussein insisted that before such negotiations began, a suitable basis had to be established. Clearly, the king would not enter into negotiations without assurance that Tel Aviv would be willing to withdraw from all of the occupied territories, including Jerusalem.[62] Accompanying the king on his British visit, Prime Minister al-Rifai stated that Jordan would not object if Egypt moved first and made an agreement with Israel. Such a step by Cairo would likely weaken Egyptian influence. The king agreed with al-Rifai but insisted that he wanted it clearly understood that he was now ready to negotiate with Israel and reach a separate agreement.[63] Foreign Office official Anthony Parsons later noted that

The Americans are fully briefed on King Hussein's attitude and, if they thought that there was mileage in starting with Jordan, they would have done so. But they recognize that the pre-conditions would be an immovable obstacle and that it would be more difficult for the Israelis to commit themselves in any way on Jerusalem and the West Bank than it would be on Sinai. This is certainly the Israeli view.[64]

While in London, the king underlined that Egypt and Syria foolishly continued to contemplate a military attack against Israel and that the Soviets were sending a considerable amount of military equipment to both Cairo and Damascus. He insisted that Amman would not join such an enterprise, except to defend Jordanian territory.[65] Meeting with several high-ranking British officials at Carlton Gardens on July 11, the king explained that President Sadat had concluded that even if Egypt went to war with Israel, and once again lost the war, the situation would be better than it was at present. Hence, the Egyptians had already made definite plans for a new round of hostilities and had set target dates. The king warned that other Arab States were involved and that the Soviet Union was supplying Iraq with high-quality equipment: "Something spectacular was being planned." The king expressed his willingness to provide HMG with technical details.[66]

King Hussein visited 10 Downing Street on July 12, where he met with Prime Minister Heath. The king told the prime minister that he considered it unlikely that Washington would provide a fresh initiative to resolve the Arab-Israeli conflict, and that he was under considerable pressure from both Cairo and Damascus to put his army under the command of the Egyptian minister of defense. The situation was very dangerous. The king repeated that dates for a new war had already been discussed. Prime Minister al-Rifai, who had accompanied Hussein to the meeting, noted that Egyptian soldiers were tired of living in ditches; they wanted either to fight or to return home.[67]

In addition to concerns about a possible new outbreak of hostilities, the Hashemite Kingdom continued to be plagued by financial worries. During a visit to Kuwait at the end of July, Prime Minister al-Rifai spoke with a Kuwaiti reporter who asked if the Kuwaiti government was now willing to restore economic assistance to Jordan, which had been cut off after Black September. Al-Rifai explained that an Arab summit conference had unanimously called for resumption of financial aid to Amman, but Kuwait had decided not to renew financial assistance in order to punish Jordan. The prime minister doubted that Kuwait would soon change its policy. He strongly objected to the Amirate's behavior, claiming that it was Kuwait's duty to assist Jordan. In an interview for the Kuwaiti newspaper *Al Rai al Am* published on July 26, al-Rifai said, "In Jordan we face estrangement, alienation and attempts at isolation, instead of receiving support and assistance. We sometimes cannot help feeling that some brothers try to make Jordan a scapegoat. Therefore my answer to any question about Jordan's attitude and view of the situation is: what are the attitudes of the "haves" among the Arab brothers?"[68]

British Consul General Snodgrass visited Amman in August where he met with Minister for the Affairs of the Occupied Territories Taher al Masri. According to al-Masri, prior to the Six-Day War, together with most Jordanians and Palestinians, he had considered the Israelis to be "inhuman monsters." Today, inhabitants of the West Bank, although anxious to see an end to the occupation, saw the Israelis as human beings, some good and some bad like the rest of mankind.[69]

At a dinner party later in the month, Ambassador Balfour-Paul and Prime Minister al-Rifai sat together secluded in a dark corner. The prime minister discussed how he handled inter-Arab relations. He claimed written communications were not effective, that Arabs considered documents to be dangerous since they became part of the record. Hence, understandings had to be reached on a personal basis requiring face-to-face contact. Prime Minister al-Rifai also explained that in excluding Jordan, Arab governments had both a declared policy and a real policy. Declared policies responded to "ephemeral pressures and currents of opinion, and were often, by that token, unfriendly to Jordan." However, their real policies, disclosed only in private, were otherwise. The British ambassador suggested that the core question was from which policy level action flowed. Al-Rifai responded that action resulted from declared policy but insisted that the goal of inter-Arab relations was to bring the declared policies closer to the real policies. To do this, a pretext was necessary.[70]

According to the prime minister, both Egypt and Syria wanted to "get off the hook" of a new round against Israel, "on which they had publicly impaled themselves." It was now Jordan's desire to supply the pretext. As a result, Prime Minister al-Rifai had visited both Sadat and Assad and had emphasized that restoring relations with Jordan would serve their common interests. They could both exploit their restored partners' military inability to enter into hostilities as an excuse for calling them off, or at least delaying them. As a result of the economic benefits that Jordan would gain if permitted to restore relations with neighboring Arab States, al-Rifai was not concerned that Amman might once again become a scapegoat for Arab failure.[71]

Syria's minister of defense visited Amman on August 29 with an oral message for King Hussein—a message from both President Assad and President Sadat— which suggested concrete steps toward unity. The king agreed to meet the two Arab leaders to discuss reconciliation but made it clear that he would be unwilling to consider permitting the *fedayeen* to return to Jordan. According to the British ambassador, "this divorcée, having aroused an interest in re-marriage, is now playing hard to get."[72]

Following a September summit meeting in Cairo, it appeared that President Sadat and President Assad were willing to cooperate with King Hussein. The Syrian-backed group, Saiqa, claimed that establishing a united Arab front against Israel was more important than *fedayeen* hatred of the Hashemite regime.[73] Prime Minister al-Rifai told Ambassador Balfour-Paul that although both Sadat and Assad had claimed to be sick of the *fedayeen*, they insisted that the king agree to permit a small number to enter his territory. Hussein refused. U.S. Ambassador Brown informed Balfour-Paul that before the king attended the Cairo meeting, his commander-in-chief, Habes Majali, stated that if His Majesty allowed even one of the *fedayeen* to return to Jordan, "Habes would shoot himself and that the army would instantaneously slaughter any that came."[74]

As both an indication of his self-confidence and a gesture to his Arab brothers, on September 18 the king announced an amnesty. More than seven hundred prisoners were released. Certainly, Nasser and Assad had pressed the king to release these prisoners; despite the reluctance of the Jordanian army and his own security services, Hussein opened the prison gates. Nevertheless, the Palestine Liberation Organization (PLO) remained dissatisfied, complaining that those released remained under surveillance. Despite such complaints, release of the prisoners improved the king's standing in the Palestinian community.[75]

A State Department memorandum noted that at the Cairo summit, King Hussein's first meeting with the leaders of Egypt and Syria since his September 1970 rout of the *fedayeen*, Jordan gained renewal of diplomatic relations with Egypt and the prospect of renewed relations with Syria. At the same time, there was no evidence that Kuwait had yet agreed to reinstate its $40 million subsidy to Jordan. Now, despite Egyptian and Syrian pressure, the Jordanians firmly refused to consider returning to the Eastern command or allowing *fedayeen* organizations back into their country. Washington stated, "Any agreement by Hussein to put his forces under foreign command, as was the case until 1970, to allow other Arab forces on Jordanian soil or to allow a return of the Fedayeen would be viewed quite seriously by Israel and would call into question the substantial military and economic assistance we have given Jordan since 1971."[76]

Hussein told Ambassador Brown that in his present position, having restored relations with Egypt, he was prepared to begin a dialogue with the PLO. Although he emphasized that he would remain firmly opposed to permitting the return of fedayeen to his kingdom. The king was pleased with the impact of his recently declared amnesty. Ambassador Brown had reservations about the king's latest activities. The American diplomat was not convinced that a future dialogue between Jordan and the PLO could be kept secret. Nor did he agree with the king's assessment that his amnesty policy was universally praised. According to Brown, the Bedouin and Jordanian security forces were unhappy with the amnesty and certainly would object to talks with the PLO: "[the] king is gambling that he can pull it off; he has done quite well so far in a high-stakes poker game with very few chips."[77]

The king later told Balfour-Paul that Assad wanted the Syrian controlled Saiqa to become the only recognized Palestinian resistance movement. Hussein and Sadat had been willing to agree because Assad was able to control Saiqa. Now the king wished to begin a dialogue with the PLO, "not as a resistance movement but as representatives of a scattered people with aspirations, rights, and human problems, which he fully understood."[78]

During his Cairo meeting with the Egyptian and Syrian leaders the king had given an interview to a journalist for a Saudi newspaper, '*Ukaz*,' which was published on September 15. The king told the reporter that Jordan was prepared to accept a unified Arab army on its soil, but only under Jordanian command. However, in time of war, the command of the Jordanian, Syrian, and Egyptian armies would go to Egyptian leadership. Discussing his attitude toward war with Israel for the liberation of Arab lands, the king explained,

War is not a picnic: it is fearsome, hazardous, bruising and destructive.
It might spread to take in parties far from the confrontation countries.
Our problem with Israel is that the Jews so far have never once had
the experience of tasting defeat. We shall enter the battle only if we are
confident of victory. The first steps in that direction are that between
us Arabs there should be full coordination in undertaking the battle.[79]

After returning to Amman, King Hussein told reporter Karsten
Prager that his reunion with the Egyptian leader had been on his
terms. He also claimed that he was not especially concerned about a
renewal of *fedayeen* activity against his kingdom. He quickly admitted, however, that a certain nuisance value would continue to cast its
shadow.[80]

As the Arabs spoke of war, President Nixon nominated his national
security adviser, Henry Kissinger, to replace William Rogers as secretary of state. Prior to Kissinger's confirmation, Chairman of the
Committee on Foreign Relations Senator William Fulbright received
a hate-filled letter from Chairman of the Palestinian Arab Delegation
at the UN Issa Nakhleh. Nakhleh referred to Kissinger's background;
he was a German Jewish refugee who favored Israel. According to
Nakhleh, many of Kissinger's influential friends—men who pro-
moted him from one position to another until he reached the office of
secretary of state—were well-known Zionist leaders. The Palestinian
claimed that Kissinger recently contributed $10,000 to Israel. Nakhleh
warned that the confirmation of the German-born Jew would ensure
an oil boycott and further bloodshed.[81] On September 21, the Senate
voted to confirm Henry Kissinger as secretary of tate. The vote was
78 to 7.[82]

King Hussein, meanwhile, continued to be concerned about a
factor that he had not discussed with reporters: the issue of a
Palestinian State. Prime Minister al-Rifai had told British Ambassador
Balfour-Paul that both Sadat and Assad had emphatically stated their
opposition to the establishment of an independent Palestinian State.[83]
However, meeting with U.S. Ambassador Brown, the king reported
that President Sadat claimed that both Washington and Moscow
intended to support the establishment of such a State. The king,
who still longed for the return of his lost territory, asked the U.S.
ambassador for a statement that would refute the Egyptian leader's
allegations. Assistant Secretary of State Sisco told Secretary of State
Kissinger that Sadat's suggestion that Washington favored establishment

of a separate Palestinian State was a "blatantly transparent attempt" to upset the king and draw him away from the United States. Sisco requested that Kissinger write a letter to Hussein that would clarify Washington's position. It was important to assure the king that the United States was not cooperating with the Soviet Union to maintain the status quo, nor was Washington interested in establishing an independent Palestinian State on the territory Hussein had lost to Israel.[84]

On the evening of September 25, King Hussein took a short helicopter ride to a building outside of Tel Aviv, which was used by Israeli intelligence, the Mossad. Prime Minister Golda Meir greeted the king. Hussein informed the Israeli prime minister that Damascus was preparing to go to war in the immediate future, and it was likely that Egypt would join Syria. However, the king's warning did not convince Prime Minister Meir that war was indeed soon to erupt.[85]

Then, during the Muslim holy month of Ramadan, on the morning of October 6, which was also the holy day of Yom Kippur, Israel informed Washington that Egypt and Syria were poised to attack. Prime Minister Meir's government assured the State Department that Israel would not strike first. By early afternoon Egyptian and Syrian forces were at war with Israeli troops. Jordanian forces did not take part.[86] Washington considered it likely that Hussein would remain on the sidelines but was concerned that if the fighting continued for more than a few days, Arab pressure would make it difficult for Jordan to refrain from participating in the hostilities.[87]

At this juncture, President Nixon was distracted by domestic affairs: the congressional investigation of the break-in to Democratic headquarters at the Watergate Hotel and on October 10—after his indictment for taking bribes and failing to pay income taxes—the resignation of Vice President Spiro Agnew. Thus in Washington, Secretary of State Kissinger had the heavy responsibility of overseeing the Middle East crisis.

Explaining that he was using diplomatic channels in an effort to quickly end the fighting, on October 10 Secretary of State Kissinger sent a message to the king to delay entering the war as long as possible—for at least another 36–48 hours. Kissinger told the king, "I do not say this lightly—I need time and your help. It is imperative you keep this in strict confidence."[88] The following evening, Kissinger spoke to Israeli Ambassador Simcha Dinitz and told him that Amman wanted to move troops into Syria, that the king did not care what action Israel took, provided that Israeli troops did not attack Jordan.[89] Soon afterward, Kissinger informed Hussein that Washington had been assured by Israel that if he kept Jordanian forces out of Syria, Israel would not move against him.[90]

Damascus, of course, demanded immediate Jordanian military involvement and requested that the king send a division to the Syrian front. Amman refused a division but agreed to a brigade to be stationed on the left flank of the Golan. According to Ambassador Brown, "in back of Jordanian minds is that this is the easiest place for them to get out and back to Jordan."[91] Prince Hassan traveled to Syria to inspect Jordanian troops. He found total confusion. Damascus wanted Jordanian troops to quickly enter the battle, but the Jordanian commander followed his instructions, which were to stall.[92]

President Assad was displeased by Jordan's hesitation and pressed the king's military to take action. According to Israeli Ambassador to the United States Simcha Dinitz, King Hussein told Prime Minister Meir that as of the morning of October 14, the eighth day of the war, Israel ought to consider the 40th Jordanian Armored Brigade a hostile force. Now the Jordanian brigade appeared to be coordinating its movements with Iraqi troops, becoming part of the Iraqi movement in the region.[93] On October 15, Tel Aviv informed Washington that Jordanian troops were approaching Israeli forces, that Jordanian and Israeli soldiers were less than ten miles apart. Israel asked the State Department to warn Jordan not to move these troops either to the west or to the north of a particular arch that had been preciously spelled out.[94] Both Israel and Jordan used Western tanks. Thus, only after Israeli officers looking through binoculars spotted small green pennants flying from antennas did they recognize that the armored vehicles approaching less than two miles away in two columns were attached to an enemy force.[95]

As the war continued, on October 16 Jerusalem's Mayor Kollek held his annual reception in honor of the Succoth holiday. The party took place at the citadel adjacent to the Jaffa Gate. Jerusalem's diplomatic community was divided about whether or not to attend. The American, Italian, and Spanish consul generals attended. The Belgian, Greek, and Turkish consul generals stayed away. The British second-in-command represented his government and a junior French official also made an appearance. The Israeli press did not report on the absences. Completely disregarding the facts, one newspaper reported that members of the consular corps attended this year's event despite their tradition of not attending. It was not a happy gathering: the guests were gloomy; many Israelis attending the reception had sons serving on the front and although in previous years numerous Arab notables were present, this year the majority—including the Christian mayors of Bethlehem and Beit Jala—declined the invitation.[96]

While the international community continued efforts to bring an end to the fighting, Secretary of State Kissinger wrote to the king expressing Washington's sympathy with his situation:

> Your Majesty, I know the dilemmas you face are surely greater than those of any other Arab leader. The president and I both know this, and we have drawn great reassurance from the strength of your leadership and the clarity of your vision of our common interests. War can cloud men's reason and weaken their grasp. You have proved equal to the task. You have our admiration, and I am convinced that history will confirm a crucial role in any fair settlement to Jordan's prudence and restraint in these difficult times.[97]

Kissinger told the king that Washington was in the midst of discussion with the Soviet Union, working to achieve an agreement that would lead to a Security Council cease-fire resolution. He assured Hussein that in the days ahead Jordanian interests would be protected. According to Kissinger, a new strategic situation had been created, which made a political settlement necessary for all of the countries of the region.[98]

Soon afterward, Secretary of State Kissinger sent a message to the king expressing Washington's appreciation for Jordanian efforts to convince Syria to accept a cease-fire. In an earlier message to Washington, the king had expressed concern about the presence of a sizable Iraqi force in Syria—a force that he considered an impediment to the cession of hostilities. Kissinger wanted Hussein to continue encouraging the Syrians to observe a cease-fire. He hoped that the king could convince Damascus to ignore Iraqi demagoguery. He also advised that the king ought to withdraw Jordanian troops from Syria at that time, both to support the future cease-fire and to eliminate the possibility of being drawn into violations by either the Iraqis or the Syrians. Kissinger also expressed his understanding of the need to replace Jordanian military equipment lost during the recent hostilities.[99]

King Hussein informed Washington that at the request of President Assad, he was withdrawing his troops slowly in order to ensure that Syrian troops had an opportunity to replace departing

Jordanian troops and prevent an Iraqi move to take over Jordanian positions. Kissinger expressed his gratitude to the king for keeping him informed. Then, following Hussein's request, the secretary of state explained to Israel why Jordanian troops were slow to leave Syrian territory.[100]

The UN Security Council passed Resolution 338 on October 22, 1973—a resolution that called on all of the countries involved in the conflict to immediately cease military activity and to implement the provisions of Security Council Resolution 242. The war was over. Unfortunately, there was no indication that peace could be achieved. Arab honor was restored, but Israel continued to occupy Arab territory.

In a letter to the British Legation to the Holy See, British official David Gore-Booth wrote that it was difficult to envision the future status of Jerusalem. Hence, London maintained that Jerusalem must remain the last of numerous issues to be addressed. Internationalization appeared to be a good idea: "But as the Israelis will never concede that Jerusalem should cease to be the capital of Israel and as King Hussein wants Jerusalem to be capital of Palestinian regions of his proposed United Arab Kingdom internationalisation of the City as a whole is obviously out of the question."[101]

Kissinger sent Ambassador Brown a message to deliver to the king. According to the secretary of state, Washington was concerned about the Palestinian people and wanted any peace settlement to take their interests into account. However, Washington had neither supported nor encouraged establishment of a Palestinian State. Kissinger assured the king that his leadership and temperate policies had brought stability and progress to Jordan and that Jordan could count on the continuation of American friendship and support.[102]

After meeting with the king in Amman on November 9, Kissinger reported to President Nixon that Hussein appeared confident. The king expressed satisfaction that during the recent war he had managed not to become totally engaged, but at the same time, had participated in a manner that allowed him to save face in the Arab World. Now the king continued to worry about the possibility that some Arab States might work out a separate peace with Israel or even try to establish a Palestinian State at his expense. Kissinger assured Hussein that the United States assumed that the Palestinians would remain in Jordan. He also told the king that Washington had not made any sort of secret agreement with the Soviets about the future of the region and that the United States would quickly provide replacements for the tanks his army had lost during the war. Before the end of his visit, Kissinger emphasized that during the coming negotiations, the future of Jerusalem would likely be the most complex issue. The king agreed and expressed his desire to work closely with Washington.[103]

From the beginning of the war, Secretary of State Kissinger had kept British officials informed and had regularly consulted them. However, a rumor circulated that he had neglected to stay in touch with HMG. Referring to Kissinger, John Graham at the British embassy in Washington told the Foreign Office, "It is certainly true that he would probably not take the advice of a local British representative, but it is a pity, I think, to have given such wide circulation to the myth that we have not been consulted at any stage."[104] Speaking to a group of Jewish intellectuals in December, Kissinger blamed both Israel and the United States for not pressing hard enough for peace immediately after the Six-Day War. He claimed that in 1971 Hussein had been ready to sign a peace treaty with Israel. As for the Palestinians, Kissinger stated that they would "have to be hungrier than they are" to accept a final status agreement. In addition, the American secretary of state repeated the often-heard mantra that it was necessary to leave the issue of Jerusalem for last. Kissinger also addressed his own Jewish faith, stating "If he had known that the Middle East situation would develop as it did soon after he became secretary, he might not have taken the job. But in it, he would do everything he could to get the best peace possible."[105]

In Tel Aviv, British Ambassador Ledwidge met with Foreign Minister Abba Eban to discuss plans for an international peace conference in Geneva, scheduled to begin on December 18. The British ambassador asked if at some future date the Israelis might consider talking to Yasser Arafat. Eban replied that there was no possibility of such talks as long as Arafat represented an organization pledged to the destruction of Israel and that under the present circumstances Israel sided with King Hussein.[106]

At the end of the year, the apostolic delegate in Jerusalem, Monseigneur Laghi, visited Jordan. Monseigneur Laghi observed that the king was trying to increase his support in the Israeli occupied West Bank but had failed to do so. The younger generation supported the PLO and anti-Hashemite pamphlets were circulating in Bethlehem. The Italian ambassador to Israel agreed with Laghi. He had independent evidence of opposition to the king in the West Bank and especially in Nablus. Monseigneur Laghi and the Italian ambassador both considered communist influence a factor. They claimed that during the upcoming UN-sponsored Geneva negotiations, "the Palestinian situation would be a trump card in Russian hands."[107]

Arab support for the PLO was among the king's constant concerns as he carefully considered who to send to Geneva to represent the Hashemite Kingdom. A November Arab summit meeting in Algiers had proclaimed the PLO the sole representative of the Palestinians. Initially, Hussein considered sending a delegation to Geneva that was composed exclusively of Palestinians, but his ministers advised that no Palestinian would risk agreeing to a settlement under UN Resolution 242—a resolution that recognized the legitimacy of Israel.[108] Meanwhile, Tel Aviv indicated that Israel wanted only one Arab State—Jordan—between its final eastern border and Iraq. Whitehall was puzzled. David Gore-Booth suggested that the more divided the Arabs were, the better off Israel would be: "Yet here we have General Dayan saying that he cannot remain in a party which is committed to the establishment of a Palestinian state on the West Bank."[109] With the UN secretary general presiding, the Geneva Peace Conference opened on December 21. Representatives of Egypt, Israel, the United States, the Soviet Union, and Jordan attended. No Syrian representative participated. Jordan and Israel now agreed to return to Geneva in January to begin talks on disengagement.[110]

Jordan had emerged from the 1973 conflict without suffering serious consequences. With support from his American and British friends, Hussein had managed to negotiate through a maze of difficulties. In addition, he had skillfully avoided alienating either his Arab brothers or Israel. There was no indication, however, that the king was any closer to regaining his lost territory.

CHAPTER 7

RELINQUISHING THE DREAM

The 1973 War had not resulted in a decisive Arab military victory. Nevertheless, it helped to restore Arab pride and confidence. Israel's Defense Minister, Moshe Dayan, wrote that the Arabs were considerably stronger than they had been during previous wars: "As for the fighting standard of the Arab soldiers, I can sum it up in one sentence: they did not run away."[1] The war also provided an opportunity for the oil-producing States to illustrate how much the West depended on Arab oil. During the hostilities Great Britain had refused to permit Washington to use its airfields to transport military equipment to Israel. As a result, together with other countries deemed friendly to the Arabs, Great Britain was rewarded with an uninterrupted supply of oil. In response to U.S. support for Israel, an embargo was imposed on oil to the United States, which resulted in frustrated drivers spending hours in long lines waiting to fill their gas tanks.

U.S. Ambassador Thomas Pickering, who took up his post in Amman in February 1974, noted that when he arrived in Jordan, despite the cease-fire, the 1973 war was not completely over. Shooting incidents continued until the spring of 1974. In June, King Hussein spoke to a reporter for *Newsweek* and reminded its readers that the Arabs had billions of dollars in oil revenue—funds that could be used to continue warfare if Tel Aviv refused to end the occupation of Arab lands.[2]

On January 20, 1974, returning from a trip to the Middle East, Secretary of State Henry Kissinger met with British officials at the London airport, including Foreign Secretary Sir Alec Douglas-Home. According to Kissinger, the Israelis still refused to agree to the stationing of Jordanian troops on the West Bank. Kissinger said that he did not wish to annoy the Israelis. However, if they continued to refuse to accept a Jordanian presence in the territory that they had occupied since 1967, he would tell them that Washington might turn to Palestine Liberation Organization (PLO) leader Yasser Arafat.[3]

As the Americans and British discussed how to obtain Israeli cooperation, Hussein and his ministers specifically pressed for at least a partial withdrawal of Israeli forces from their positions on the Jordan River. Concerning the issue of Palestinian self-determination, the king held firm to his view that the first step toward restoring the rights of the Palestinians had to be Israeli withdrawal. Hussein truly hoped that after Israel withdrew from the West Bank, the Palestinians would decide to remain part of Jordan. However, he indicated that whatever their choice, he would support their decision. As for Jerusalem, the king steadfastly maintained that Arab sovereignty over the old city had to be restored.[4]

Visiting London at the end of March 1974, the king underlined that the future of the West Bank depended on Israel's willingness to negotiate with him. In the event that Israel continued to stall, Hussein said that he would concentrate on the East Bank of his kingdom. Yet during moments of frustration, the king declared that he would leave the future of the West Bank to the Israelis and Palestinians to sort out.[5]

Ambassador Balfour-Paul met with his American counterpart, Thomas Pickering on April 5, and both agreed that after its creation, a West Bank state would decide to unite with Jordan. However, the U.S. ambassador was not certain that the Hashemites could survive such a union. Following his meeting with Pickering, Balfour-Paul had a long discussion with the king. Hussein had hardened his position and now appeared determined to be in complete charge of negotiations leading to an Israeli withdrawal. The king told Balfour-Paul that he was interested in an Israeli agreement to withdraw from territory that Jordan could reoccupy, and that he had no interest in discussing a withdrawal that would benefit the PLO. However, the king doubted that progress was possible as long as the inflexible Israeli prime minister, Golda Meir, remained in office. During his meeting with the king, Balfour-Paul asked Hussein what he thought of Yitzhak Rabin, the military leader, now serving as his government's labor minister. Although he would later change his perspective, the king then described Rabin as "an arrant Nazi." According to Hussein, General Dayan was the only Israeli leader able to deliver a settlement.[6]

Later, discussing Hussein, General Dayan noted the king's charm and his courage. Nevertheless, from Dayan's perspective, when considering a future settlement with Israel, Hussein viewed "reality in fanciful terms." Dayan emphasized that Israel would not return to its 1948 borders.[7]

Discussing the future of the occupied territory, some British officials, however, expressed surprise at Hashemite confidence in West Bank support. Balfour-Paul suggested that perhaps West Bank Palestinians who had access to the king had misled him and his advisers. He looked for a parallel that Whitehall would appreciate and suggested that the chancellor of the exchequer occasionally declared confidence in the strength of the pound sterling. In May the king continued to expect support from Egypt and Syria for his proposed constitutional link between the East and West Banks. Balfour-Paul warned that the alternative to the king's United Arab Kingdom plan was a PLO controlled state, which would be unwilling to accept Israel's existence.[8]

Despite British support for Hussein, London's ability to help him was now extremely limited. Great Britain had not been a participant in the December 1973 Geneva Conference. According to Whitehall, if London had been represented at that United Nations–sponsored conference, the British might have been able to support the king's position. Looking for the silver lining, Foreign Office official Michael Weir noted that regardless of what transpired regarding the West Bank, at least the king had the East Bank to fall back on.[9]

Clearly, the king longed for an end to Israel's occupation but did not want the PLO to take control of what, prior to June 1967, had been his territory. King Hussein had worked hard to counter Arab pressure to recognize the PLO as heir to the Israeli occupied West Bank. He had failed. U.S. Ambassador to Egypt Hermann Eilts recalled that in October 1974—the very evening before President Anwar Sadat departed for an Arab summit meeting in Rabat—Cairo informed the U.S. embassy that the Egyptian leader would continue to support Hussein as the spokesman for the Palestinians.[10]

Once at the Rabat conference, however, President Sadat bowed to the majority view to recognize not Jordan, but the PLO as the representative of the Palestinians. For the first time, the PLO was officially recognized by all of the Arab states as the "sole legitimate representative of the Palestinian people." The Arab heads of state now called for close cooperation between the front-line states and the PLO and prohibited interference by other Arab States in Palestinian

affairs. The Rabat Declaration conferred the mantle of legitimacy onto
the PLO. It gave official Arab recognition to the PLO's claim to the
West Bank and clearly put the fate of the Palestinian people in PLO
hands. King Hussein opposed the Rabat Declaration, but after the
Arab oil-producing states promised to provide Jordan with an annual
subsidy of $300 million, he signed it.[11]

Both Sadat and Hussein had capitulated, and thus, the PLO
achieved a major diplomatic victory. President Sadat sent an apologetic
note to Washington explaining that he had accepted the will of the
conference.[12] Hence, at Rabat, King Hussein was pressed to accept
the PLO as "the sole legitimate representative of [the] Palestinian
people."[13] As a result, the king was cut out of the process of actually
negotiating for the return of the West Bank. The king, however, had
a consolation prize. Jordan was included in the conference's annual
military aid allocation for all of the Arab States bordering Israel.[14]

Among the additional frustrations the king faced after the 1973
War was the issue of American Hawk Missiles, which Hussein wanted
to purchase in the event they were needed, not against Israel but
against one of his Arab neighbors. Negotiations about the purchase of
these missiles were arduous. Initially, Washington appeared reluctant
to sell the missiles, and Congress supported Israel's insistence that the
missiles be set in concrete silos targeted away from Israel. In addition,
although King Hussein had been under the impression that he had an
agreement with King Faisal stipulating that Saudi Arabia would pay
for the missiles, the Saudis were not forthcoming with the funds.
Finally, the Saudi government agreed that the United States could
charge their surplus account at the U.S. Defense Department to pay
for the missiles.[15]

Given the serious obstacles the king continued to encounter, U.S.
Ambassador Pickering noted that during his tenure in Amman, his
embassy had to develop a variety of strategies concerning how to
work together with a very small kingdom that truly wanted to play a
positive role in bringing about a peace settlement. Pickering emphasized that the king was committed to resolving the conflict. But, unfortunately, Hussein did not have much influence in the Arab World, and
as a result with either Israel or the United States.[16]

Pickering recalled that the situation was frustrating for the king,
but he had grown up with frustrations and handled them very well.
Although he was unhappy, he had the personality, the determination,
and the sense of commitment that permitted him to carry on.[17] The

king did not lose hope and was an inspiration to those who worked with him.

After three years of service in Amman, Ambassador Balfour-Paul continued to be impressed with the king's courage. The British ambassador claimed that despite strong opposition from his Arab neighbors, Hussein continued to play an important role. Balfour-Paul admitted that in previous years the king had been "double-crossed by the Egyptians, boycotted by the Syrians, accused of treason by Algerians and Libyans, while Tunisians have denied the very existence of his country and Palestinians his own personal right to exist at all." However, the British ambassador noted that in 1975 numerous Arab leaders, including the Shah of Iran, Egyptian leader Anwar Sadat, Syrian President Hafaz Assad, and Saudi Prince Fahd had visited Jordan. Once again Balfour-Paul expressed the hope that insofar as it was able, Great Britain would continue to support the Hashemite Kingdom.[18]

Hussein remained unhappy with the decisions made at the 1974 Rabat Conference. British officials reported to London that the king assumed that if he sat back and did nothing the other Arab leaders would approach him and ask for his involvement. Hussein did not give up. He continued to champion federation between Jordan and a West Bank Palestinian State. He also talked about the possibility of creating a joint Israeli-Jordanian-Palestinian administration for Jerusalem.[19] In March 1975 the king claimed that if sovereignty over the Arab part of the city was returned to him, the city would not be divided but would become a city of all believers.[20]

As the king continued to focus on strategy, high policy, military, and security developments, his brother Hassan concentrated on economic development. Ambassador Pickering mused that Hassan had a quick mind and sometimes talked in shorthand. He moved rapidly from one subject to another, thinking everyone could follow him. Pickering claimed that as he got to know the prince, he found him to be a very interesting person—someone who had creative ideas but also always supported his brother.[21]

During a visit to the United States in May 1975, the king claimed that the major Arab States were ready to make peace with Israel. Speaking at the South Carolina Citadel Military College, he explained that the Arabs had two conditions: Israeli withdrawal from Arab territory and Israeli recognition of the rights of the Palestinians to their homeland. The king stated that Washington had to participate in peacemaking efforts. Cairo agreed. According to the Egyptian embassy in Amman, when in the United States the king had permission to speak for all of the confrontation states.[22]

Promoting British support for Amman, Ambassador Balfour-Paul noted that since the beginning of his reign, King Hussein had provided stability. Despite myriad problems, Jordan was not "an unhappy country." Of course, together with the Americans, the British were pleased that thanks to the Hashemites' Jordan remained fundamentally favorable to the West. Balfour-Paul underlined that despite past problems, Amman continued its close relationship with Great Britain.[23]

However, neither London nor Washington could help Hussein alleviate tensions between the Palestinians and the Jordanians. Palestinian animosity toward the Hashemites continued to be a serious concern for Amman and its supporters. The memory of Black September remained vivid. Attempting to address the problem, the king worked hard to improve relations. He continued efforts to demonstrate his interest in including Palestinian representatives. As a result, some Palestinians served in his cabinet. According to Ambassador Pickering, Palestinians were more comfortable in Jordan than in either Lebanon or Syria. However, Pickering noted that groups of Palestinian diehards remained active in the kingdom. Nevertheless, during his years in Amman, Pickering did not find it necessary to take any special security precautions. Traveling through the desert Pickering used a lightly armored 4-wheel drive vehicle. The Jordanian authorities insisted that he take one of their side arms, which he practiced with but fortunately never had to use.[24]

The new British ambassador to Jordan, John Moberly, met with Hussein in October 1975 to discuss future Jordanian elections. Hussein was concerned that if the Arab residents of the Israeli-occupied West Bank were excluded, he would be accused of abandoning them to Tel Aviv. However, if he allowed West Bank participation in elections he would be accused of rejecting the Rabat Conference decision. The king also complained to Ambassador Moberly about Washington's agreement to supply Israel with massive quantities of military equipment. In addition, he expressed unhappiness about the American reluctance to move the search for Middle East peace forward until after the next presidential election. Following his meeting with the king, Ambassador Moberly talked with Ambassador Pickering. The U.S. ambassador assured his British colleague that both President Gerald Ford and Secretary of State Kissinger were concerned about President Sadat's isolation from other Arab leaders as a result of his peace-making efforts. The State Department wished to improve the situation. Pickering claimed that Washington was trying to work out a proposal relating to the Israeli-occupied Golan Heights, a proposal that would entice President Assad to agree to negotiate.[25]

Diplomatic efforts to achieve some sort of a breakthrough continued. British Foreign Secretary David Ennals visited Amman in November 1975. During a meeting with Prime Minister Zaid al-Rifai, the Jordanian told Ennals that peace was impossible unless the Israelis withdrew from all Arab territory. He emphasized that no Arab leader could concede territory to Israel. Al-Rifai explained that immediately after the Rabat conference, for a brief period, Arab support for the PLO increased. He insisted, however, that the PLO was no longer a major political force. Al-Rifai claimed that Amman supported Palestinian involvement in negotiations to achieve an end to the Arab-Israeli conflict. At the same time, Jordan did not consider the PLO the sole representative of the Palestinian people. According to Ennals, Her Majesty's Government (HMG) agreed.[26] Foreign Secretary Ennals favorably impressed his hosts when he asked to visit a refugee camp and decided to be interviewed on Jordanian television. Whitehall was pleased at the warm welcome that Ennals received.[27] However, London alone could not achieve any sort of a breakthrough.

International attention once again focused on the king's private life, when on February 9, 1977, the king experienced yet another personal tragedy. Hussein's third wife, Queen Alia, was returning to Amman from a visit to a hospital in the south of Jordan. Her pilot, a close friend of the king's, had considerable experience. Nevertheless, the helicopter crashed. All aboard were killed. The death of Queen Alia left Hussein seriously depressed.[28]

Fortunately, after Alia's death Hussein met a young American woman who pleased him. In June 1978, the king married his fourth wife, Elizabeth Halaby, a Princeton University–educated American of Arab and Swiss descent. The king was forty-two and the father of eight children. His twenty-six year old bride had not been previously married. Hussein proclaimed his new wife, Queen Noor (light of Hussein). According to Noor, her name was the "most precious gift" that she ever received from the king.[29]

Before the king's marriage to Queen Noor in November 1977, a dramatic breakthrough in the Arab-Israeli conflict occurred when Egyptian President Sadat announced his willingness to visit Israel. Israeli Prime Minister Menachem Begin, a hard-line expansionist, quickly extended an invitation. Sadat flew to Israel and as an astonished public listened, he spoke to the Israeli *Knesset.* "I have come to Jerusalem, the city of peace, which will always remain as a living embodiment of coexistence among believers of the three religions. It is inadmissible that anyone should conceive the special status of the city of Jerusalem within the framework of annexation or expansionism. It should be a free and open city for all believers."[30]

Following Sadat's journey to Israel, at the invitation of President Carter, President Sadat and Prime Minister Begin met with him at the presidential retreat, Camp David. Working steadily from September 5 to 17, 1978, Sadat and Begin reached an agreement. President Sadat had not consulted King Hussein before embarking on his peace-seeking saga. On September 19, Amman issued a statement reaffirming support for a comprehensive solution to the conflict, condemned Egypt's actions, and demanded an Israeli withdrawal from all of the Occupied Territories. After the signing of the Camp David Accords, Jordan accepted an Iraqi invitation to attend a conference in Baghdad, which the Iraqis called the "Confrontation Front Summit." Held in November 1978, the Arab states emphatically rejected the Camp David Accords and expelled Egypt from the Arab League. Prior to King Hussein's arrival in Baghdad, savvy Baath party officials sent workers to the royal cemetery to cut the grass that covered the neglected graves of Hussein's Hashemite relatives.[31]

President Jimmy Carter was unhappy that Hussein openly opposed the Camp David agreement. Neither Hussein's disapproval nor the condemnation of the Arab League deterred Sadat. As a result, Egypt and Israel signed a peace treaty on March 26, 1979. Hosted by President Carter, the dramatic signing ceremony took place on the White House lawn.[32] Tied to the anti-Sadat camp, Hussein was now unable to move toward peace.

Hussein visited the United States in September 1979 in order to attend United Nations meetings; however, he kept his distance from the White House. President Carter requested that Secretary of State Cyrus Vance explore the possibility that the king might be willing to travel to Washington to discuss the Camp David Accords. President Carter later wrote, "The report to me was that no good purpose would be served by an official meeting between me and Jordan's monarch."[33]

While in New York, Hussein talked to reporter Robert MacNeil. Asked if he had been invited to the White House, the king replied that he had not sought an invitation nor was one offered. However,

Hussein confirmed that he had met with Secretary of State Vance. MacNeil suggested that relations between Washington and Amman had cooled; the king agreed. MacNeil then asked if rather than a federation between both banks of the Jordan River, the king would support an independent Palestinian state. According to the king, "If that is their choice, by all means."[34]

Soon after, Washington and Amman renewed their close connection. Although the Camp David Accords remained an issue, Carter and Hussein were both profoundly disturbed by ongoing events in Iran: the end of the Shah's rule, the establishment of a fundamentalist Islamic state, and the seizure of American hostages. Then in December 1979, the Soviets invaded Afghanistan, providing further reason to reestablish the warm relationship between Washington and Amman.[35]

Following President Ronald Reagan's second election victory in 1984, his administration was ready and eager to take the stalled Middle East peace process forward. At the end of May 1985, King Hussein traveled to Washington. President Reagan wrote in his diary that the king was "doing a great & courageous thing in his efforts to bring about peace in the Middle East."[36] At this juncture, a PLO-Jordanian position had been worked out: an agreement to negotiate as a joint delegation at an international conference. Neither Israeli Prime Minister Yitzhak Shamir nor Secretary of State George Shultz wanted to accept the PLO as a partner in peace talks. Washington was cool to the concept of an international conference and asked the king to agree to direct negotiations with Israel. The deadlock continued.[37]

Although London's role in Jordan had gradually been reduced, HMG continued to exercise influence. Great Britain's new ambassador to Jordan, Sir John Coles, arrived in Amman in November 1984. Prior to his appointment, Coles had served three years as private secretary to Prime Minister Margaret Thatcher. Coles explained that the king admired Prime Minister Thatcher and wanted her to visit Amman. According to Coles, London's ambassador still maintained a unique position in Jordan. Despite the decline of British power, Coles was confident that he would have a direct relationship with Hussein.[38]

Washington, of course, now had the power and the U.S. ambassador was closest to Hussein. However, the British ambassador had second place positioning. From the beginning of his tenure in Amman, Coles considered it important to establish a good relationship with U.S. Ambassador Paul H. Boeker: "Luckily that feeling was reciprocated." Coles and Boeker played tennis together and took trips into the desert with their families. As Coles settled in Amman, he became socially close to the king. He probably knew Queen Noor better than any other ambassador. Ambassador Coles and his wife Anne spent a weekend with Hussein and Noor at their palace in Aqaba. Coles was very impressed with Queen Noor. The queen was an excellent hostess, "very accomplished socially." She had the ability to help her guests and her husband relax. "Everyone knows that the marriage was controversial in Jordan and more widely." According to Ambassador Coles, Hussein needed a wife who could respond to his serious side but who could also help him to enjoy life. Coles claimed that Hussein's American wife carried out her role very well. At the same time, Coles distrusted any Westerner who assumed that he knew Queen Noor and really understood the relationship between the king and the queen.[39] Lady Anne Coles, who regularly called on Queen Noor, considered her a very private person, difficult to know well: "You certainly didn't forget she was Queen." It was apparent that she was concerned about the Jordanian people and especially devoted to improving the conditions of Jordan's underprivileged population.[40]

Ambassador Coles underlined that the Palestinians formed a majority of the Jordanian population. Some Palestinians were very successful businessmen. Others were educated professionals. However, a large number remained displaced refugees living in camps. Emotionally connected, the Palestinians were keenly aware of what was going on concerning the Arab-Israeli issue. Memories of Black September continued to be very strong. Prominent Jordanians reminisced about the period and stated that Jordan came close to disappearing. Nevertheless, at the end of 1984 King Hussein invited the Palestine National Congress to meet in Amman. According to Coles, "That was a pretty remarkable thing to do." The king had concluded that in order to progress toward peace between Jordan and Israel, there had to be real cooperation between the Jordanians and the Palestinians. The king saw indications that under Arafat a moderate Palestinian movement was emerging and that it would now be possible for the United States to embark on yet another peace initiative. Hence, the king was ready to form a relationship with Arafat's PLO: "It was a very bold move, very controversial."[41]

The king's goal was an international conference with a joint Palestinian-Jordanian delegation. He planned to persuade Arafat to accept the concept of land for peace. The king made it clear to his closest Western allies that he wanted them to encourage this process. His first request was that Washington receive a joint Palestinian-Jordanian delegation. This was not a simple matter, since the PLO had not yet renounced terrorism. The president and his secretary of state could not sit down with members of a terrorist organization. Prime Minister Thatcher had expressed willingness to receive the joint Palestinian-Jordanian delegation that the king wished to create, but American agreement remained uncertain. [42]

Movements toward peace continued. During a radio address on September 21, 1985, President Reagan announced that Egyptian President Husni Mubarak, who had succeeded the assassinated Sadat in October 1981, was arriving in Washington, DC, and that the following week King Hussein would visit as well. President Mubarak explained King Hussein's vision for a Jordanian-Palestinian delegation and stated that the king wished to begin negotiations quickly. President Reagan underlined that Washington supported the king's efforts and was trying "to make this vision a reality."[43]

Difficulties mounted at the beginning of 1986 after Congress refused to pass legislation providing arms to Jordan. Since 1979 the king had unsuccessfully tried to obtain the American Stinger anti-aircraft missile system. The unhappy king decided to turn to the Soviet Union for assistance and arranged a $3 million package while visiting Moscow.[44] According to Ambassador Coles, the king did not at all enjoy turning to the Soviet Union, but when Washington became a disappointment, he considered it essential to reach out to the Soviets.[45]

Unfortunately, despite his persistence, the king's plan for a joint Palestinian-Jordanian delegation collapsed, following a series of terrorist incidents and the refusal of key PLO players to accept United Nations Resolution 242. The king concluded that the PLO was not a valid negotiating partner for Jordan. In Amman, Prime Minister al-Rifai developed a program for West Bank development that he intended to carry out without consulting the PLO. He also attempted to ascertain whether or not West Bank moderates were willing to maintain a direct relationship with Jordan: "The answer was no. The PLO was too solidly entrenched." The king's vision of a joint confederation that included both Palestinians and Jordanians did not have Palestinian support.[46]

Ambassador Coles was aware that during his attempts to create a joint Palestinian-Jordanian delegation, the king's relations with Israel continued: "I only became aware because he took me into his confidence

and it's not a confidence that I am prepared to break." Referring to
Hussein, Coles said, "The important thing about him was his moderation as compared to other Arab leaders." Contacts with Israel had to
be secret and the king took considerable risks, but they were risks
that he was prepared to take in order to achieve a negotiated peace.[47]

Hussein never lost his willingness to take risks. Despite the king's
ongoing problems with his Arab neighbors, in 1986 after the death
of Glubb Pasha, Hussein insisted on attending a memorial service
for the late Arab Legion commander. At the memorial service, which
took place in Westminster Abbey on April 17, the king honored the
British solider he had so unceremoniously fired two decades before.[48]

American diplomat, Roscoe Suddarth, who served as ambassador
to Jordan from 1987 to 1990, noted that when he took up his post,
the king was not yet completely prepared to relinquish his claim to the
Israeli-occupied West Bank. Before Ambassador Suddarth arrived in
Amman, the king had attended meetings in London with Israeli
Foreign Minister Shimon Peres. They had come to an agreement on
how to get peace talks started, but "their plans were shot down by
Prime Minister Yitzak Shamir." The king was unhappy with the United
States, and specifically with Secretary of State George Schultz, for
accepting Shamir's position. Schultz tried again to work on Shamir.
He noted that Washington had an official stationed in Jerusalem who
would go back and forth between Amman and Tel Aviv but did not
achieve a breakthrough. The Israelis wanted a public announcement
that after an U.S.-Soviet Summit there would be direct talks between
Jordan and Israel. According to Ambassador Suddhart, "This was very
offensive to King Hussein. It was sprung on him. I was there." The
king was first shocked than offended. "Ambassadors have often to
break the ice. It was really frigid." Hussein appeared "to be playing
hard to get," but pressed from all sides, reluctantly agreed to do so.[49]

Meanwhile, the confidence of Palestinians living under Israeli occupation had grown. At the end of 1987 they began a spontaneous upris-
ing against the occupation—the *intifada*. Israel was unable to put
down the *intifada*. Finally, it appeared that King Hussein truly understood that his role had diminished that he could not speak for the
Palestinians.[50] Speaking solely for Jordan, the king insisted that his
kingdom was not Palestine. However, the Israeli right continued to
advocate the view of their former Defense Minister Ariel Sharon: that
Jordan become the Palestinian homeland and that Israel annex the
West Bank.[51]

The king announced cancellation of a massive development program for the West Bank in July 1988. He also announced the dissolution of the Lower House of Jordan's parliament, where a large number of members represented West Bank constituencies. According to a Jordanian diplomat, the king wished to emphasize that he was not competing with the PLO.[52] In a speech to his nation on July 31, the king stated that his goal was to assist the Palestinians:

> Jordan, dear brothers, has not nor will it give up its support and assistance to the Palestinian people, until they achieve their national goals, God willing. No one outside Palestine has had, nor can have, an attachment to Palestine or its cause, firmer than that of Jordan or my family. Moreover, Jordan is a confrontation state, whose borders with Israel are longer than those of any other Arab state, longer even than the combined borders of the West Bank and Gaza with Israel.[53]

During a press conference on August 7, 1988, Hussein declared that Jordan would never again speak on behalf of the Palestinians. Sitting under a portrait of his great-grandfather, Sharif Hussein, the king spoke to his people on Jordanian television, explaining that he was bowing to the wishes of the PLO and the Arab States.[54] Following Hussein's broadcast, the prime minister issued instructions saying that all Jordanian citizens who were residents of the West Bank would henceforth be considered Palestinian nationals. Nevertheless, on the evening news, Jordanian television continued to a show a map of Jordan that included both banks. In addition, the bridges connecting the two banks remained open and West Bank schools remained under Jordanian supervision.[55] After the king distanced Amman from the West Bank, the Jordanian dinar fell rapidly and there was a run on Jordanian banks.[56]

Hussein made the decision to relinquish Jordan's right to the Israeli occupied West Bank without first consulting either the Jordanian Assembly or his appointed senate. He had long been under pressure from his fellow Arab States to accept the Palestinian right to the West Bank but had steadfastly resisted that pressure. Speculating about why finally the king capitulated, political scientist Hillel Frisch points to the success of the *intifada*. According to Frisch, the *intifada* undermined the Hashemite position on the West Bank to such an extent that the unhappy king had to accept the reality of PLO leadership.[57]

King Hussein directed his displeasure toward the United States, when at a dinner for the visiting British Foreign Secretary, Sir Geoffrey

Howe, U.S. Ambassador Suddarth was seated in the back of the dining room, exiled from the most prominent guests. Recalling American financial assistance to Amman, Suddarth said, "We were giving them two or three hundred million dollars a year, but I was consigned to the outer space."

After dinner, Suddarth asked to see the king but was turned down; this was the only occasion when Hussein refused to see him. Fortunately, the ambassador was entertaining a guest at the embassy, a guest he referred to as an outstanding peace advocate—Rabbi Arthur Hertzberg. Ambassador Suddarth went to the palace accompanied by the rabbi and together they entered Crown Prince Hassan's office. There the two Americans met the king. Hence, Ambassador Suddarth was able to talk to Hussein prior to the king's public announcement that he was relinquishing his right the West Bank. Suddarth reminisced that Washington and Amman were on very cordial terms: "one could certainly get away with that sort of thing." During his meeting with the king, Ambassador Suddarth emphasized that Washington wanted Jordan to continue playing a role in the peace process. Yes, Amman had cut all of its ties to the West Bank. Nevertheless, the king continued to hope for a future confederation, but of course, understood that the Palestinians had to achieve sovereignty, "even for only one minute."[58]

Relinquishing the dream of restoration of the West Bank had been a difficult process. Hussein had done his very best to restore the legacy of his grandfather, King Abdullah. He had failed, but nevertheless, he had the satisfaction of retaining firm control of the East Bank and the continued support of his Anglo-American friends.

CHAPTER 8

THE FINAL YEARS

For three years, until the end of the Reagan administration, the king did not visit Washington. Then in April 1989, Hussein met with President George H. W. Bush at the White House. After their meeting the president referred to Hussein as an old friend and noted that the relationship between Washington and Amman had substantial roots. The president emphasized that both countries were committed to negotiating a Middle East peace. President Bush also assured the king that Washington would provide Jordan with economic and military assistance.[1]

After he called at the White House, the king spoke to PBS reporter Robert MacNeil and noted his respect and admiration for the president. Asked if the Israeli government had sufficiently rewarded the Palestine Liberation Organization (PLO) for recognizing Israel's right to exist, the king said "not yet," but that he hoped Israel would change its position.[2] The following day the king spoke to CNN, claiming that the Jordanian decision to disengage from the West Bank had led to the Palestinian decision to renounce violence and accept United Nations (UN) Security Council Resolutions 242 and 338. Expressing his confidence in President Bush, the king stated, "I feel more comfortable and much happier and much more optimistic on this visit to Washington than I have felt in a long time over many years that have passed."[3]

Then the slow movement toward peace was abruptly interrupted by the August 1990 Iraqi invasion of Kuwait. Before the invasion, Jordan had considered Iraq "an economic godsend."[4] During the 1980s, Baghdad had become Amman's most important trading partner. Oil was a vital factor; the Hashemite Kingdom received almost 85 percent of its oil from Iraq. Payment for that oil was charged against the debt that Iraq had accumulated during the 1980–88 Iran-Iraq War. In addition, Amman and Baghdad had worked out areas of military cooperation, including reconnaissance flights along the border between Jordan and Israel.[5]

Jordanians employed in the Gulf States, who resented how their wealthy Gulf brothers had treated them, firmly supported Saddam Hussein. These Jordanians appreciated the Iraqi leader's call to share Arab wealth. In addition, Jordanians considered Iraq their leader on the road to unity and the sole Arab State likely to deter Israel.[6]

Washington and London, however, adamantly opposed the Iraqi occupation of Kuwait. On August 2 Prime Minister Margaret Thatcher and President George H. W. Bush spoke to reporters in Aspen, Colorado. Both condemned Saddam Hussein's aggression. According to Prime Minister Thatcher, Iraq—a member of the UN—had violated the territory of another UN member. Iraqi behavior was totally unacceptable, and if allowed to endure, would endanger the security of other small countries.[7]

Now the king's relationship with Saddam Hussein offended the United States and members of the American-led coalition, which later liberated the Amirate.[8] The Saudis were again reminded that King's Hussein's great-grandfather had been Sharif of Mecca. Members of the Saudi royal family were concerned that King Hussein's support for the Iraqi dictator was an indication of Hashemite ambition to recapture Arabia.[9] Jordanians, however, were pleased with their king and angry with Washington and its allies, who had transformed what they considered to be an inter-Arab dilemma into an international conflict.[10]

Reflecting the opinion of the majority of his subjects, King Hussein referred to Saddam Hussein as an Arab patriot. During an Arab League meeting of foreign ministers, the king opposed a resolution condemning the Iraqi invasion. Despite the king's objection, the resolution was approved.[11] On August 5 a reporter asked President Bush if perhaps King Hussein was trying to arrange discussions between Washington and Baghdad. The president said "no," but stated that the king wanted to be helpful and that despite their differences on Iraq he hoped relations between Amman and Washington would improve. The president also stated that the king had agreed to prohibit the flow of Iraqi goods through the port of Aqaba.[12]

United in their opposition to Iraqi aggression, on August 6 the members of the UN Security Council declared Baghdad's annexation of Kuwait illegal and imposed economic sanctions. Ten days later, President Bush met with King Hussein who had earlier announced his support for those sanctions. Following their meeting, President Bush told reporters that the king, who had recently met in Baghdad with the Iraqi dictator, received no indication that Saddam Hussein was willing to cooperate with the international community.[13]

King Hussein was in a difficult position. Following the Iraq invasion, PLO leader Yasser Arafat sided with Saddam Hussein. Both King Hussein and Arafat attempted to assume the role of peacemaker. From the perspective of Washington and London, the king was supporting Iraqi aggression. Accepting one of Saddam Hussein's arguments, on December 9 King Hussein stated that there ought to be a connection between the settlement of the Kuwaiti-Iraqi dispute and the Israeli-Palestinian dispute—an idea that was "pure honey" to Jordan's large Palestinian population.[14]

As international pressure escalated, the king attempted to mediate between Iraq and the West. On January 3, 1991, King Hussein and British Prime Minister John Major discussed the problem. Realizing that compromise with Iraq was unlikely, the king sought to insure Jordan's security. At the same time, Israel was fully aware of Jordan's importance as a stable State, ruled by a moderate king, located on its eastern border, and separating it from Iraq. Concerned about what action Israel would take during the approaching American-led war to liberate Kuwait, King Hussein invited Israeli Prime Minister Yitzhak Shamir secretly to meet with him in London. The king wanted to obtain a guarantee that when war began, Israel would not violate Jordanian territory. Shamir and several of his close advisers, including Deputy Chief of the General Staff Ehud Barak, gathered in the king's North London residence. During the visit the hospitable king provided kosher meals. Prime Minister Shamir agreed that Israel would not violate Jordanian airspace and King Hussein promised to ban passage of Iraqi planes through his airspace and to refuse to allow Iraqi forces to enter Jordanian territory.[15]

Despite his best efforts to handle the complex situation, King Hussein remained uncomfortable. At the start of the first Gulf War, BBC reporter John Simpson dined with the king and heard him speak in gloomy terms about his likely future. According to Simpson, the king expected that he would have to flee Jordan and spend the rest of his life on his estate outside London.[16] Addressing his nation on January 15, the king assured his people that he had done everything within his power to achieve a political settlement; he had tried his best to resolve the Iraqi-Kuwaiti quarrel "within the Arab context."[17]

The American-led action to drive Iraq from Kuwait—Operation Desert Storm—began on January 17. Soon after, on February 6 King Hussein made a speech denouncing Allied efforts to destroy Iraq and divide the Arab World. An angry President Bush composed a letter to the king expressing his disappointment at King Hussein's "vitriolic attack" on the coalition forces. The president told the king that "[his] words exculpate Saddam Hussein for the most serious and most brazen crime against the Arab nation by another Arab in modern times."[18] Responding to a question about the king's speech in parliament, Prime Minister John Major said that Whitehall had conveyed its misgivings to Hussein's government.[19]

After Iraqi forces were driven from Kuwait, relations between Jordan and the United States remained strained. At a news conference on March 1, President Bush explained that it would take time to resolve the differences between Amman and Washington. The president said that he did not feel any animosity toward the king and had no wish to destabilize Jordan. At the same time, the Jordanians had not yet accepted the reality of Saddam Hussein's defeat: "And I see people dancing around in the streets still talking about a victory or still saying that we've sued for peace because we were done in by Saddam."[20]

Both Jordan and the PLO attempted to repair relations with Washington.[21] Speaking to journalists from the Middle East in March 1991, President Bush did not criticize King Hussein but expressed his disappointment with the Palestinians who had so lavishly praised Saddam Hussein. Chairman Arafat had lost all credibility. According to the president, the Palestinians had "bet on the wrong horse for the wrong reasons, the wrong motives. I mean, they did not stand up and condemn that aggression."[22]

During the crisis, an estimated quarter-million Palestinians had fled from Kuwait to Jordan. Bending under the new population burden, the kingdom's economy was on the verge of collapse. Unemployment was estimated at 45 percent. Every day additional shops and restaurants closed. It appeared that malnutrition and infant mortality would soon dramatically increase. Yet, the king remained very popular: "Now with the war lost, Saddam Hussein humiliated, Iraq in ruins, and their own economy a wreck, Jordanians are blaming everyone but their king and his government."[23]

Ironically, Saddam Hussein's aggression, which the PLO had so wholeheartedly supported, now left the impoverished Palestinians with no alternative but to enter into negotiations. The king quickly agreed to the formation of a joint Jordanian-Palestinian delegation, which would be authorized to attend a Madrid Peace Conference. The reluctant Israeli prime minister, Yitzhak Shamir, had to be pressed. Washington prevailed and an international conference convened on October 30, 1991, under the chairmanship of both President Bush and Soviet Prime Minister Mikhail Gorbachev.[24]

Following elections in Israel and the United States, the new leaders continued efforts to achieve peace. Hosted by President William Clinton on September 13, 1993, Israeli Prime Minister Rabin and PLO Chairman Arafat shook hands before cheering crowds on the White House lawn. The handshake marked the signing of a Declaration of Principles for peace between the Palestinians and the Israelis. Thus, clearing the way for King Hussein to publicly move toward a peace treaty with Israel.

After years of struggle, King Hussein finally achieved his goal, an end to the Israeli-Jordanian aspect of the Arab-Israeli conflict. On July 25, 1994, Hussein and Prime Minister Rabin signed the Washington Declaration, which formally ended the state of belligerency between

Figure 3. King Hussein at the White House in October 1998, attempting to help President Clinton bring Yasser Arafat and Benjamin Netanyahu together. Photograph courtesy of the William J. Clinton Presidential Library.

their two countries. Hussein was especially pleased with Israel's acceptance of his guardianship of Jerusalem's Muslim holy sites. Article 9 of the treaty stated, "Israel respects the present role of the Hashemite Kingdom of Jordan in Muslim holy shrines in Jerusalem."[25] In honor of the occasion, both Israeli Prime Minister Rabin and King Hussein spoke to a joint session of Congress.

Diplomat Baruck Binah, who served as the Israeli embassy's congressional liaison, remembered the excitement of July 26, 1994, the day that Hussein and Rabin addressed Congress. The House was completely full. Some of those attending had to stand. Binah recalled meeting the king in Speaker of the House Tom Foley's chambers. According to Binah, it was a very exciting occasion: "The king's hand shake was strong and I [can't] find another word, but brave." The Israeli diplomat told Hussein that both their grandfathers had met after World War II, when an earlier Baruch Binah—who served under General Allenby as an intelligence officer in the British army—was a member of a Zionist delegation that made an agreement with Abdullah. "It made it so personal and so real."[26]

During his address to Congress, Hussein recalled his family's history:

> My family has also paid a heavy price. My great-grandfather, the leader of the Great Arab Revolt for Freedom, Independence and unity, lies buried next to the blessed Al Aqsa Mosque in Jerusalem. I was by the side of my grandfather, King Abdullah, at the doors of Al Aqsa Mosque when he was martyred. He was a man of peace who gave his life for an ideal. I have pledged my life to fulfilling his dream. He too is here today.[27]

Afterward, together with President Clinton, Hussein and Rabin held a press conference.[28] A final peace agreement between Jordan and Israel was signed the following October. Prior to leaving for the Middle East to attend the signing ceremony from the White House Rose Garden, the president reminded the press that the peace treaty between Israel and Jordan would be only the second such treaty concluded between Israel and an Arab State. Many Jordanians, however, remained bitterly opposed to Israel and were unhappy with the peace treaty. In the following years, some Jordanians even expressed resentment at the influx of Israeli tourists.[29] President Clinton was not discouraged; his goal was to convince all of the Arab States "to follow the brave and hopeful inspiration of Israel and Jordan."[30]

President Clinton later traveled to Jordan to attend a signing ceremony in Wadi Araba. Speaking to the assembled crowd, the king
thanked the United States, calling President Clinton Jordan's partner
and friend. The king stated, "No one will ever forget this day and, in
particular, they will always remember the fact that you, personally,
came to be with us here on this most happy of occasions, at the end of
a chapter of darkness and the opening of a book of light."[31] From
Wadi Araba, the American president traveled to Amman, where he
spoke to the Jordanian parliament. Clinton explained that Americans
refuse to accept "that our civilizations must collide." He later wrote
that the king had survived several assassination attempts and realized
the risks he was taking when he agreed to a peace treaty with Israel.[32]

Ironically, although King Hussein survived peacemaking, Prime
Minister Rabin did not. In November 1995, a Jewish extremist assas-
sinated the Israeli leader. King Hussein and Queen Noor traveled to
Jerusalem to attend Rabin's funeral. This was Hussein's first visit to
the holy city since Jordan's devastating defeat in 1967.[33] Speaking at
Rabin's grave on Mount Herzl military cemetery, Hussein said,

> Standing here, I commit myself before you, before my people in
> Jordan, before the world, to myself to continue with our utmost
> effort, to ensure that we leave a similar legacy. We are not ashamed,
> nor are we afraid nor are we anything but determined to fulfill the
> legacy for which my friend fell, as did my grandfather in this very city,
> when I was with him and but a young boy.[34]

Washington continued to support Hussein. On April 2, 1997,
Secretary of Defense William Cohen welcomed the king to the
Pentagon, an institution Hussein had visited on many previous
occasions. Cohen discussed Washington's program to enhance
Jordan's military strength and underlined the lease of sixteen F16
fighter jets to the Hashemite Kingdom. Delighted, the king
responded that he was proud to be a friend of the United States.[35]

Settling in Amman in 1997, the newly appointed British Ambassador
Christopher Battiscombe, who had served in a number of Arab
countries, settled in Amman in 1997. Soon after Battiscombe arrived
in Jordan, the king's health began to decline. On one occasion the
king apologized to Battiscombe for postponing appointments with
him. Hussein explained that he was ill and that his doctor did know
what was wrong with him. Despite the king's illness, the U.S.

ambassador continued regularly to see him. When the king wanted
something done, "he would ring up the Americans and say please help
me."[36]

Unwilling to permit his illness to deter him, the king continued to
move the peace process forward. Visiting Washington in March 1998,
he held a joint press conference with Secretary of State Madeleine
Albright. The two discussed Saddam Hussein's obligation to permit
the United Nations Special Committee (UNSCOM), which had
been established after the liberation of Kuwait to oversee the elimination of Iraqi arms, to proceed with its inspections. The king emphasized the need for a dialogue between Washington and Baghdad. He
also expressed the hope that in the future Iraq would become a democratic country, "an example of pluralism."[37]

While serving in Amman, British Ambassador Battiscombe established an excellent relationship with Israeli Ambassador Oded Eran,
"who was quite keen to come to us." Battiscombe considered the
Israeli ambassador to be one of the most effective diplomats in Jordan.
Battiscombe had never visited Israel; he had feared that traveling there
might damage his career. But since Jordan and Israel had established diplomatic relations, accompanied by Israeli Ambassador Eran, Battiscombe
toured the Jewish state.[38]

Despite earlier agreements, a Palestinian state remained an unreal-
ized dream as friction between the PLO and Israel continued. President
Clinton tried to bring the two sides together in October 1998 at the
Wye River Conference Center in Maryland. Neither Chairman Arafat
nor Prime Minister Benjamin Netanyahu appeared prepared to make
the necessary compromises. Although gravely ill with what he now
knew was cancer, King Hussein, who was being treated at the Mayo
Clinic, interrupted his chemotherapy treatment to attend the meeting. He traveled from Minnesota to Maryland to address the assembled leaders. Prior to the king's entry, Secretary of State Madeleine
Albright passed around a disinfecting liquid and asked that everyone
clean their hands to protect the king who "had reached the stage in his
illness where it was a risk for him to meet with a large group."[39] The
king's presence failed to end the deadlock, but it added to his legacy.
Meanwhile in Amman, Ambassador Battiscombe made friends with
many Palestinians, who remained critical of the king. These unhappy
Palestinians claimed that the king had tried too hard to please Israel.
Some Palestinians living in Jordan continued to advocate extreme

views. They wanted to eliminate Israel. Hence, they were hostile toward the king.[40]

Shortly before his death on January 25, 1999, the ailing king announced that his brother, Crown Prince Hassan, would not succeed him, but that he had appointed his eldest son, Prince Abdullah, as heir to the throne. British Ambassador Battiscombe had a close relationship with Prince Hassan because during the king's illness, the crown prince had served as Jordan's "effective ruler." Battiscombe was completely surprised that the king did not appoint his brother as heir to the throne. However, in the two months before the announcement, the British ambassador had received several clues from Jordanian friends that Prince Hassan would be ousted. Nevertheless, until Hussein's actual announcement, Battiscombe had refused to believe that the able Prince Hassan would not become king. With the benefit of hindsight, Battiscombe said that it was likely Hussein had always intended to replace his brother with one of his own sons. Battiscombe speculated that if Prince Hassan did not have a son it might have been easier for King Hussein to allow him to become king.[41] According to political scientist Russell Lucas, three major issues influenced the king's selection of his oldest son: (1) Abdullah

Figure 4. King Hussein and his wife Queen Noor, surrounded by his children. Photograph courtesy of the Embassy of Jordan

was a military man; (2) Abdullah's wife was Palestinian; and finally, (3) Washington preferred Abdullah.[42]

The new thirty-six-year-old crown prince, son of Hussein's former British wife, Princess Muna, was a military officer in the Jordanian army. U.S. Ambassador Roscoe Suddarth later told a reporter that he was convinced that Abdullah would carry out his father's policies: "The trouble is carrying out the king's policies requires very fancy footwork."[43] The ousted Prince Hassan reacted with dignity, expressing respect for his older brother's wish. "For me," Hassan said, "you are a father, a brother, and a friend. I do acquiesce, submit to, and obey your command Sir."[44]

Soon after appointing Crown Prince Abdullah, on February 7, 1999, King Hussein died. Jordanian television announced his death at 12:30 PM. Outside the hospital where the king's body rested, the scene was turbulent. Hundreds of Jordanians gathered in a torrential rain. Groups of women wailed and held their hands to the sky. Men gathered in clusters, waving Jordanian flags, pictures of the king and pieces of torn black cloth. They shouted, "Our blood and our soul is sacrificed for you" and proclaimed, "There is no God but God."[45]

Following the announcement of King Hussein's death, his oldest son, now King Abdullah, appeared on television. He said,

> Hussein's spirit will remain with us. He will not be absent from our hearts and minds. We shall keep to al-Hussein's pledge of building and giving honestly and loyally for dear Jordan. We stand with all faith together as one heart and one family. Children of the Jordanian family, people and family. Hussein was a father and a brother to each and every one of you as he was my father.[46]

From the White House Rose Garden, President Clinton expressed his sorrow. He praised the late king's courage, his commitment to peace, and his devotion to Jordan. He emphasized the king's efforts to strengthen Jordan's relations with the United States and his pursuit of peace between Israel and the Arab World. Addressing Queen Noor, the president said, "You are a daughter of America and a Queen of Jordan. You have made two nations very proud."[47] Later, while visiting a Harley-Davidson plant, the president reminisced about the king, stating that Hussein was a very satisfied Harley customer. Clinton recalled that during a visit to Washington, DC, Hussein gave him a picture of himself and Queen Noor riding a Harley in the Jordanian desert.[48]

Numerous world leaders traveled to Jordan to pay their respects. Ambassador Battiscombe called the king's funeral the "most extraordinary event" he had ever attended. The funeral was a tribute both to King Hussein and to Jordan. Among the mourners were four American presidents, four Israeli prime ministers, the vice president of Iraq, both the Syrian and the Egyptian presidents, and European royalty. "It was like walking through Madam Tussauds, except that all of the people were alive!" Led by Prime Minister Tony Blair, the British delegation was assigned a room in the palace complex. Ambassador Battiscombe circulated among those assembled and invited them to visit with his prime minister. The British ambassador noted the presence of the ruler of Bahrain, the German chancellor, and the French president. Of course, Battiscombe had to exercise caution. For example, it would have been unwise for Prime Minister Blair to appear with the Iraqi vice president. Since Ambassador Battiscombe did not know what the Iraqi looked like, he was concerned that by mistake his prime minister and the Iraqi vice president might shake hands.[49] Journalist Robert Fisk noted that large crowds of simple Jordanians also gathered to say their good-byes: "Then there was the other Jordan. Outside the gate, sweating and shrieking to God, smashed back by gun butts, sworn at by the descendants of Glubb Pasha's Arab Legion as they clawed their way towards King Hussein's coffin, the other Jordan did not quite fit in with the pageantry on the other side of the palace wall."

Evaluating King Hussein's legacy, U.S. Ambassador Suddarth stated that Hussein had wanted the monarchy to encompass both Jordanians and Palestinians. He looked back to Sharif Hussein and to Abdullah, and understood that the Israelis were there to stay. He recognized that war and strife would be detrimental to everyone in the region. This gave him a confidence that allowed him to transcend the limitations of "a desperately resource-poor country, a country that had been carved out of the desert, a country with a huge displaced Palestinian population grafted on. He can be proud of his legacy."[50]

Suddarth claimed that Jordan was one of the most modern countries in the Middle East. The Jordanians inherited constitutional and administrative apparatus, which the British had provided. Young military officers grew the same kind of mustaches and assumed the stiff-upper-lip style of the king. The king's power base was the East

Bank. When he signed the peace treaty with Israel, he fell back on that bedrock of support. According to Ambassador Suddarth, the king "hated and had no respect for Arafat." He had an ambivalent relationship with the Palestinians but protected the Palestinian community. He continued, "I think he will go down in history as a great man."[51]

A memorial service for the late king was held in London's St. Paul's Cathedral on July 6, 1999. It was attended by members of both the British and the Jordanian royal families. In addition to Prime Minister Tony Blair, three former prime ministers were present, Edward Heath, Margaret Thatcher, and John Major. Heir to the British throne, Prince Charles, noted that King Hussein's background had provided him with both "the virtues of a bedouin Arab and . . . an English gentleman."[52]

Despite a multitude of problems, during his long reign, King Hussein had earned the gratitude and the respect of both London and Washington. Throughout the Cold War years, Jordan had steadfastly supported the West. In addition, although the king had longed for the return of his lost territory, the West Bank and East Jerusalem, he had finally accepted the Palestinian claim to the still Israeli-occupied West Bank. Finally, despite his failed attempt to work out an Arab solution to the Iraqi invasion of Kuwait, he had been able to repair the damage to U.S.-Jordanian relations and to make peace with Israel. Although Hussein's son, King Abdullah II, inherited a smaller kingdom than his father had, he also inherited a powerful legacy—a legacy that includes the support and respect of both Great Britain and the United States.

BIBLIOGRAPHY

ARCHIVES

British

Cabinet The National Archives, Kew, London Cabinet (CAB)
Foreign and Commonwealth Office (FCO 17)
Foreign Office (FO)
Prime Minister's Office (PREM 15)
Public Records Office, London
War Office (WO)

Israeli

Dayan Institute, Tel Aviv (Newspaper Archives)
Israel State Archives, Jerusalem (ISA)

U.S.

National Archives, College Park, MD
DEF Israel
POL 7, Jordan
POL 15, Jordan.
POL 23, Jordan
POL 28, Jerusalem
1962, 786.5/2–762

DOCUMENTS (PUBLISHED)

Foreign Relations of the United States
1951, Vol. V
1959, Vol. XI
1964–67, Vol. XVIII

1964–68, Vol. XX
Public Papers of the Presidents, Richard Nixon, 1970. Washington, DC: Government Printing Office, 1971.

INTERVIEWS BY AUTHOR

Christopher Battiscombe
Baruch Binah
Lady Anne Coles
Sir John Coles
Morris Draper
Carter Hills
Robert Keeley
Thomas Pickering
Talcott Seeyle
John Snodgrass
Roscoe Suddarth
Ziad Abu Ziad

INTERVIEW BY ASSOCIATION FOR DIPLOMATIC STUDIES AND TRAINING, ARLINGTON, VA, ADST

Ambassador Harrison M. Symmes

MEMOIRS

Abdullah, King. *My Memoirs Completed: "Al–Takmilah."* London: Longman, 1978.
Albright, Madeleine. *Madam Secretary.* New York: Miramax, 2003.
Brinkley, Douglas, ed. *The Ronald Reagan Diaries.* New York: HarperCollins, 2007.
Carter, Jimmy. *The Blood of Abraham.* Boston: Houghton Mifflin, 1985.
Clinton, William. *My Life.* New York: Knopf, 2004.
Crossman, Richard. *The Diaries of a Cabinet Minister.* Vol. II. New York: Holt, Rinehart and Winston, 1976.
Dayan, Moshe. *Story of My Life.* New York: William Morrow, 1976.
Eban, Abba. *An Autobiography.* New York: Random House, 1977.
Eden, Anthony. *Full Circle.* London: Cassell, 1960.

Glubb, Sir John. *The Changing Scenes of Life: An Autobiography*. London: Quartet Books, 1983.

Hussein, King. *Uneasy Lies the Head*. New York: Bernard Geis, 1962.

Kirkbride, Sir Alec. *From the Wings: Amman Memoirs, 1947–1951*. London: Frank Cass, 1976.

Kissinger, Henry. *Crisis*. New York: Simon & Schuster, 2003.

———. *White House Years*. Boston: Little Brown, 1979.

Kollek, Teddy and Amos Kollek. *For Jerusalem*. New York: Random House, 1978.

Noor, Queen. *Leap of Faith*. New York: Miramax, 2003.

Rusk, Dean. *As Told to Richard Rusk: As I Saw It*. New York: Norton, 1999.

Sadat, Anwar. *In Search of Identity*. New York: Harper & Row, 1977.

Shultz, George. *Turmoil and Triumph: My Years as Secretary of State*. New York: Scribner's, 1993.

Sultan, Khaled bin. *Desert Warrior*. New York: HarperCollins, 1995.

Thatcher, Margaret. *The Path to Power*. London: Harper Collins, 1995.

SECONDARY SOURCES

Adelson, Roger. *London and the Invention of the Middle East: Money, Power, and War, 1902–1922*. New Haven, CT: Yale University Press, 1995.

Ajami, Fouad. *The Arab Predicament*. New York: Cambridge University, 1993.

Anderson, Betty. *Nationalist Voices in Jordan*. Austin: University of Texas Press, 2005.

Ashton, Nigel J. "A 'Special Relationship' Sometimes in Spite of Ourselves." *The Journal of Imperial and Commonwealth History* 33, no.2 (May 2005): 221–24.

Bailey, Clinton. *Jordan's Palestinian Challenge, 1948–1983*. Boulder, CO: Westview, 1984.

Benvenisti, Meron. *Jerusalem: The Torn City*. Jerusalem: Isratypeset, 1976.

Brenchley, Frank. *Britain and the Middle East: An Economic History 1945–1987* London: Lester Crook, 1989.

Byford-Jones, W. *Adventures with Two Passports*. London: Robert Hales, 1956.

Carr, Winifred. *Hussein's Kingdom*. London: Leslie Frewin, 1966.

Citino, Nathan. *From Arab Nationalism to OPEC*. Bloomington: Indiana University Press, 2002.

Craig, Gordon A., and Francis L. Loewenheim. *The Diplomats, 1939–1979*. Princeton, NJ: Princeton University Press, 1994.

Dallas, Roland. *King Hussein: A Life on the Edge*. New York: Fromm, 1999.

Dann, Uriel. *King Hussein and the Challenge of Arab Radicalism: Jordan, 1955–1967*. New York: Oxford University Press, 1989.

Dearden, Ann. *Jordan*. London: Robert Hale, 1958.

Dumper, Michael. *The Politics of Jerusalem since 1967*. New York: Columbia, 1997.

Edwards, Beverly Milton, and Peter Hinchcliffe. *Jordan: A Hashemite Legacy*. London: Routledge, 2001.

Fisk, Robert. *The Great War for Civilisation*. New York: Knopf, 2006.

Frisch, Hillel. "Fuzzy Nationalism: 'The Case of Jordan.'" *Nationalism and Ethnic Politics* 8 (Winter 2002): 87–103.

Gat, Moshe. *Britain and the Conflict in the Middle East, 1964–1967*. Westport, CT: Praeger, 2003.

Gelber, Yoav. *Israeli-Jordanian Dialogue, 1948–1953*. Brighton: Sussex Academic Press, 2004.

Graves, Robert. *Lawrence and the Arabs*. New York: Paragon House, 1991.

Hahn, Peter L. *Caught in the Middle East: U.S. Policy toward the Arab-Israeli Conflict, 1945–1961*. Chapel Hill: University of North Carolina Press, 2004.

Haron, Miriam Joyce. *Palestine and the Anglo-American Connection, 1945–1950*. New York: Peter Lang, 1986.

Heikal, Mohamed. *The Road to Ramadan*. New York: Ballantine, 1975.

Hourani, Albert. *A History of the Arab Peoples*. Cambridge, MA: Harvard University Press, 1991.

Hurewitz, J. C. *The Struggle for Palestine*. New York: Schocken, 1976.

Isaacson, Walter. *Kissinger*. New York: Simon & Schuster, 1992.

Johnston, Charles. *The Brink of Jordan*. London: Hamish Hamilton, 1972.

Joyce, Miriam. *Kuwait, 1945–1996: An Anglo-American Perspective*. London: Frank Cass, 1998.

Katz, Kimberly. *Jordanian Jerusalem*. Gainesville: University Press of Florida, 2005.

Keeley, Louise S. "Racing King Hussein." *Foreign Service Journal* (June 1999): 54–55.

Klein, Menachem. *Jerusalem: The Contested City*. New York: New York University Press, 2001.

Klieman, Aaron S. *Foundations of British Policy in the Arab World: The Cairo Conference of 1921*. Baltimore: Johns Hopkins University Press, 1970.

Lucas, Russell E. *Institutions and the Politics of Survival in Jordan: Domestic Responses to External Challenges, 1988–2001*. Albany: State University of New York Press, 2005.

Lunt, James. *The Arab Legion: 1923–1957*. London: Constable, 1999.

———. *Hussein of Jordan*. New York: William Morrow, 1989.

Marlowe, John. *Arab Nationalism and British Imperialism*. London: Cresset, 1961.

Mishal, Shaul. *West Bank/East Bank: The Palestinians in Jordan*. New Haven, CT: Yale University Press, 1978.

Monroe, Elizabeth. *Britain's Moment in the Middle East*. Baltimore: Johns Hopkins, 1963.

Morris, Benny. *Israel's Border Wars, 1949–1956*. Oxford: Clarendon, 1993.

Mutawi, Samir A. *Jordan in the 1967 War*. New York: Cambridge University Press, 2002.

Nevo, Joseph. *King Hussein and the Evolution of Jordan's Perception of a Political Settlement with Israel, 1967–1988*. Brighton: Sussex Academic Press, 2006.

Oren, Michael. *Six Days of War*. New York: Oxford University Press, 2002.

Parker, Richard, ed. *The October War*. Gainesville: University of Florida Press, 2001.

Podeh, Elie. "The Struggle over Arab Hegemony after the Suez Crisis." *Middle Eastern Studies* 29 (January 1993): 91–110.

Quandt, William B. *Peace Process*. Washington, DC: The Brookings Institution, 1993.

Rabinovich, Abraham. *The Yom Kippur War*. New York: Shocken, 2004.

Robins, Philip. *A History of Jordan*. Cambridge: Cambridge University, 2004.

Rubin, Barry. *The Arab States and the Palestine Conflict*. Syracuse, NY: Syracuse University Press, 1981.

Sachar, Howard. *Europe Leaves the Middle East, 1936–1954*. New York: Knopf, 1972.

Salibi, Kamal. *The Modern History of Jordan*. London: Tauris, 1993.

Schenker, David. *Dancing with Saddam*. Lanham, MD: Washington Institute for Near East Policy, 2003.

Seale, Patrick, ed. *The Shaping of an Arab Statesman*. London: Quartet Books, 1983.

Shlaim, Avi. *The Iron Wall*. New York: Norton, 2000.

Smith, Simon C. *Britain's Revival and Fall in the Gulf*. London: Routledge Curzon, 2004.

Snow, Peter. *Hussein*. Washington, DC: Robert B. Luce, 1972.

Spiegel, Steven L. *The Other Arab-Israeli Conflict: Making American's Middle East Policy, from Truman to Reagan*. Chicago: University of Chicago Press, 1985.

Susser, Asher. *On Both Banks of the Jordan: A Political Biography of Wasfi al-Tall*. London: Frank Cass, 1994.

Tal, Lawrence. "Britain and the Jordan Crisis of 1958." *Middle Eastern Studies* (January 1995): 39–57.

Wilson, Mary C. *King Abdullah, Britain and the Making of Jordan*. Cambridge: Cambridge University Press, 1987.

Wasserstein, Bernard. *Divided Jerusalem*. New Haven, CT: Yale University Press, 2002.

Yaqub, Salim. *Containing Arab Nationalism: The Eisenhower Doctrine and the Middle East.* Chapel Hill: University of North Carolina Press, 2004.

PERIODICALS

Al–Ahram
Financial Times (London)
Jordan Times
Life
New York Times
Newsweek
Palestine News
Time
Washington Post

WEB SITES

http://www.jordanembassyus.org
http://meria.idc.ac.il/journal/2002/issue4/jv6n4a2.html
http://www.pbs.org.newshour
http://bushlibrary.tamu.edu/
http://www.Kinghussein.gov
http://domino.un.org
http://www.margaretthatcher.org
http://www.publications.parliament.uk/pa/cm199091/cmhansrd/1991
http://www.boston.com/news/
http://clinton6.nara.gov
http://www.defenselink.mil/transcripts/1997/t040397
http://news.bbc.uk
http://www.jewishvirtuallibrary.org

NOTES

INTRODUCTION

1. James Lunt, *Hussein of Jordan* (New York: William Morrow, 1989), xxi.
2. John Marlowe, *Arab Nationalism and British Imperialism* (London: Cresset, 1961), 20.
3. Lunt, *Hussein of Jordan*, xxii.
4. J. C. Hurewitz, *The Struggle for Palestine* (New York: Schocken, 1976), 18.
5. Marlowe, *Arab Nationalism and British Imperialism*, 21–23.
6. Philip Robins, *A History of Jordan* (Cambridge: Cambridge University, 2004), 17.
7. James Lunt, *The Arab Legion: 1923–1957* (London: Constable, 1999), 13.
8. Ibid., 19.
9. Aaron S. Klieman, *Foundations of British Policy in the Arab World: The Cairo Conference of 1921* (Baltimore: Johns Hopkins Press, 1970), 129.
10. Roger Adelson, *London and the Invention of the Middle East: Money, Power, and War, 1902–1922* (New Haven, CT: Yale, 1995), 200.
11. Uriel Dann, *King Hussein and the Challenge of Arab Radicalism, Jordan, 1955–1967* (New York: Oxford University Press, 1989), 3.
12. Elizabeth Monroe, *Britain's Moment in the Middle East* (Baltimore, Johns Hopkins, 1963), 68.
13. Peter Snow, *Hussein* (Washington, DC: Robert B. Luce, 1972), 22.
14. King Abdullah, *My Memoirs Completed: "Al-Takmilah"* (London: Longman, 1978), 73.
15. Kimberly Katz, *Jordanian Jerusalem* (Gainesville: University Press of Florida, 2005), 26.
16. Robert Graves, *Lawrence and the Arabs* (New York: Paragon House, 1991), 400–401.
17. Ibid., 32.
18. Ibid., 29.
19. Avi Shlaim, *The Iron Wall* (New York: Norton, 2001), 29.
20. Robins, *A History of Jordan*, 50.
21. Charles Johnston, *The Brink of Jordan* (London: Hamish Hamilton, 1972), 18.
22. Mary C. Wilson, *King Abdullah, Britain and the Making of Jordan* (Cambridge: Cambridge University, 1987), 129
23. Robins, *A History of Jordan*, 53–54.
24. Howard Sachar, *Europe Leaves the Middle East, 1936–1954* (New York: Knopf, 1972), 408.
25. Sir Alec Kirkbride, *From the Wings: Amman Memoirs, 1947–1951* (London: Frank Cass, 1976), 84.
26. Avi Shlaim, *The Iron Wall*, 29.
27. Kirkbride, *From the Wings*, 4–5.
28. Ibid., 28.

29. Miriam Joyce Haron, *Palestine and the Anglo-American Connection, 1945–1950* (New York: Peter Lang, 1986), 120.
30. Shaul Mishal, *West Bank/East Bank: The Palestinians in Jordan* (New Haven, CT: Yale, 1978), 2–3.
31. Bernard Wasserstein, *Divided Jerusalem* (New Haven, CT: Yale, 2002), 167.
32. Kirkbride, *From the Wings*, 34–35.
33. Moshe Dayan, *Story of My Life* (New York: William Morrow, 1976, p. 136.
34. Kirkbride, *From the Wings*, 140–41.
35. Haron, *Palestine and the Anglo-American Connection, 1945–1950*, 155.
36. Benny Morris, *Israel's Border Wars, 1949–1956* (Oxford: Clarendon, 1993), 4–5.
37. Despatch, "The Charge in Jordan (Fritzlan) to the State Department," Foreign Relations of the United States (Amman), March 29, 1951, p. 5:977; hereafter referred to as FRUS.
38. Morris, *Israel's Border Wars, 1949–1956*, 15.
39. Barry Rubin, *The Arab States and the Palestine Conflict* (Syracuse, NY: Syracuse University Press, 1981), 214.
40. Lunt, *Hussein of Jordan*, 3.
41. Roland Dallas, *King Hussein: A Life on the Edge* (New York: Fromm, 1999), 2–3.
42. Hussein, *Uneasy Lies the Head* (New York: Bernard Geis, 1962), 17.
43. Ibid., 12–13.
44. Telegram, "Drew to the State Department," (Amman), July 31, 1951, pp. 5:990–91, FRUS.
45. Hussein, *Uneasy Lies the Head*, 43–44.
46. "The Minister in Jordan (Drew) to the State Department," (Amman), September 20, 1951, 5:994–96, FRUS.
47. Snow, *Hussein*, 45.
48. Lunt, *Hussein of Jordan*, 14–15. After his death in 1972, King Talal's body was returned to Jordan for burial in Amman.
49. Hussein, *Uneasy Lies The Head*, 36–37.

CHAPTER 1

1. Letter, Bowker to Furlonge (London), January 31, 1953, FO 371/104890, The National Archives, Kew, England (formerly Public Records Office); hereafter referred to as TNA.
2. Letter, Furlonge to Bowker (Amman), March 5, 1953, FO 371/104890, TNA.
3. Letter, Furlonge to Ross (Amman), March 12, 1953, FO 371/104890, TNA.
4. Letter, Furlonge to Bowker (Amman), March 19, 1953, FO 371/104890, TNA.
5. Interview with Carter Hills (Washington, DC), March 17, 2004.
6. Letter, Furlonge to Bowker (Amman), April 14, 1953, FO 371/104890, TNA.
7. W. Byford-Jones, *Adventures with Two Passports* (London: Robert Hales, 1956), 58.
8. Letter, Furlonge to Bowker (Amman), April 14, 1953, FO 371/104890, TNA.
9. Interview with Talcott Seeyle (Washington, DC), March 18, 2004.
10. Letter, Furlonge to Bowker (Amman), April 28, 1953, FCO 371/104890, TNA.
11. Telegram 242, Furlonge to Foreign Office (Amman), May 6, 1953, FCO 371/104890, TNA.
12. Snow, *Hussein* (Washington, DC: Robert B. Luce, 1972), 54.
13. Interview with Talcott Seeyle (Washington, DC), March 18, 2004.
14. Ibid.
15. Memorandum, Political Situation in Jordan (London), December 3, 1953, FO 371/104890, TNA.

16. Letter, Furlonge to Allen (Amman), October 21, 1953, FCO 371/104890, TNA.
17. Sir John Glubb, *The Changing Scenes of Life: An Autobiography* (London: Quartet Books, 1983), 172.
18. Ibid.
19. Telegram 572, Furlonge to Foreign Office (Amman), November 2, 1953, FO 371/104890, TNA.
20. Letter, Furlonge to Eden (Amman), November 4, 1953, FO 371/104890, TNA.
21. Memorandum, Falla, Iraqi Offer of Troops to Aid Jordan, April 12, 1954, FO 371/111100, TNA.
22. Yoav Gelber, *Israeli-Jordanian Dialogue, 1948–1953* (Brighton: Sussex, 2004), 272.
23. James Lunt, *The Arab Legion, 1923–1957* (London: Constable, 1999), 137.
24. Note on Egyptian Activities in Jordan, February 2, 1956, WO 216/912, TNA.
25. Miriam Joyce, *Kuwait, 1945–1996: An Anglo-American Perspective* (London: Frank Cass, 1998), 32.
26. Nigel J. Ashton, "A 'Special Relationship' Sometimes in Spite of Ourselves," *The Journal of Imperial and Commonwealth History* 33, no. 2 (May 2005): 225.
27. Ann Dearden, *Jordan* (London: Robert Hale, 1958), 116.
28. Gordon A. Craig and Francis L. Loewenheim, *The Diplomats, 1939–1979* (Princeton, Princeton University, 1994), 182.
29. Anwar el-Sadat, *In Search of Identity* (New York: Harper and Row, 1977), 136.
30. Uriel Dann, *King Hussein and the Challenge of Arab Radicalism* (New York: Oxford University Press, 1989), 31.
31. King Hussein, *Uneasy Lies the Head* (New York: Random House, 1962), 143.
32. Telegram 276, Duke to Foreign Office (Amman), March 1, 1956, FO 800/724, TNA.
33. Telegram 278, Duke to Foreign Office (Amman), March 1, 1956, FO 800/724, TNA.
34. Telegram 346, Foreign Office to Amman (London), March 2, 1956, FO 800/724, TNA.
35. Anthony Eden, *Full Circle* (London: Cassell, 1960), 348.
36. Telegram 280, Duke to Foreign Office (Amman), March 2, 1956, FO 800/724, TNA.
37. Letter, Duke to Rose (Amman), March 28, 1956, WO 216/912, TNA.
38. Ashton, "A 'Special Relationship,'" 226.
39. Elie Podeh, "The Struggle over Arab Hegemony after the Suez Crisis," *Middle Eastern Studies* 29 (January 1993): 95.
40. Robert H. Ferrell, ed., *The Eisenhower Diaries* (New York: Norton, 1981), 331–32.
41. Ashton, "A 'Special Relationship,'" 227.
42. Charles Johnston, *The Brink of Jordan* (London: Hamish Hamilton, 1972), 36–37.
43. Ibid., 46–47.
44. Johnston to Selwyn Lloyd (Amman), June 26, 1957, CAB 21/4632, TNA.
45. Snow, *Hussein*, 104.
46. Philip Robins, *A History of Jordan* (Cambridge University, 2004), 97.
47. Salim Yaqub, *Containing Arab Nationalism: The Eisenhower Doctrine and the Middle East* (Chapel Hill: University of North Carolina, 2004), 140.
48. Robins, *A History of Jordan*, 99.
49. King Hussein, *Uneasy Lies the Head*, 176–79.
50. Quoted in Yaqub, *Containing Arab Nationalism*, 138.
51. Dann, *King Hussein*, 65.
52. Nathan Citino, *From Arab Nationalism to OPEC* (Bloomington: Indiana University Press, 2002), 132.
53. Peter L. Hahn, *Caught in the Middle East: U.S. Policy toward the Arab-Israeli Conflict, 1945–1961* (Chapel Hill: University of North Carolina Press, 2004), 237.
54. Letter, Troutbeck to Eden (Baghdad), March 10, 1954, FO 371/110952, TNA.

55. Johnston, *The Brink of Jordan*, 91.
56. King Hussein, *Uneasy Lies the Head*, 193.
57. Dann, *King Hussein*, 87.
58. Ibid., 187.
59. King Hussein, *Uneasy Lies the Head*, 184–85.
60. Lawrence Tal, "Britain and the Jordan Crisis of 1958," *Middle Eastern Studies* (January 1995): 44.
61. Betty Anderson, *Nationalist Voices in Jordan* (Austin: University of Texas, 2005), 193.
62. Political Directive, Chiefs of Staff to Commander-in-Chief (London), July 18, 1958, PREM 11/2380, TNA.
63. Memorandum (London), July 17, 1958, CAB 21/4632, TNA.
64. Telegram 1946, Barbour to Foreign Office (Washington, DC) July 18, 1958, PREM 11/2380, TNA.
65. Letter, Eisenhower to Macmillan (Washington, DC), July 18, 1958, PREM 11/2380, TNA.
66. Telegram 4794, Foreign Office to Washington, DC (London), July 19, 1958, PREM 11/2380, TNA.
67. Yaqub, *Containing Arab Nationalism*, 234.
68. Ibid., 206.
69. Telegram 952, Johnston to Foreign Office (Amman), July 21, 1958, PREM 11/2380, TNA.
70. Telegram 987, Johnston to Foreign Office (Amman), July 23, 1958, Amman, PREM 11/2380, TNA.
71. Telegram 2260, Foreign Office to Amman (London), July 24, 1958, PREM/11/2380, TNA.
72. Johnston, *The Brink Of Jordan*, 104.
73. Record of Meeting (London), July 27, 1958, PREM 11/2380, TNA.
74. Telegram 537, Foreign Office to Tel Aviv (London), August 2, 1958, PREM 11/2380, TNA.
75. Telegram 2534, Foreign Office to Amman (London), August 4, 1958, PREM 11/2380, TNA.
76. Telegram 1792, Johnston to Foreign Office (Amman), October 4, 1958, PREM1/3028, TNA.
77. Dann, *King Hussein*, 101–2
78. Louise S. Keeley, "Racing King Hussein," *Foreign Service Journal* (June 1999): 54–55.
79. King Hussein, *Uneasy Lies the Head*, 233.
80. Memorandum of a Conversation, White House (Washington, DC) March 1959, Vol. XI, pp. 700–704, Foreign Relations of the United States; hereafter referred to as FRUS.
81. Letter, Hussein to Prime Minister (Amman), April 3, 1960, PREM 11/3028, TNA.
82. Letter, Johnston to Lord Home (Amman), September 8, 1960, CAB 21/4632, TNA; King Hussein, *Uneasy Lies the Head*, 245–53.
83. W. Byford-Jones, *Adventures with Two Passports*, 74–75.
84. Financial Times, "Obituary: Lord Henniker," *Financial Times* (London), May 3, 2004.
85. Quoted in Winifred Carr, *Hussein's Kingdom* (London: Leslie Frewin, 1966), 24.
86. Simon C. Smith, *Britain's Revival and Fall in the Gulf* (London: Routledge Curzon, 2004), 17.
87. Despatch 120, Mak to State Department (Kuwait), February 7, 1962, 786.5/2-762, National Archives, College Park, MD; hereafter referred to as NA.
88. Asher Susser, *On Both Banks of the Jordan: A Political Biography of Wasfi al-Tall* (London: Frank Cass, 1994), 70–71.

89. Moshe Gat, *Britain and the Conflict in the Middle East, 1964–1967* (Westport, CT: Praeger, 2003), 163. According to Gat, in light of the relationship between Israel and Jordan the raid on Samu was puzzling.

90. Moshe Dayan: *Story of My Life* (New York: Morrow, 1976), 289.

91. Memorandum from the President's Special Assistant (Walt Rostow) to President Johnson (Washington, DC), December 12, 1966, Arab-Israel Dispute, 1964–1967, Vol. XVIII, pp. 711–12, FRUS.

92. Michael Oren, *Six Days of War* (New York: Oxford University Press, 2002), 33–34.

93. Samir A. Mutawi, *Jordan in the 1967 War* (New York: Cambridge University Press, 2002), 80–81.

94. Telegram, Embassy to State Department (Amman), December 11, 1966, Arab-Israel Dispute, 1964–1967, Vol. XVIII, pp. 707–11, FRUS.

95. Memorandum from Acting Secretary of State Katzenbach to President Johnson (Washington, DC) December 12, 1966, Arab-Israel Dispute, 1964–1967, Vol. XVIII, pp. 714–15, FRUS.

96. Tal, *Politics, the Military, and National Security in Jordan, 1955–1967*, 110–11.

97. Susser, *On Both Banks*, 119.

98. Oren, *Six Days of War*, 35–37.

CHAPTER 2

1. Steven L. Spiegel, *The Other Arab-Israeli Conflict: Making American's Middle East Policy, From Truman to Reagan* (Chicago: University of Chicago Press, 1985), 137.

2. Frank Brenchley, *Britain and the Middle East: An Economic History 1945–1987* (London: Lester Crook, 1989), 148.

3. *The Palestine News*, Dayan Institute, Tel Aviv University, May 25, 1967, p.1.

4. Asher Susser, *On Both Banks of the Jordan: A Political Biography of Wasfi al-Tall* (London: Routledge, 1994), 123.

5. *The Palestine News*, Dayan Institute, Tel Aviv University, May 31, 1967, p.1.

6. Abba Eban, *An Autobiography* (New York: Random House, 1977), 380.

7. Peter Snow, *Hussein: A Biography* (Washington, DC: Robert B. Luce, 1972), 173.

8. Dean Rusk, *As Told to Richard Rusk, As I Saw It* (New York: Norton, 1999), 387.

9. Queen Noor, *Leap of Faith* (New York: Miramax, 2003), 70.

10. *The Palestine News*, Dayan Institute, Tel Aviv University, June 1, 1967, p. 3.

11. Ibid., June 1, 1967, p. 4.

12. Ibid., p. 1.

13. Ibid., June 3, 1967, p. 3.

14. William Dale, "An Embassy in Wartime: The Six Day War," http://www.unc.edu/depts/diplomat/archives, American Diplomacy.org.

15. Teddy Kollek and Amos Kollek, *For Jerusalem* (New York: Random House, 1978), 191.

16. The Second Arab-Israel War, 1967: The Battle, Hadow (Tel Aviv), July 6, 1967, PREM 13/1622, The National Archives, Kew, England (formerly Public Records Office); hereafter referred to as TNA.

17. Menachem Klein, *Jerusalem: The Contested City* (New York: New York University Press, 2001), 53.

18. Interview with Ziad Abu Ziad (Jerusalem), June 12, 1988.

19. Richard Crossman, *The Diaries of a Cabinet Minister*, Vol. II (New York: Holt, Rinehart and Winston, 1976).

20. Quoted in Snow, *Hussein*, 195.
21. Letter, Balfour-Paul to Callaghan (Amman), September 12, 1975, FCO 93/665, TNA.
22. Interview with Ziad Abu Ziad (Jerusalem), June 12, 1988.
23. Telegram 789, Adams to Foreign Office (Amman), June 30, 1967, FCO 17/240, TNA.
24. Telegram 796, Adams to Foreign Office (Amman), July 1, 1967, FCO 17/240, TNA.
25. Memorandum, Rostow to President Johnson (Washington, DC), June 27, 1967, Lyndon B. Johnson Library.
26. Record of a Conversation (London), June 30, 1967, PREM 13/1622, TNA.
27. Telegram 789, Adams to Foreign Office (Amman), June 30, 1967, PREM 13/1622, TNA.
28. Memorandum, Morris (London), July 1, 1967, FCO 17/240, TNA.
29. Telegram 731, Hadow to Foreign Office (Tel Aviv), July 1, 1967, FCO 17/240, TNA.
30. Telegram 732, Hadow to Foreign Office (Tel Aviv), July 1, 1967, FCO 17/240, TNA.
31. Visit of King Hussein, Prime Minister's Working Lunch (London), July 3, 1967, FCO 17/240, TNA.
32. Record of a conversation (London), July 3, 1967, PREM 13/1622, TNA.
33. Letter, Urwick to Morris (Washington, DC), July 7, 1967, FCO 17/11, TNA.
34. William B. Quandt, *Peace Process* (Washington, DC: The Brookings Institute, 1993), 46.
35. Klein, *Jerusalem: The Contested City*, 60.
36. Meron Benvenisti, *Jerusalem: The Torn City* (Jerusalem, Isratypeset, 1976), 277–78.
37. Telegram 4460, U.S. Embassy to State Department (Amman), April 22, 1968, DEF 8 ISR, National Archives, College Park, MD; hereafter referred to as NA.
38. Telegram 156513, State Department to Tel Aviv (Washington, DC), May 1, 1968, XR POL 28 Jerusalem, NA.
39. Airgram 319, Hall to State Department (Jerusalem), August 23, 1968, POL 28 Jerusalem, NA.
40. Telegram from the Embassy in Jordan to the Department of State (Amman), December 9, 1968, Arab-Israel Dispute, 1964–1968, Vol. XX, pp. 682–83, Foreign Relations of the United States; hereafter referred to as FRUS.
41. Telegram from the Embassy in Jordan to the Department of State (Amman), December 30, 1968, Arab-Israel Dispute, 1964–1968, Vol. XX, pp. 732–33, FRUS.
42. Telegram From the Department of State to the Embassy in Jordan (Washington, DC), December 25, 1968, Arab-Israel Dispute, 1964–1968, Vol. XX, pp. 723, FRUS.
43. Memorandum, Seeyle to Hart (Washington, DC), January 8, 1969, POL Jordan, NA.
44. Memorandum, Walsh to the Kissinger, Official Visit of King Hussein, Briefing Book (Washington, DC), April 1969, Nixon Papers, NA.
45. Memorandum to the President, Official Visit of King Hussein, Briefing Book (Washington, DC), April 1969, Nixon Papers, NA.
46. Ibid.
47. Telegram 3323, Symmes to State Department (Amman), July 12, 1969, POL 23 Jordan, NA.
48. Research Memorandum, Hughes to Secretary of State (Washington, DC), July 16, 1969, POL 23, Jordan, NA.
49. Airgram 130, Embassy to State Department (Amman), September 4, 1969, POL 13-2 Jordan, NA.
50. Telegram 3688, Country Team to State Department (Amman), August 4, 1969, POL 23 Jordan, NA.
51. Telegram 4012, Embassy to State Department (Amman), August 23, 1969, POL 23-8, Jordan, NA.
52. Letter, Rifai to Secretary General (Amman), August 21, 1969, http://domino.un.org.

53. British Consul-General to the Foreign Office (Jerusalem), January 20, 1970, FCO 17/1369, TNA.
54. Telegram 312, Foreign Office to Amman (London), October 3, 1969, FCO 17/830/1, TNA.
55. Telegram 312, Foreign Office to Amman (London), October 3, 1969, FCO 17/830/1, TNA.
56. Telegram 5316, Embassy to State Department (Amman), November 3, 1969, POL 15-1 Jordan, NA.
57. Telegram 5424, Symmes to Sisco (Amman), November 8, 1969, POL 23-3 Jordan, NA.
58. Interview with John Snodgrass (London), January 11, 2000.
59. Letter, Lewen to Yarnold (Jerusalem), February 10, 1970, FCO 17/1366, TNA.
60. Letter, Yarnold to Dunn (London), March 5, 1970, FCO 17/1366, TNA.
61. Telegram 1589, U.S. Embassy to Secretary of State (Amman), April 15, 1970, POL 23-8, NA.
62. Interview, Ambassador Harrison M. Symmes, February 25, 1989, Association for Diplomatic Studies and Training, Arlington, VA; hereafter referred to as ADST.
63. Telegram 1589, U.S. Embassy to Secretary of State (Amman), April 15, 1970, POL 23-8, NA.
64. Interview, Ambassador Harrison M. Symmes, February 25, 1989, ADST.
65. Patrick Seale, ed., *The Shaping of an Arab Statesman* (London: Quartet Books, 1983), 12.
66. Telegram 56129, State Department to U.S. Embassy in Amman (Washington, DC), April 15, 1970, POL 23-8, NA.
67. Telegram 1618, U.S. Embassy to Secretary of State (Amman), April 16, 1970, POL 23-8, NA.
68. Interview with Morris Draper (Washington, DC), October 4, 2004.
69. Telegram 1629, U.S. Embassy to Secretary of State (Amman), April 16, 1970, POL 23-8, NA.
70. Clinton Bailey, *Jordan's Palestinian Challenge, 1948–1983* (Boulder, CO: Westview, 1984), 50–51.
71. Norvell De Atkine, "Amman 1970: A Memoir," Middle East Review of International Affairs, http://meria.idc.ac.il/journal/2002/issue4/jv6n4a2.html, p. 3.
72. Talking Points for Meeting between the Secretary of State and King Hussein, Background (London), May 6, 1970, FCO 17/308, TNA.
73. Memorandum of a Conversation (Washington, DC), May 14, 1970, POL 7 Jordan, NA, pp. 1–2.
74. Memorandum of a Conversation (Washington, DC), May 14, 1970, POL 7 Jordan, NA, p. 3.
75. Memorandum of a Conversation (Washington, DC), May 14, 1970, POL 7 Jordan, NA, pp. 1–4.
76. Memorandum for the President, William P. Rogers (Washington, DC), May 18, 1970, POL 7 Jordan, NA.
77. Telegram 530, Barnes to Foreign Office (Tel Aviv), June 5, 1970, FCO 17/1066, TNA.
78. Telegram 225, Adams to Foreign Office (Amman), June 5, 1970, FCO17/1066, TNA.
79. *New York Times*, June 10, 1970, p. 1.
80. Memorandum for Henry Kissinger (Washington, DC), June 11, 1970, POL 23, NA.
81. Telegram 289, Stewart to Tel Aviv (London), June 11, 1970, FCO 17/1066, TNA.
82. *Newsweek*, June 22, 1970, p. 34.
83. Memorandum for Henry Kissinger (Washington, DC), June 11, 1970, POL 23, NA.
84. Telegram 90492, State Department to Beirut (Washington, DC), June 11, 1970, POL 23, NA. AUB indicates the American University in Beirut.
85. Memorandum For Henry Kissinger (Washington, DC), June 11, 1970, POL 23, NA, p. 2.

86. Memorandum For Henry Kissinger (Washington, DC), June 11, 1970, POL 23, NA, p. 3.
87. Telegram, State Department to U.S. Embassy Rome (Washington, DC), June 11, 1970, POL 23, NA.
88. Telegram 91713, State Department to U.S. Embassy in Amman (Washington, DC) June 12, 1970, POL 23, NA.
89. *Newsweek*, June 22, 1970, p. 34.
90. Telegram 91662, State Department to U.S. Embassy Ankara (Washington, DC), June 12, 1970, POL 23, NA.
91. Telegram 1306, Bergus to Secretary of State (Cairo), June 12, 1970, POL 23, NA.
92. Telegram 3021, Barbour to Secretary of State (Tel Aviv), June 12, 1970, POL 23, NA.
93. Telegram 2726, Odell to Secretary of State (Amman), June 14, 1970, POL 23, NA, p.2.
94. Telegram 560, Barnes to Foreign Office (Tel Aviv), June 12, 1970, FCO 17/1066, TNA.
95. Telegram 557, Barnes to Foreign Office (Tel Aviv), June 12, 1970, FCO 17/1066, TNA.
96. Telegram, 4642, Annenberg to State Department (London), June 15, 1970, POL 23, Jordan, NA.
97. Telegram 2682, Odell to Secretary of State (Amman), June 14, 1970, POL 23, NA.
98. Telegram 2726, Odell to Secretary of State (Amman), June 14, 1970, POL 23, NA, p. 3.
99. Telegram 2915, U.S. Embassy to Secretary of State (Amman), June 23, 1970, POL 23, N..A.

CHAPTER 3

1. Telegram 2985, U.S. Embassy to Secretary of State (Amman), June 25, 1970, POL 23, National Archives, College Park, MD; hereafter referred to as NA.
2. Graeme Zielinski, "Diplomat L. Dean Brown Dies," *Washington Post*, May 10, 2001, p. B7, http://www.jordanembassyus.org/05102001009.htm.
3. Service at Embassy Amman, 1970, Extract From Oral History of Ambassador Hume, Foreign Service Institute, October 2000–January 2001, p. 8, http://www.unc.edu/depts/diplomat/archives-roll/2002.
4. Kamal Salibi, *The Modern History of Jordan* (London: Tauris, 1993), 234.
5. Norvell De Atkine, "Amman 1970: A Memoir," *Middle East Review of International Affairs*, pp. 1–2, http://meria.idc.ac.il/journal/2002/issue4/jv6n4a2.html.
6. *Newsweek*, July 13, 1970, p. 44.
7. Telegram 3245, Draper to Secretary of State (Amman), July 11, 1970, POL 23, NA.
8. Telegram 128623, State Department to U.S. Embassy Tehran (Washington, DC), POL 23, NA.
9. Letter, Hussein to Wilson (Amman), August 5, 1968, FCO 17/830/1, The National Archives, Kew, England (formerly Public Records Office); hereafter referred to as TNA.
10. Telegram 4209, Odell to Secretary of State (Amman), August 31, 1970, POL 23, NA.
11. Telegram 143328, State Department to U.S. Embassy Moscow (Washington, DC), September 2, 1970. POL 23, NA.
12. Telegram 6984, Annenberg to Secretary of State (London), September 2, 1970, POL 23, NA. The Four-Powers refer to Great Britain, France, the Soviet Union, and the United States.
13. Telegram 4335, Odell to Secretary of State (Amman), September 4, 1970, POL 23, NA.
14. Interview with Morris Draper (Washington, DC), October 4, 2004.
15. Ibid.
16. James Lunt, *Hussein of Jordan* (New York: William Morrow, 1989), 131–32.
17. *Life*, September 18, 1970, p. 30.
18. Ibid., p. 36.

19. Interview with Talcott Seeyle (Washington, DC), March 18, 2004.

20. Telegram 4375, Odell, to Secretary of State (Amman), September 7, 1970, POL 23, NA.

21. Telegram 4477, Odell to Secretary of State (Amman), September 9, 1970, POL 23, NA.

22. Telegram 4492, Odell to Secretary of State (Amman), September 9, 1970, POL 23, NA.

23. Telegram 147707, Rogers to U.S. Embassy in London (Washington, DC), September 9, 1970, POL 23, NA, pp. 1–2.

24. Telegram 147707, Rogers to U.S. Embassy in London (Washington, DC), September 9, 1970, POL 23, NA, p. 4.

25. Telegram 147707, Rogers to U.S. Embassy in London (Washington, DC), September 9, 1970, POL 23, NA, p. 5.

26. Telegram 4549, U.S. Embassy to State Department (Amman), September 10, 1970, POL 23 Jordan, NA.

27. SITREP AT 0800, September 14, 1970, PREM 15/24, TNA.

28. Telegram 4683, Brubeck to Secretary of State (Amman), September 13, 1970, POL 23, NA.

29. Telephone Discussion between Sir Denis Greenhill, Dr. Kissinger, and Mr. Sisco, September 16, 1970, PREM 15/24, TNA.

30. Report of Telephone Conversation, September 17, 1970, PREM 15/124, TNA.

31. SITREP AT 0800, September 14, 1970, PREM 15/24, TNA.

32. Note of Action Taken, Sir Denis Greenhill (London), September 19, 1970, PREM 15/124, TNA.

33. Report, Reddaway to Graham, September 18, 1970, PREM 15/124, TNA.

34. Mohamed Heikal, *The Road to Ramadan* (New York: Ballantine, 1975), 94.

35. Benny Morris, *Righteous Victims* (New York: Vintage, 2001), 374.

36. Telegram 2783, Washington, DC, to Foreign Office, September 21, 1970, FCO 17/1050, TNA.

37. Letter, Thomson to Trend (London), September 21, 1970, PREM 15/24, TNA.

38. Cabinet, Evacuation and Emergency Aid Committee (London), September 21, 1970, FCO 17/1050, TNA. Israelis offered their cooperation. See Telegram 905, Tel Aviv to Foreign Office, September 25, 1970, FCO 17/1051, TNA.

39. Memorandum, Ibbott to Tripp (Amman), September 21, 1970, PREM 15/24, TNA.

40. Memorandum of a Conversation (Washington, DC), September 21, 1970, PREM 15/24, TNA.

41. Telex Conversation between Amman and London, September 22, 1970, PREM 15/124, TNA.

42. Text of Proposed Message to Nasser (London), September 22, 1970, PREM 15/124, TNA.

43. SITREP AT 0800, September 14, 1970, PREM 15/24, TNA.

44. Margaret Thatcher, *The Path to Power* (London: Harper Collins, 1995), 198.

45. Memorandum, Middle East Crisis, September 22, 1970, PREM 15/124, TNA, pp. 1–3.

46. Telegram 1250, Foreign Office to UK Mission (London), September 23, 1970, FCO 17/1051, TNA.

47. Telegram 375, London to Amman, September 22, 1970, FCO 17/1050, TNA.

48. Letter, Whitehall to McCluney (London), September 23, 1970, TNA.

49. Telegram 500, Beirut to Foreign Office, September 24, 1970, FCO 17/1051, TNA.

50. Telegram 2129, Foreign Office to Washington, DC (London), September 23, 1970, FCO 17/1050, TNA.

51. Cabinet, The Relief Situation (London), September 24, 1970, FCO 17/1051, TNA.

52. Telegram 2840, State Department to Foreign Office (Washington, DC), September 25, 1970, FCO/17/1051, TNA.

53. Telegram 1264, Foreign Office to UK Mission (New York), September 24, 1970, FCO 17/1051, TNA.

54. Telegram 394, Douglas-Home to Amman (London), September 25, 1970, FCO/17/1051, TNA.
55. Telex Conference with Amman, 0515Z, September 24, 1970, FCO 17/1051, TNA.
56. *Time*, October 5, 1970, p.38.
57. Asher Susser, *On Both Banks of the Jordan: A Political Biography of Wasfi al-Tall* (London: Frank Cass, 1994), 139–40.
58. Salibi, *The Modern History of Jordan*, 235–41.
59. Letter, Woodrow to Evans (Jerusalem), October 5, 1970, FCO 17/1361,TNA.
60. Telegram 5574, Brown to Secretary of State (Amman), October 3, 1970, POL 23, NA.
61. Ibid., 2.
62. Salibi, *The Modern History of Jordan*, 235–41.
63. Record of Conversation between King Hussein of Jordan and HM Ambassador (Paris), December 15, 1970, FCO/17/1101/91888, TNA.
64. Henry Kissinger, *White House Years* (Boston, Little Brown, 1979), 631.
65. Fouad Ajami, *The Arab Predicament* (New York: Cambridge University, 1993), 177.
66. Telegram 4974, Calhoun to State Department (Tunis), October 14, 1971, POL 23-9 Jordan, NA.
67. Telegram 6818, Brown to Secretary of State (Amman), October 30, 1970, POL 7 Jordan, NA.
68. Letter, Woodrow to Evans (Jerusalem), October 5, 1970, FCO 17/1361, TNA, pp. 1–2.
69. Letter, Woodrow to Evans (Jerusalem), October 5, 1970, FCO 17/1361, TNA, p. 3.
70. Record of a Conversation between the Minister of State for Foreign and Commonwealth Affairs and the Deputy Prime Minister of Israel (Jerusalem), November 3, 1970, FCO 17/1331, TNA.
71. Record of a Conversation between the Minister of State for Foreign and Commonwealth Affairs and the Director of Israeli Military Intelligence (Jerusalem), November 3, 1970, FCO 17/1331, TNA.
72. Telegram 6393, Brown to Secretary of State (Amman), November 5, 1970, POL 7, Jordan, NA. Al-Tall had assumed the post of prime minister on October 28, 1970.
73. Telegram 6463, Brown to State Department, November 9, 1970, POL 23 Jordan, NA,
74. Richard Nixon, *Public Papers of the Presidents, Richard Nixon, 1970* (Washington, DC: Government Printing Office, 1971), 1076.
75. Memorandum, Acting Secretary to the President, State Department (Washington, DC), December 4, 1970, POL 7 Jordan, NA.
76. Brief for the Secretary of States Meeting with King Hussein (London), December 21, 1970, FCO 17/1101/91888, TNA, p. 1.
77. Record of the Prime Minister's Meeting with King Hussein, December 4, 1970, FCO 17/1101/91888, TNA.
78. Record of the Prime Minister's Meeting with King Hussein, December 4, 1970, FCO 17/1101/91888, TNA.
79. Telegram 203323, State Department to Amman (Washington, DC), December 11, 1970, POL 7 Jordan, NA, p. 1.
80. Telegram 6814, Embassy to State Department (Amman), November 30, 1970, POL 3 Pal Entity, POL 7 Jordan, NA.
81. Telegram 203323, State Department to Amman (Washington, DC), December 11, 1970, POL 7 Jordan, NA, p. 1.
82. Telegram 203323, State Department to Amman (Washington, DC), December 11, 1970, POL 7 Jordan, NA, pp. 2–6. Four days later in Paris King Hussein stated that: for the first time in speaking to the Egyptians, he was hearing several voices speak up that he had never heard before. Previously it had always been Nasser who did the talking, and the others sat around silent, but now plenty of people were prepared to express their points of view. Record of

Conversation between King Hussein of Jordan and HM Ambassador (Paris), December 15, 1970, FCO/17/1101/91888, TNA, p. 2.

83. Telegram 203323, State Department to Amman (Washington, DC), December 11 1970, POL 7 Jordan, NA, pp. 2–6.

84. Telegram 203323, State Department to Amman (Washington, DC), December 11, 1970, POL 7 Jordan, NA, pp. 6–10.

85. Telegram 202532, State Department to Amman (Washington, DC), December 11, 1970, POL 7 Jordan, NA, pp.1–4.

86. Telegram 202532, State Department to Amman (Washington, DC), December 11, 1970, POL 7 Jordan, NA, pp. 5–7.

87. Telegram 202613, State Department to Amman (Washington, DC), December 11, 1970, POL 7 Jordan, NA.

88. Telegram 3681, British Embassy to Foreign Office (Washington, DC), December 11, 1970, FCO 17/1101/91888, TNA.

89. Record of Conversation between King Hussein of Jordan and HM Ambassador (Paris), December 15, 1970, FCO/17/1101/91888, TNA.

90. Near Eastern Department Memo, Adams (London), December 18, 1970, FCO 17/1066/9188, TNA.

91. Telegram 1147, Barnes to Foreign Office (Tel Aviv), December 31, 1970, FCO/17/1066/91888, TNA.

92. Press Release (London), November 17, 1970, FCO 17/1066, TNA.

93. Telegram 1006, Phillips to Foreign Office (Amman), December 31, 1970, FCO 17/1066, TNA.

94. Beverley Milton Edwards and Peter Hinchcliffe, *Jordan: A Hashemite Legacy* (London: Routledge, 2001), 45.

95. Summary of 1970, Phillips to Foreign Office, January 6, 1971, FCO 17/1411, TNA

CHAPTER 4

1. Letter, Phillips to Evans (Amman), December 22, 1970, FCO 17/1099, The National Archives, Kew, England (formerly Public Records Office); hereafter referred to as TNA.

2. Telegram 5, Phillips to Foreign Office (Amman), January 4, 1971, FCO 17/1410, TNA.

3. Minute, Strachan (Amman), January 6, 1971, FCO 17/1410, TNA.

4. Letter, Carter to Long (Amman), January 29, 1971, FCO 17/1410, TNA.

5. Letter, Barrington to Stephens (London), January 18, 1971, FCO 17/1419, TNA.

6. Memorandum, Adams (London), January 26, 1971, FCO 17/1419, TNA.

7. Letter, Moon to Graham (London), February 23, 1971, PREM 15/507, TNA.

8. Telegram A-118 Wolle to State Department (Amman), September 7, 1971, POL 15-1, National Archives, College Park, MD; hereafter referred to as NA.

9. Memorandum of a Conversation, State Department (Washington, DC), March 1, 1971, POL 15-1 Jordan, NA.

10. Memorandum of a Conversation, State Department (Washington, DC), March 1, 1971, POL 15-1 Jordan, NA.

11. Telegram 37256, State Department to Amman (Washington, DC), March 4, 1971, POL 7 Jordan, NA, pp. 1–3.

12. Telegram 37256, State Department to Amman (Washington, DC), March 4, 1971, POL 7 Jordan, NA, pp. 4–5.

13. Telegram 37256, State Department to Amman (Washington, DC), March 4, 1971, POL 7 Jordan, NA, pp. 5–6.

NOTES

14. Telegram 36856, State Department to Amman (Washington, DC), March 3, 1971, POL 7 Jordan, NA, p. 5.
15. Telegram 37256, State Department to Amman (Washington, DC), March 4, 1971, POL 7 Jordan, NA, pp. 12–13.
16. Telegram 37256, State Department to Amman (Washington, DC), March 4, 1971, POL 7 Jordan, NA, p. 14.
17. Letter, Phillips to Evans (Amman), March 18, 1971, FCO 17/1410, TNA.
18. Letter, Phillips to Evans (Amman), March 19, 1971, FCO 17/1419, TNA.
19. Letter, Brubeck to Seelye (Amman), March 11, 1971, POL Jordan-UK, NA.
20. Letter, Seelye to Brubeck (Washington, DC), March 25, 1971, POL Jordan-UK, NA.
21. Letter, Phillips to Evans (Amman), March 17, 1971, FCO 17/1600, TNA.
22. Ibid.
23. Telegram 1989, Brown to Secretary of State (Amman), April 23, 1971, POL 15-1, NA.
24. Intelligence Note (Washington, DC), April 23, 1971, XR POL 15-1, NA.
25. *New York Times*, April 1, 1971, p. 16.
26. Ibid., April 3, 1971, p. 13.
27. Telegram 176, Phillips to Foreign Office (Amman), April 4, 1971, FCO 17/1410, TNA.
28. *New York Times*, April 7, 1971, p. 5.
29. Letter, Champion to Long (Amman), April 6, 1971, FCO 17/1410, TNA.
30. Telegram 239, Phillips to Foreign Office, May 21, 1971, FCO 17/1410, TNA.
31. Letter, Champion to Long (Amman), April 30, 1971, FCO 17/1438, TNA.
32. Memorandum, Harrison (Amman), April 29, 1971, FCO 17/1438, TNA.
33. King Hussein's Recorded Message (London), May 18, 1971, FCO 17/1600, TNA.
34. Letter, Snodgrass to Laver (Jerusalem), November 30, 1971, FCO 7/1604, TNA.
35. Letter, Snodgrass to Douglas-Home (Jerusalem), March 3, 1972, FCO 7/1795, TNA.
36. Interview with John Snodgrass (London), January 11, 2000. On March 12, 1973, an Israeli diplomat called at the Foreign Office to complain about Consul General Snodgrass. Whitehall rejected the complaint, omitting it from the record. Memorandum, Long to Craig and Parsons (London), March 15, 1973, FCO 93/132, TNA.
37. Airgram A-46, Brown to State Department (Amman), May 21, 1971, POL 23-8 Jordan, NA.
38. Airgram A-60, American Embassy to State Department (Amman), June 8, 1971, POL 13-10, NA.
39. Airgram A-60, American Embassy to State Department (Amman), June 8, 1971, POL 13-10, NA.
40. Letter, Carter to Long (Amman), June 4, 1971, FCO 17/1410, TNA.
41. Telegram 2767, Brown to State Department (Amman), June 14, 1971, POL 15-1 Jordan, NA.
42. Letter, Champion to Evans (Amman), June 15, 1971, FCO 17/1410, TNA.
43. lTelegram 2869, Brown to Secretary of State (Amman), June 18, 1971, POL15-1, NA.
44. Letter, Phillips to Evans (Amman), June 18, 1971, FCO 17/1410, TNA.
45. Telegram 303, Amman to Foreign Office, June 18, 1971, FCO 17/1414, TNA.
46. Telegram 250600Z, Phillips to Foreign Office (Amman), June 24, 1971, FCO 17/1410, TNA.
47. Benny Morris, *Righteous Victims* (New York: Vintage, 2001), 375.
48. Telegram 599, Barnes to Amman (Tel Aviv), July 22, 1971, FCO 17/1410, TNA.
49. Cabinet (London), July 22, 1971, FCO 17/1410, TNA.
50. Telegram 1793, Bergus to State Department (Cairo), July 20, 1971, POL Jordan-UAR, NA.
51. Telegram 382, Phillips to Foreign Office (Amman), July 22, 1971, FCO 17/1410, TNA.

52. Telegram 2228, U.S. Mission to Secretary of State (New York), August 12, 1971, POL 17 Jordan-United States, NA.

53. Telegram 4086, Brubeck to State Department (Amman), August 31, 1971, POL 15-1 Jordan, NA.

54. Telegram 4355, Brown to Secretary of State (Amman), September 12, 1971, POL 15-1 Jordan, NA.

55. http://www.jewishvirtuallibrary.org/jsource/UN/unres298.html.

56. Letter, al-Tall to Phillips (Amman), October 3, 1971, FCO 17/1604, TNA.

57. Diplomatic Report 531/71, Her Majesty's Ambassador at Amman to the Secretary of State for Foreign and Commonwealth Affairs (Jordan), November 12, 1971, FCO 17/1415, TNA.

58. Letter, Gore-Booth to Evans (London), December 22, 1971, FCO 17/1422, TNA.

59. Asher Susser, *On Both Banks Of The Jordan: A Political Biography of Wasfi al-Tall* (London: Frank Cass, 1994), 168.

60. Memorandum For Henry Kissinger (Washington, DC), November 29, 1971, POL 15-1, NA.

61. Letter, Cater to Gore-Booth (Amman), January 1, 1972, FCO 17/1683, TNA.

62. *New York Times*, November 30, 1971, p. 20.

63. Telegram 5346, American Embassy to Secretary of State (Amman), November 29, 1971, POL 15-1, NA.

64. Telegram 1604, Beaumont to Foreign Office (Cairo), December 3, 1972, FCO 17/1410, TNA.

65. Telegram 5396, Brown to Secretary of state (Amman), December 1, 1971, POL 15-1, NA, p. 1.

66. Telegram 4, Phillips to Foreign Office (Amman), December 2, 1971, FCO 17/1410, TNA.

67. Telegram 1211, Balfour Paul to Foreign Office (Baghdad), December 2, 1971, FCO 17/1410, TNA.

68. Letter, Young to Holding (Cairo), December 10, 1971, FCO 17/1410, TNA.

69. Telegram 5561, American Embassy to Secretary of State (Amman), December 10, 1971, POL 15-1, NA.

70. Telegram 5561, American Embassy to Secretary of State (Amman), December10, 1971, POL 15-1, NA, p.2.

71. Memorandum, Jordanian Ambassador's Concern over Jack Anderson Newspaper Article (Washington, DC), December 20, 1971, POL 15-1, NA.

72. Telegram 5710, Brown to Secretary of State (Amman), December 21, 1971, POL 15-1, NA.

73. Letter, Gore-Booth to Evans (London), December 22, 1971, FCO 17/1422, TNA.

74. Telegram 4312, Tebbit to Foreign Office (Washington, DC), December 21, 1971, FCO 17/1422, TNA.

75. Telegram 742, Phillips to Foreign Office, December 25, 1971, FCO 17/1422, TNA.

76. Telegram 5742, American Embassy to Secretary of State (Amman), December 22, 1971, POL 15-1, NA.

77. Memorandum For Henry Kissinger (Washington, DC), December 24, 1971, POL 15, NA.

78. Letter, President Nixon to King Hussein (Washington, DC), December 23, 1971, POL 15-1, NA.

Chapter 5

1. Telegram 11465, American Embassy to Secretary of State (London), December 16, 1971, POL 17, National Archives, College Park, MD; hereafter referred to as NA.
2. Telegram 11407, Annenberg to Secretary of State (London), December 15, 1971, POL 17 Jordan, NA.
3. Telegram 5647, Brubeck to Secretary of State (Amman), December 16, 1971, POL 17, NA.
4. Letter, Carter to Gore-Booth (Amman), January 1, 1972, FCO 17/1683, The National Archives, Kew, England (formerly Public Records Office); hereafter referred to as TNA.
5. Annual Review (Jordan), January 13, 1972, FCO 371/1685, TNA.
6. Letter, Snodgrass to Evans (Jerusalem), February 8, 1972, FCO 17/1683, TNA.
7. Letter, Carter to Gore-booth (Amman), January 21, 1972, TNA.
8. Telegram 11005Z, Brown to Secretary of State, January 11, 1972, POL 17-7 Jordan, NA.
9. Telegram 5978, State Department to American Embassy in Amman (Washington, DC), January 11, 1972, POL 17-7 Jordan–United States, NA.
10. Telegram 556, Greene, to Secretary of State (Cairo), February 23, 1972, POL 15-1, NA.
11. Telegram 905, Brown to Secretary of State (Amman), March 1, 1972, POL 15-1, NA.
12. Telegram 6220, Greene to Secretary of State (Cairo), March 1, 1972, POL 15-1 Jordan, NA.
13. Telegram 905, Embassy to State Department (Amman), March 1972, POL 23-8 Jordan, NA.
14. Memorandum for the President (Washington, DC), March 23, 1972, POL 15-1, NA.
15. The United Arab Kingdom, Cabinet (London), March 16, 1972, FCO 17/1687, TNA.
16. Text of Message, Prime Minister to King Hussein (London), n.d., FCO 17/1687, TNA.
17. Telegram 237, Barnes to Foreign Office (Tel Aviv), March 17, 1972, FCO 17/1687, TNA.
18. Memorandum, Sisco to Secretary of State (Washington, DC), March 20, 1972, POL 15-1, NA.
19. Telegram 230, Barnes to Foreign Office (Tel Aviv), March 16, 1972, FCO 17/1687, TNA.
20. Letter, Parsons to Evans (London), March 15, 1972, FCO, 17/1687, TNA
21. Letter, Callan to Beckett (Beirut), March 18, 1972, FCO 17/1687, TNA.
22. Telegram 434, Beaumont to Foreign Office (Cairo), March 20, 1972, FCO 17/1687, TNA.
23. Telegram 308, Stoltzfus to State Department (Kuwait), February 28, 1972, POL Jordan-Kuwait, NA.
24. *Newsweek*, April 17, 1972, p. 46.
25. Telegram 1516, American Embassy to State Department (Amman), April 7, 1972, POL 17 Egypt-Jordan, NA.
26. Memorandum for the President (Washington, DC), March 23, 1972, POL 15-1, NA.
27. Special Reports, Foreign Office (Jordan), April 25, 1972, FCO 17/1688, TNA.
28. Minute, Gore-Booth (London), May 5, 1972, FCO 17/1692, TNA.
29. Letter, Phillips to Craig (Amman), May 9, 1972, FCO 17/1692, TNA.
30. Minute, Shea (London), May 15, 1972, FCO 17/1692, TNA.
31. Report (Jordan), May 3, 1972, FCO 17/1683, TNA.

32. Letter, Callan to Beckett (Beirut), May 19, 1972, FCO 17/1686, TNA.
33. Letter, Al-Rifai to Kissinger (Amman), May 15, 1972, Nixon Papers, NA.
34. Letter, Champion to Goore-Booth (Amman), June 15, 1972, FCO 17/1683, TNA.
35. Telegram 2678, American Embassy to State Department (Amman), June 27, 1972, POL 7 Oman, NA.
36. Letter, Al-Rifai to Kissinger (Amman), July 15, 1972, Nixon Papers, NA.
37. Telegram 147425, Sisco to Brown (Washington, DC), August 14, 1972, POL Jordan–United States, NA.
38. Telegram 3404, Brown to Sisco (Amman), August 16, 1972, POL Jordan–United States, NA.
39. Memorandum, Haig to Kissinger (Washington, DC), August 2, 1972, Nixon Papers, NA.
40. Telegram 3651, Brown to State Department (Amman), August 31, 1972, POL Jordan–United States, NA.
41. *New York Times*, September 6, 1972, p. 19.
42. Telegram 668, Day to State Department (Jerusalem), September 15, 1972, POL 23-10 Jordan, NA.
43. Telegram 3974, Wolle to State Department (Amman), September 20, 1972, POL 23-10 Jordan, NA.
44. Telegram 3539, Rogers to State Department (New York), September 28, 1972, POL Jordan–United States, NA.
45. Telegram 733, Day to State Department (Jerusalem), September 29, 1972, POL 28 Jerusalem, NA.
46. Telegram 731, Day to State Department (Jerusalem), September 29, 1972, POL 28 Jerusalem, NA.
47. Letter, Champion to Hope (Amman), September 18, 1972, FCO 17/1683, TNA.
48. Memorandum, Helms to Kissinger (Washington, DC), September 14, 1972, Nixon Papers, NA.
49. Letter, Champion to Hope (Amman), September 26, 1972, FCO 17/1683, TNA.
50. Telegram 591, Balfour Paul to Foreign Office (Amman), September 11, 1972, FCO 17/1683, TNA.
51. Minute, Kay (London), November 14, 1972, FCO 17/1683, TNA.
52. Telegram 3850, Wolle to Secretary of State (Amman), September 13, 1972, POL 15-1, NA.
53. Telegram 169685, State Department to Amman (Washington, DC), September 14, 1972, POL 15-1, NA.
54. Telegram 175215, Irwin to Sisco (New York), September 26, 1972, POL 15-1, NA.
55. Airgram A-124, Brubeck to State Department (Amman), September 30, 1972, SOC 12-1, NA.
56. Letter, Balfour-Paul to Foreign Office (Amman), September 26, 1972, FCO 17/1690, TNA.
57. Interview, Ambassador Roscoe Suddarth (Washington, DC), March 19, 2004.
58. Memorandum of a Conversation (Washington, DC), October 3, 1972, Nixon Papers, NA.
59. Telegram 4282, Brubeck to Secretary of State (Amman), October 2, 1972, POL 23-8, NA.
60. Telegram 4350, Brubeck to Secretary of State (Amman), October 5, 1972, POL 23-8, NA.
61. Telegram 4877, Brown to Secretary of State (Amman), November 4, 1972, POL 23-8, NA.
62. Letter, Champion to Craig (Amman), October 17, 1972, FCO 17/1683, TNA.
63. Letter, Carter to Hope (Amman), October 24, 1972, FCO 17/1683, TNA.

64. Letter, Carter to Hope (Amman), November 3, 1972, FCO 17/1683, TNA.
65. Letter, Wallis to Pike (Amman), November 20, 1972, HW 12/243, TNA.
66. Record of Mr. Craig's Conversations (Jerusalem), November 21, 1972, FCO 17/1749, TNA.
67. Letter, Balfour-Paul to Foreign Office (Amman), November 20, 1972, FCO 59/981, TNA.
68. Telegram 5287, Brown to Secretary of State (Amman), November 29, 1972, POL 15-1, NA.
69. Ibid.
70. Telegram 5736, Brown to Secretary of State (Amman), December 21, 1972, POL 15-1, NA.
71. Telegram 5786, Brown to Secretary of State (Amman), December 26, 1972, POL 15-1, NA.
72. Telegram 5287, Brown to Secretary of State (Amman), November 29, 1972, POL 15-1, NA.
73. Letter, Wallis to Pike (Tel Aviv), December 12, 1972, FCO 17/1692, TNA. According to Peter Wallis, "Smith is most helpful to us and we should prefer that he not be quoted to his U.S. colleagues elsewhere."
74. Telegram 8090, U.S. Embassy to State Department (Tel Aviv), December 8, 1972, POL Israel-Jordan, NA.
75. Record of Conversation Between HM Ambassador and Mrs. Meir (Jerusalem), December 13, 1972, FCO 17/1749, TNA.
76. Letter, Ledwidge to Parsons (Tel Aviv), December 20, 1972, FCO 17/1749, TNA.
77. Letter, Moberly to Parsons (Washington, DC), December 29, 1972, FCO 93/319, TNA.
78. Ibid.
79. Letter, Parker to Balfour-Paul (Amman), January 1, 1973, FCO 93/87, TNA.
80. Letter, Balfour-Paul to Douglas-Home (Amman), January 13, 1973, FCO 93/87, TNA.
81. Annual Review, Balfour-Paul to Douglas-Home (Amman), January 8, 1973, FCO 93/79, TNA.
82. Letter, Craig to Balfour-Paul (London), January 22, 1973, FCO 93/79, TNA.

CHAPTER 6

1. Telegram 47, Brown to State Department (Amman), January 3, 1973, POL 15-1 Jordan, National Archives, College Park, MD; hereafter referred to as NA.
2. Telegram 2622, Brown to State Department (Amman), May 15, 1973, POL 15-1 Jordan, NA.
3. Letter, Balfour Paul to Williams (Amman), August 28, 1973, FCO 93/81, The National Archives, Kew, England (formerly Public Records Office); hereafter referred to as TNA.
4. Letter, Ledwidge to Parsons (Tel Aviv), January 3, 1973, FCO 93/319, TNA.
5. Memorandum, Pike (London), January 18, 1973, FCO 93/79, TNA.
6. Letter, Balfour-Paul to Craig (Amman), January 27, 1973, FCO93/82, TNA.
7. Letter, Balfour-Paul to Craig (Amman), February 5, 1973, FCO 93/97, TNA.
8. Memorandum, Hope (London), February 1, 1973, FCO 93/87, TNA.
9. Ibid.

10. Telegram 384, Brown to State Department (Amman), January 22, 1973, POL Jordan, NA.
11. Telegram 4511, Sisco to Brown (Washington, DC), January 9, 1973, POL 7 Jordan, NA.
12. Telegram 5024, State Department to Amman (Washington, DC), January 10, 1973, POL 7 Jordan, NA.
13. Telegram 10741, Rogers to Amman (Washington, DC), January 18, 1973, POL 7 Jordan, NA.
14. Telegram 16319, State Department to Amman, January 27, 1973, POL 7 Jordan, NA.
15. Telegram 30, Defense Department to Ottawa (Amman), January 31, 1973, POL 7 Jordan, NA.
16. Intelligence Note, State Department (Washington, DC), February 2, 1973, POL 7 Jordan, NA, pp. 1–6.
17. President's Monday Briefing (Washington, DC), February 3, 1973, Nixon Papers, NA.
18. Telegram 25110, Rogers to American Embassy Amman (Washington, DC), February 9, 1973, POL 7 Jordan, NA, pp. 1–3.
19. Ibid., 3–6.
20. Memorandum, ME/4171/A/5, December 15, 1972, FCO 17/1749, TNA.
21. Telegram 25110, Rogers to American Embassy Amman (Washington, DC), February 9, 1973, POL 7 Jordan, NA, pp. 7–8.
22. Telegram 25110, Rogers to American Embassy Amman (Washington, DC), February 9, 1973, POL 7 Jordan, NA, p. 9.
23. Memorandum of a Conversation (Washington, DC), February 9, 1973, POL 7 Jordan, TNA.
24. Telegram 1182, American Embassy to State Department (Tel Aviv), February 14, 1973, Nixon Paper, NA.
25. Letter, Balfour Paul to Craig (Amman), February 19, 1973, FCO 93/98, TNA.
26. Letter, Snodgrass to Pike (Jerusalem), January 10, 1973, FCO 93/319, TNA.
27. Letter, Snodgrass to Long (Jerusalem), January 17, 1973, FCO 93/316, TNA.
28. Letter, Snodgrass to Gore-Booth (Jerusalem), February 21, 1973, FCO 93/316, TNA.
29. Letter, Snodgrass to Gore-Booth (Jerusalem), August 21, 1973, FCO 93/316, TNA.
30. Telegram 210, Brown to State Department (Amman), January 13, 1973, POL 7 Jordan, NA.
31. Memorandum, Visit of the Minister of State to Jordan, March 12–15, 1973, TNA.
32. Letter, Balniel to Wood (London), February 12, 1973, FCO 9/86, TNA.
33. Letter, Wood to Balniel (London), February 20, 1973, FCO 9/86, TNA.
34. Record of a Conversation (Amman), March 13, 1973, FCO 59/981, TNA.
35. Ibid.
36. Conversation between the Minister of State and the Israeli Ambassador (London), April 3, 1973, FCO 93/144, TNA.
37. Letter, Balniel to Wood (London), March 22, 1973, FCO 59/981, TNA.
38. Letter, Balfour-Paul to Craig (Amman), March 20, 1973, FCO 93/241, TNA.
39. Letter, Balfour-Paul to Craig (Amman), April 2, 1973, FCO 93/241, TNA.
40. Letter, Dalton to Hope (Amman), April 10, 1973, FCO 93/81, TNA.
41. Telegram 1446, American Embassy to State Department (Amman), March 19, 1973, POL 28 Jerusalem, NA.
42. Airgram 024, Day to State Department (Jerusalem), March 15, 1973, POL 18 Israel, NA.

43. Letter, Parsons to Pike (London), April 18, 1973, FCO 93/317, TNA.
44. Letter, Teulon to Pike (London), April 24, 1973, FCO 93/317, TNA.
45. Memorandum, Gore-Booth (London), April 26, 1973, FCO 93/317, TNA.
46. Letter, Giffard to Craig (Tel Aviv), February 23, 1973, FCO 93/317, TNA.
47. Diplomatic Report No. 289/73, Snodgrass to Foreign Office (Jerusalem), May 9, 1973, FCO 93/317, TNA.
48. Letter, Snodgrass to Gore-Booth (Jerusalem), May 9, 1973, FCO 93/317, TNA.
49. Letter, Sharaf to UN (New York), May 8, 1973, FCO 93/317, TNA.
50. Diplomatic Report 266/73 (Ledwidge, Israel), April 30, 1973, FCO/93/124, TNA.
51. Letter, Balfour-Paul to Craig (Amman), April 30, 1973, FCO 93/241, TNA.
52. Letter, Tait to Hope (Amman), May 11, 1973, FCO 93/81, TNA.
53. Telegram 2817, Brown to Secretary of State (Amman), May 25, 1973, POL 15-1 Jordan, NA.
54. Letter, Tait to Hope (Amman), June 5, 1973, FCO 93/81, TNA.
55. Ibid.
56. Memorandum, Sisco to Rogers (Washington, DC), May 29, 1973, POL 15-1 Jordan, NA.
57. Telegram 6335, Houghton to State Department (Beirut), May 31, 1973, POL 15-1 Jordan, NA.
58. Letter, Tait to Hope (Amman), June 12, 1973, FCO 93/81, TNA.
59. Speech, Freij (Bethlehem), June 18, 1973, FCO 93/316, TNA.
60. Letter, Snodgrass to Craig (Jerusalem), June 13, 1973, FCO 93/317, TNA.
61. Letter, Balfour-Paul to Doulas-Home (Amman), May 29, 1973, FCO 93/80, TNA.
62. Minute, Parsons (London), July 18, 1973, FCO 93/97, TNA.
63. Letter, Amery to Secretary of State (London), July 17, 1973, FCO 93/94, TNA.
64. Minute, Parsons (London), July 18, 1973, FCO 93/97, TNA.
65. Letter, Acland to Bridges (London), July 17, 1973, FCO093/94, TNA.
66. Record of a Conversation (London), July 11, 1973, FCO 93/97, TNA.
67. Record of a Conversation (London), July 12, 1973, PREM 15/2146, TNA.
68. Letter, Kealy to Gore-Booth (Kuwait), August 8, 1973, FCO 93/98, TNA.
69. Letter, Snodgrass to Foreign Office (Amman), August 14, 1973, FCO 93/316, TNA.
70. Letter, Balfour-Paul to Craig (Amman), August 27, 1973, FCO 93/82, N.A.
71. Ibid.
72. Letter, Balfour-Paul to Craig (Amman), September 3, 1973, FCO 93/82, TNA.
73. Airgram A-170, Embassy to State Department (Beirut), September 11, 1973, POL Jordan, NA.
74. Telegram 458, Balfour-Paul to Foreign Office (Amman), September 17, 1973, FCO 93/82, TNA.
75. Letter, Balfour-Paul to Craig (Amman), September 24, 1973, TNA.
76. Memorandum, Pickering to Scowcroft (Washington, DC), September 18, 1973, POL 7 Jordan, NA, pp. 1–2.
77. Telegram 5040, Brown to Secretary of State (Amman), September 19, 1973, Nixon Papers, NA.
78. Telegram 468, Balfour-Paul to Foreign Office (Amman), September 20, 1973, FCO 93/82, TNA.
79. Translation of an Article (Jedda), September 16, 1973, FCO 93/241, TNA.
80. *Time*, October 8, 1973, p. 47.
81. Letter, Nakhleh to Fulbright (New York), September 7, 1973, 5296/2, State of Israel Archives, Jerusalem; hereafter referred to as ISA.
82. Walter Isaacson, *Kissinger* (New York: Simon & Schuster, 1992), 505.

83. Telegram 458, Balfour-Paul to Foreign Office (Amman), September 17, 1973, FCO 93/82, TNA.
84. Memorandum, Sisco to Secretary of State (Washington, DC), September 24, 1973, POL 15-1 Jordan, NA.
85. Abraham Rabinovich, *The Yom Kippur War* (New York: Shocken, 2004), 49–50.
86. Telegram, Kissinger to All Diplomatic and Consular Posts (Washington, DC), October 6, 1973, Nixon Papers, NA.
87. Telegram 5343, American Embassy to State Department (Amman), October 7, 1973, Nixon Papers, NA.
88. Telegram 201118, Kissinger to American Embassy Amman (Washington, DC), October 10, 1973, Nixon Papers, NA.
89. Henry Kissinger, *Crisis* (New York: Simon & Schuster, 2003), 190.
90. Telegram 203591, Kissinger to American Embassy Amman (Washington, DC), October 13, 1973, Nixon Papers, NA.
91. Telegram 5436, Brown to State Department (Amman), October 11, 1973, Nixon Papers, NA.
92. Telegram 5510, Brown to State Department (Amman), October 15, 1973, Nixon Papers, NA.
93. Telegram 203885, Kissinger to American Embassy Amman (Washington, DC), October 15, 1973, Nixon Papers, NA.
94. Telegram 203686, Kissinger to American Embassy Amman (Washington, DC), October 15, 1973, Nixon Papers, NA.
95. Rabinovich, *The Yom Kippur War*, 434.
96. Airgram 121, Day to State Department (Jerusalem), October 19, 1973, NA.
97. Telegram 207370, Kissinger to U.S. Embassy in Amman (Washington, DC), October 19, 1973, Nixon Papers, NA.
98. Ibid.
99. Telegram 210442, Kissinger to U.S. Embassy in Amman (Washington, DC), October 25, 1973, Nixon Papers, NA.
100. Telegram 212589, State Department to Embassy in Amman (Washington, DC), October 27, 1973, Nixon Papers, NA.
101. Letter, Gore-Booth to Purcell (London), October 29, 1973, FCO 93/319,TNA.
102. Message from Secretary to Brown (Washington, DC), November 2, 1973, POL 15-1 Jordan, NA.
103. Memorandum, Scowcroft to the President (Washington, DC), November 9, 1973, Nixon Papers, NA.
104. Letter, Graham to Craig (Washington, DC), December 7, 1973, FCO 93/220, #220213, TNA.
105. Report on Discussion between Henry Kissinger and a group of "Jewish Intellectuals (unknown location), December 6, 1973, ISA.
106. Telegram, Ledwidge to Foreign Office (Tel Aviv), December 6, 1973, FCO 93/219, #220213, TNA.
107. Telegram 081200Z, Ledwidge to Foreign Office (Tel Aviv), December 8, 1973, FCO 93/219 #220213, TNA.
108. Telegram 101140Z, Balfour Paul to Foreign Office (Amman), December 10, 1973, FCO 93/219, #220213, TNA.
109. Letter, Gore-Booth to Wallis (London), December 10, 1973, FCO 93/220 #220213, TNA.

110. Jordan: Annual Review for 1973 (Melhuish, Jordan), January 2, 1974, FCO 93/417 #220213, TNA.

CHAPTER 7

1. Moshe Dayan, *Story of My Life* (New York: William Morrow, 1976), 510.
2. *Newsweek*, June 17, 1974, p. 44.
3. Record of a Conversation (London), January 20, 1974, PREM 15/2153, TNA.
4. Husayn and Rifai Spell Out Negotiating Position (London), March 20, 1974, FCO 93/540, TNA.
5. Community Briefing (London), March 29, 1974, FCO 93/540, TNA.
6. Letter, Balfour-Paul to Craig (Amman), April 5, 1974, FCO 93/540, TNA.
7. Dayan, *Story of My Life*, 432–33.
8. Letter, Balfour-Paul to Craig (Amman), May 10, 1974, FCO 93/540, TNA.
9. Letter, Weir to Balfour-Paul (London), July 30, 1974, FCO 93/540, TNA.
10. Quandt, *Peace Process* (Washington, D.C.: The Brookings Institution, 1993), 159.
11. Ibid.
12. Richard Parker, ed., *The October War* (Gainesville: University of Florida Press, 2001), 271–72.
13. Robins, *A History of Jordan* (Cambridge: Cambridge University, 2004), 139.
14. Ibid.
15. Interview with Ambassador Thomas Pickering (Arlington, VA), October 7, 2004.
16. Ibid.
17. Ibid.
18. Letter, Balfour-Paul to Callaghan (Amman), September 12, 1975, FCO 93/665, TNA.
19. Memorandum, Acland (London), March 20, 1975, FCO 93/585, TNA.
20. Interview with Ambassador Thomas Pickering (Arlington, VA), October 7, 2004.
21. Ibid.
22. Letter, Burton to Williams (Amman), May 16, 1975, FCO 93/787, TNA.
23. Diplomatic Report 265/75, Balfour-Paul to the Foreign Office (Amman), June 23, 1975, FCO 93/664.
24. Interview with Ambassador Thomas Pickering (Arlington, VA), October 7, 2004.
25. Letter, Moberly to Urwick (Amman), October 24, 1975, FCO/93/787, TNA.
26. Record of Mr. Ennals' Call on Jordanian Prime Minister (Amman), November 12, 1975, FCO 93/669, TNA.
27. Letter, Moberly to Callaghan (Amman), November 25, 1975, FCO 93/669, TNA.
28. James Lunt, *Hussein of Jordan* (New York: William Morrow, 1989), 181.
29. Queen Noor, *Leap of Faith: Memoirs of an Unexpected Life* (New York: Miramax, 2003), 94–95.
30. Anwar Sadat, *In Search of Identity* (New York: Harper & Row, 1977), 338–39.
31. Robert Fisk, *The Great War for Civilisation* (New York: Knopf, 2006), 149–50.
32. Roland Dallas, *King Hussein: A Life on the Edge* (New York: Fromm International, 1999), 168–69.
33. Jimmy Carter, *The Blood of Abraham* (Boston: Houghton Mifflin, 1985), 139.
34. Interview with King Hussein, September 26, 1979, http://www.pbs.org/newshour/bb/middle_east/hussein_9-26-79.html.
35. Robins, *A History of Jordan*, 149.

36. Douglas Brinkley, ed., *The Ronald Reagan Diaries* (New York: HarperCollins, 2007), 331.
37. William B. Quandt, *Peace Process* (Washington, DC: The Brookings Institution, 1993), pp. 352–55.
38. Talk by Sir John Coles at St. Anthony's College (Oxford), Autumn 1999.
39. Interview with Sir John Coles (Beaulieu), January 9, 2006.
40. Interview with Lady Anne Coles (Beaulieu), January 9, 2006.
41. Interview with Sir John Coles (Beaulieu), January 9, 2006.
42. Ibid.
43. Public Papers of the Presidents, Ronald Reagan, Reagan Radio Address on Peace between Israel, Egypt, and Jordan, September 21, 1985, http://www.jewishvirtuallibrary.org.
44. Lunt, *Hussein of Jordan*, 200–201.
45. Interview with Sir John Coles (Beaulieu), January 9, 2006.
46. Ibid.
47. Ibid.
48. Lunt, *Hussein of Jordan*, 201.
49. Interview Roscoe Suddhart (Washington, DC), March 19, 2004.
50. Albert Hourani, *A History of the Arab Peoples* (Cambridge, MA: Harvard University Press, 1991), 433.
51. *Time*, August 15, 1988, p. 23.
52. l *New York Times*, July 31, 1988, p. 9.
53. Address to the Nation (Amman), July 31, 1988, http://www.kinghussein.gov.
54. *Time*, August 15, 1988, p. 22.
55. Hillel Frisch, "Fuzzy Nationalism: The Case of Jordan," *Nationalism and Ethnic Politics* 8 (Winter 2002): 99.
56. George Shultz, *Turmoil and Triumph: My Years as Secretary of State* (New York: Scribner's, 1993), 1033.
57. Frisch, "Fuzzy Nationalism," 97–98.
58. Interview with Roscoe Suddhart (Washington, DC), March 19, 2004. The late Rabbi Hertzberg declined to be interviewed.

CHAPTER 8

1. Remarks Following Discussions with King Hussein I of Jordan (Washington, DC), April 19, 1989, http://bushlibrary.tamu.edu/researchpapers/1989/89041900 .html.
2. *NewsHour* Online, King Hussein, April 21, 1989, http://www.pbs.org.
3. Robert Novak and John Wallach, CNN Interview with King Hussein, April 22, 1989, http://www.kinghussein.gov.
4. David Schenker, *Dancing with Saddam* (Lanham, MD: Washington Institute for Near East Policy, 2003), 30.
5. Ibid., 12.
6. Russell E. Lucas, *Institutions and the Politics of Survival in Jordan: Domestic Responses to External Challenges, 1988–2001* (Albany: State University of New York, 2005), 45.
7. Remarks and a Question-and-Answer Session with Reporters (Aspen), August 2, 1990, http://bushlibrary.tamu.edu/research/papers/1990/90080202.html.
8. Philip Robins, *A History of Jordan* (Cambridge: Cambridge University, 2004), 184–87.
9. Khaled bin Sultan, *Desert Warrior* (New York: HarperCollins, 1995), 210.

10. Lucas, *Institutions and the Politics of Survival*, 45.
11. Roland Dallas, *King Hussein: A Life on the Edge* (New York: Fromm, 1999), 217.
12. Remarks and an Exchange with Reporters on the Iraqi Invasion of Kuwait, August 5, 1990, http://bushlibrary.tamu.edu/research/papers/1990/90080502.html.
13. The President's News Conference on the Persian Gulf (Washington, DC), August 16, 1990, http://bushlibrary.tamu.edu/research papers/1990/90081600.html.
14. Dallas, *King Hussein: A Life on the Edge*, 219.
15. Avi Shlaim, *The Iron Wall* (New York: Norton, 2001), 477–79.
16. *BBC News*, November 14, 2005, http//news.bbc.co.uk.
17. Address to the Nation, January 15, 1991, http://www.kinghussein.gov.jo/91_Jan15.html.
18. National Security Council, Memorandum, from (whsr_router@whsr), February 9, 1991, Bush Archives, http://www.margaretthatcher.org/search/.
19. Written Answers to Questions, February 14, 1991, British Parliament, http://www.publications.parliament.uk/pa/cm199091/cmhansrd/1991.
20. The President's News Conference on the Persian Gulf Conflict, March 1, 1991, http://bushlibrary.tamu.edu/research/papers/1991/91030103.html.
21. Robins, *A History of Jordan*, 184–87.
22. Interview with Middle Eastern Journalists, March 8, 1991, http://bushlibrary.tamu.edu/research/papers/1991/91030805.
23. "Jordanians Share Pain of Iraqi Loss," *The Boston Globe*, March 25, 1991, http://www.boston.com/news/packages/iraq/globe_stories 032491_postwar_jordan.htm.
24. William Quandt, *Peace Process* (Washington, DC: Brookings Institution, 2001), 310.
25. Dallas, *King Hussein: A Life on the Edge*, 217.
26. Interview with Consul General Baruch Binah (Chicago), July 20, 2006.
27. Address to the Joint Session of the U.S. Congress (Washington, DC), July 26, 1994, http://www.kinghussein.gov.jo/94_july 26.html.
28. William Clinton, *My Life* (New York: Knopf, 2004), 609.
29. Quandt, *Peace Process*, 33.
30. Remarks by the President (Washington, DC), October 25, 1994, http://clinton6.nara.gov.
31. Address at the Signing of the Jordan-Israel Treaty of Peace, October 26, 1994, http://www.kinghussein.gov.jo/94_Oct26.html.
32. Clinton, *My Life*, 625–26.
33. Fouad Ajami, *The Dream Palace of the Arab* (New York: Pantheon, 1998), 294.
34. Queen Noor, *Leap of Faith* (New York: Miramax, 2003), 384.
35. Department of Defense News Briefing, Secretary of Defense William S. Cohen, April 2, 1997, http://www.defenselink.mil/transcripts/1997/.
36. Interview with Ambassador Christopher Battiscombe (London), January 10, 2006.
37. Press Conference, His Majesty King Hussein and U.S. Secretary of State Madeleine Albright (Washington, DC), March 19, 1998, http://www.kinghussein.gov.jo/98_ march 19.html.
38. Interview with Ambassador Christopher Battiscombe (London), January 10, 2006.
39. Madeleine Albright, *Madam Secretary* (New York: Miramax, 2003), 314.
40. Interview with Ambassador Christopher Battiscombe (London), January 10, 2006.
41. Ibid.
42. Lucas, *Institutions and the Politics of Survival*, 128
43. Interview with Roscoe Suddarth, February 8, 1999, http://www.pbs.org/newshour.
44. Quoted in *Al-Ahram Weekly*, January 28–February 3, 1999, p. 1.
45. *Washington Post*, February 8, 1999, p. 1.

46. http://news.bbc.co.uk, February 7, 1999.
47. Remarks of the President on the Death of King Hussein (Washington, DC), February 7, 1999, http://clinton5.nara.gov.
48. Remarks by President Clinton to Harley-Davidson Employees (York, PA), February 7, 1999, http://clinton5.nara.gov.
49. Interview with Ambassador Christopher Battiscombe (London), January 10, 2006.
50. Interview with Ambassador Roscoe Suddarth (Washington, DC), March 19, 2004.
51. Ibid.
52. *Jordan Times*, July 6, 1999, http://www.jordanembassyus.org/070699001.htm.

INDEX

Page numbers in *italics* indicate illustrations.

186 INDEX